MW00413125

Marguerite Long

A Life in French Music, 1874–1966

Cecilia Dunoyer

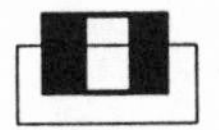

Indiana University Press
Bloomington and Indianapolis

The paper used in this publication meets the minimum requirements of American National Standard for Information Sciences—Permanence of Paper for Printed Library Materials, ANSI Z39.48-1984.

Manufactured in the United States of America

Library of Congress Cataloging-in-Publication Data

Dunoyer, Cecilia, —
Marguerite Long : a life in French music, 1874–1966 / Cecilia Dunoyer.
p. cm.
Discography: p.
Includes bibliographical references and index.
ISBN 0-253-31839-4
1. Long, Marguerite. 2. Pianists—France—Biography. I. Title.
ML417.L85D86 1993
786.2'092—dc20
[B] 93-9354

1 2 3 4 5 97 96 95 94 93

Frontis: Marguerite Long in the 1930s. Bibliothèque Musicale Gustav Mahler, Paris; Marguerite Long Archives.

To my
three beloved boys,
the big one,
the little one, and
the newest one,
who had a race with this book
and won.

Contents

PART TWO

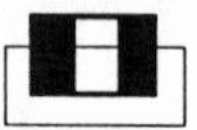

Pedagogue and Ambassador of French Music 105

Illustrations

Preface

It is perhaps a form of nostalgia for the Old World that inspired me, after having lived in the United States for ten years, to undertake a biography of Marguerite Long. Immersing myself in the life of this exceptional artist was also a journey through one of the most fascinating artistic periods of history: Paris from the end of the last century to the 1960s.

Marguerite Long (1874–1966), the most important French woman pianist of our century, marked a whole epoch of musical life in Paris with the indelible stamp of her personality, artistry, and achievement. Part I of this biography focuses on her blossoming career and her collaboration with composers up to 1939; Part II concentrates on her eminence as a pedagogue and an ambassador of French music from 1939 to her death.

Early on, Long's career was guided and inspired by her inexhaustible desire to discover French contemporary music. The circumstances of her life, notably her marriage to the eminent musicologist Joseph de Marliave, only strengthened her collaborations and friendships with the composers of her time. Among them, Fauré, Debussy, and Ravel occupied a central place in her personal, musical, and artistic development. She associated Fauré with the blossoming of her career, her youth, and her blissful marriage to Marliave, during which Fauré and the young couple shared an intimate friendship. World War I brought the tragic loss of her husband; but during this same period, her collaboration with Debussy earned her the reputation of being the one whose playing most closely expressed the composer's aesthetic ideals. Her career reached a climax in the 1930s, when, with Ravel himself, Long played the première performance of the G major Concerto, which was written for and dedicated to her. She and Ravel subsequently toured throughout Europe with the new work.

Appointed Professor at the Paris Conservatoire in 1906, Long was the first woman to teach a Classe Supérieure at that institution; she taught there until 1940. World War II marked a turning point in her formidable pedagogical activity. In 1943, determined to boost young careers, she founded, with the collaboration of Jacques Thibaud, the competition which bears both their names. During the two decades following the war, her weekly master classes became the *rendez-vous* of pianists from all over the world; these artists sought her guidance for international contests as well as for their first important engagements. Her role as ambassador of French music was repeatedly recognized and celebrated by the innumerable titles and honors she received from both French and foreign governments.

The circumstances surrounding this biographical study were somewhat unusual and thus deserve a few words of explanation. Marguerite Long left no heirs. Married in 1906 and widowed in 1914, she had no children and never remarried. Whatever wealth she possessed she invested in the foundation established in 1962 to ensure the long-term support of the competition she created during World War II, the Concours Marguerite Long–Jacques Thibaud. According to her wish, all her belongings of any monetary value were to be auctioned, after her death, to raise more funds for the foundation. The sale, executed by Maître Ader, took place at the Hôtel des Ventes Salle Drouot, the largest auction house in Paris. Unfortunately for future historians, more than her jewelry and furs were sold. Numerous autograph letters were auctioned, and her correspondence with Fauré, Debussy, Ravel, and other composers was dispersed among collectors, making it virtually impossible to trace, as these much-coveted items frequently change hands.

Nevertheless, there remained a substantial quantity of personal papers, concert programs and reviews, newspaper clippings, photographs, autograph letters, official documents conferring national honors and decorations, Long's own music scores with their composers' autograph dedications and sometimes annotations, notebooks of lectures, classes and speeches, and "Le Livre d'or" (see chapter 12), all of which provide ample documentation on the life of the "Grande Dame." Autograph letters from composers, friends, pupils, and collaborators give us particularly valuable details of or insight into the events of Long's life.

Curiously enough, none of what was left, to which I refer as the Long Archives, was entrusted to a library or an archivist. Instead, these original sources were packed in a dozen or so cardboard boxes and stored at the office of her competition, the Concours Long–Thibaud, which by then had gained international status. When the office was moved in the early 1980s from a modest corner in the building of the Salle Gaveau to a sunny and roomy three-room apartment at 32 Avenue Matignon (a mere three blocks from the Champs-Elysées), so were the boxes containing Long's Archives.

Preface

When I knocked on the door of the office of the Concours Marguerite Long–Jacques Thibaud, I was warmly greeted by the executive director, Chantal Bernard, and her helpful and friendly assistant, Sylvie Crabos. Rather surprised by my request, they showed me to the "gold mine": the sought-after boxes of documents were piled up in the bathtub and balanced atop the bidet of the unused *salle-de-bain* of the apartment. Reacting to the bewildered expression on my face, they explained that they needed every closet and file space available for documents pertaining to the competition, and that Long memorabilia ended up by default in the only unusable room of the apartment. They assured me that no one had ever looked through the materials, and neither they nor anyone else had any idea what was there. My work was cut out for me. Bernard and Crabos very kindly gave me a table and a chair, and made room for me to spread out my papers.

I spent weeks in Paris, thanks to a grant from the French Embassy in the United States, leafing through the boxes containing the Long Archives and reconstructing the pianist's life. Unfortunately, as her papers were randomly gathered and never organized, there was no systematic way to refer to the various documents. Although I separated materials by categories (letters, photographs, newspapers, etc.), the only way to find a specific document was to leaf through the whole thing again. Finally, because of my research and persistent interest in the cause, an agreement was made in 1991 between the Concours Long–Thibaud and the Bibliothèque Musicale Gustave Mahler (BMGM) in Paris to appraise and professionally archive these abundant materials. The Long Archives will therefore be conveniently available to anyone for reference in the near future. Since this book relies for a large part on these materials, which are not yet catalogued, sources from this collection are simply identified as "Long Archives, BMGM, Paris."

Two other important sources are behind this research project: the Institut National de l'Audio-Visuel (I.N.A.) Archives, and numerous personal interviews.

Long gave a series of weekly half-hour interviews, or rather radio talks, between October 12, 1954 and February 22, 1955. Entitled "Mes maîtres, mes amis, mes élèves," these programs were conceived and implemented by four journalists: Claude Rostand, Bratislow Horowitz, Christian Mégret, and Gérard Michel. Throughout the twenty broadcasts, Long delightfully reminisced about her life, keeping to a predetermined subject during each session. Through these talks I was able to hear first-hand not only about her collaborations with Fauré, Debussy, and Ravel but also her opinions on subjects ranging from teaching to competitions, from contemporary music to her childhood memories. The tapes of these broadcasts are stored with the French Radio Archives in Paris, at the Institut National de l'Audiovisuel. I refer to this source as "I.N.A. Archives, Paris."

Finally, I conducted many interviews with Long's friends, former pupils, and collaborators, including her physician, who provided a nonmusician's viewpoint. These interviews were extremely valuable in constructing a portrait of Marguerite Long that would be as objective as possible, since not all those associated with her had only fond memories. Conversing over several months with a wide range of individuals between the ages of 45 and over 90, I began to grow into the personage and appreciate her in all of her facets, above and beyond tangible and historical facts.

The abundance of detail in the resources available to me made it possible to portray the rich character of Long's multifarious activities. All the sources were originally in French; the English translations are mine, including quotations from books originally published in French. Quotations from published English translations of French authors are identified.

Acknowledgments

Many strands from my life in the "old" and "new" worlds came together in my work about Marguerite Long. I would like to thank all those who made this project not only possible but enjoyable every step of the way, especially Chantal Bernard, Executive Director of the Concours Marguerite Long–Jacques Thibaud, who gave me free access to the entire Long Archives before they were entrusted to the Bibliothèque Musicale Gustav Mahler. The atmosphere in her office was always cheerful, thanks to her great sense of humor. I am indebted to all who candidly shared with me their personal recollections of Marguerite Long, in particular Daniel Wayenberg and the late Pierre Barbizet for being so honest, colorful, and romantic in their portrayal of their mentor. My sincere thanks to the I.N.A. Archives for making all of Long's 1954–55 radio interviews available to me, and to Marie-Gabrielle Soret at the Bibliothèque Musicale Gustav Mahler for assisting me in selecting and reproducing valuable photographs. I am grateful for a grant from the French Embassy's Cultural Services which supported months of research in Paris. Monique and Etienne Dalemont deserve my most heartfelt thanks for hosting me in their home during weeks of research in Paris, for providing numerous dinners, and for listening to my stories.

Eugene Helm gave me the confidence needed to start such a project; it was his idea that I write a book! His unflagging support and warm encouragement have been invaluable all along. Thomas Schumacher is also at the root of this work. When, early on, I shared my thoughts with him, his immediate and enthusiastic response propelled me into action. In addition, I was fortunate to benefit from the interest and friendship of many members of the faculty at the University of Maryland. I also cherish my long conversations with Charles Timbrell, during which we commiserated on the trials and tribulations of getting our books ready for publication. His advice and suggestions have always been extremely helpful.

My deepest appreciation goes to my parents, who read every word of the manuscript, offered editorial advice, and shared with me their keen interest in the subject matter. Most important, they have always showed unabated faith in me and thus have given me the strength to overcome hurdles and moments of doubt in my life. I owe my father a huge debt of gratitude for taking on with such passion the French translation of this book, which is about to be published in Paris.

Last but not least, the patient and loving presence of my husband, Taylor Greer, is behind every page of this work. He has weathered the ups and downs of all my undertakings unscathed, and my gratitude toward him grows every day. As with every task I complete, I have included him, consulted with him, and asked his advice. Finally, no matter how great the challenges, I am filled with wonder at *petit* François for beginning every day with the most radiant and affectionate smile, and for being such an infinite source of inspiration.

PART ONE

The Artist

Le soleil de Nîmes, couvert ou radieux, selon le déroulement des années a toujours, malgré tout, rayonné sur ma vie. Au terme d'une existence aussi remplie que la mienne, les souvenirs d'enfance reviennent impérieux, et c'est avec une grande émotion que j'évoque ceux qui se rattachent à ma chère et noble cité, au parfum des grands pins de sa tour Magne, au bruit obsédant des cigales ainsi qu'à mes études musicales et autres dont la récompense était pour moi le drame sonore des corridas.

—Marguerite Long

Throughout the passing of years, the sun of Nîmes, radiant or overcast, has always shone over my life. At the end of a life as filled as mine, my childhood memories come back, very powerful, and it is with great emotion that I evoke those that are connected to my dear and noble city, to the fragrance of the tall pine trees surrounding the Tour Magne, to the obsessive noise of crickets, as well as to my musical and other studies, for which my reward was the sonorous drama of the bullfights.

Marguerite Long's hands. Bibliothèque Musicale Gustav Mahler, Paris; Marguerite Long Archives.

1

Marguerite Long's Youth

Childhood in Nîmes: 1874–1886

Marguerite Long's earliest childhood memories are inseparable from the sunny skies, the fragrance, and the beauty of her native Nîmes, an old Roman town in the south of France, where she spent the first thirteen years of her life. She was born on November 13, 1874 at 14 Grande Rue, but shortly thereafter her family moved to Rue Pavée, where her father, who had a passion for flowers, cultivated a beautiful garden. Throughout her life, she could close her eyes and conjure up the intoxicating perfume of honeysuckle, jasmine, and clematis, which were particularly pungent after her father's evening watering. As a toddler, nothing could stop her from crawling down the few steps to inhale voluptuously the fragrance of the earth. To watch the *belles de nuit* close at night was for her a great mystery. This is where her lifelong passion for flowers was born, and where her imagination began its rapid development. When her father would scold her because she was walking around at night with her face up in the air, she would answer that she was looking at the stars. In fact she was trying to count them.

Marguerite's parents were not musicians. Her father, Pierre, originally from the Drôme region, somewhat north of Nîmes, worked for the railroad. But her mother, Anne Marie Antoinette, who was a native of the Ardèche region, also north of Nîmes, had a good musical instinct, and little Marguerite was not allowed to play wrong notes.

If her father had given her a love for flowers, it was her sister, Claire, eight years older, who planted the seed of musical passion. Claire Long was a splendid pianist; at age seventeen she was appointed Professor of Piano at the

Marguerite Long's parents. Bibliothèque Musicale Gustav Mahler, Paris; Marguerite Long Archives.

Nîmes conservatory. She had studied with a German master, Amédée Mager, who had settled in Nîmes. Mager had earned a Premier Prix at the Paris Conservatoire in the class of the famed Antoine Marmontel, whose pupils included Bizet, Debussy, d'Indy, Francis Planté, and Louis Diémer. Claire's fragile health prevented her from leaving home to pursue her studies at the Paris Conservatoire, but still permitted a successful career. Claire was Marguerite's first teacher:

> I owe her everything, my sister whose piano was my first piano and whose sensitive and knowledgeable fingers guided the fingers of her baby sister. . . . She, who was my first teacher, and probably the best and most loving of all my mentors.[1]

From Claire, Marguerite received a firm base of Franco-German principles of piano playing. She could not remember when she first played the piano: "I feel as though I have always played, as I feel I could always read and write."

Read and write she did at an early age. A touching collection of letters the very young Marguerite wrote to her parents on every New Year were meticulously kept. From the earliest one, dated 1880, to later ones, we can see the shaping of her distinctive handwriting. As a six- and seven-year-old, she was already concerned with the health of both her mother and her sister, and with being a conscientious daughter. On December 31, 1882, she wrote in an already remarkably mature handwriting:

> Dear parents,
>
> I am happy to be able to write to you on this happy day. I am committed to be well behaved and to practice my piano and do my homework this year, because now I am old enough to obey you. I pray to God every day that he will keep you here for a long time. I love you very much and to prove it to you I want to be very nice. . . . I love Claire and Mommy very much and I pray for God to let them live forever. I hope Claire will not worry anymore and that we will become good friends. I kiss you with all my heart.
>
> Your little girl who loves you,
>
> Marguerite Long[2]

Her earliest musical recollections go back to the days when, at the age of two or three, she would climb onto a stool next to her sister while she practiced. Imitating Claire, Marguerite would turn pages with great speed but without understanding what was on them. Nevertheless, music stirred very strong emotions in her, both happy and melancholic. When Claire played a certain piece by Weber, which was fashionable at the time, Marguerite would be filled with sadness. She would run to her mother's arms in tears and say, "Maman, I don't want you to die." In retrospect, the scene is all the more touching since her "Maman" died when Marguerite was not quite seventeen, a few weeks before she won her Premier Prix at the Paris Conservatoire.

As she grew up, her interests were many and her curiosity unlimited. Marguerite would climb into trees and read for hours. She was at the head of her class in school, and yet, when asked if she liked to work hard, she would answer sarcastically with a famous quotation by the French playwright Tristan Bernard, who once said that work is not made for man because it tires him.

In 1883, when Claire was appointed to the Nîmes conservatory, Marguerite entered her class and pursued academic and musical studies simulta-

Marguerite and her sister, Claire, in front of their home. Bibliothèque Musicale Gustav Mahler, Paris; Marguerite Long Archives.

neously. Their parents were very supportive and frequently took their daughters to the theatre and the opera. Marguerite had seldom played with dolls until this time. Now she enjoyed dressing them in costumes: she set up her own miniature stage and imagined Romeo and Juliet, Marguerite and Faust, and Othello and Desdemona. Before she was ten she knew *Aida, Les Huguenots, William Tell, Lohengrin,* and many other operas by memory and would compose paraphrases of her favorite scenes at the piano.

Francis Planté, in a photograph inscribed in 1912, "To Marguerite Long de Marliave, her enthusiastic and fervent friend." Bibliothèque Musicale Gustav Mahler, Paris; Marguerite Long Archives.

The great Théâtre de Nîmes was an exceptional musical resource. When Marguerite was still young, she would go with her sister to operas and concerts by visiting virtuosos. She remembered in particular a concert by Francis Planté, who was then one of Europe's most acclaimed pianists. Born in 1839, he had played as a child prodigy in every capital and court. His career lasted 90 years, during which he earned the friendship and affection of all the greats: Liszt, Thalberg, Anton Rubinstein, Paderewski, Rossini, Massenet, Saint-Saëns. Planté had great charisma on stage, and he made a lasting impression on the eight-year-old Marguerite Long. She met him later, and never missed a chance to hear him play. For his part, he wrote a number of endearing letters to Long, whose career he followed through the years.

The stage fascinated her, and it was with tremendous exaltation that she made her first public appearance in 1886, at the age of eleven. Having just obtained a Prix d'Honneur at the Nîmes Conservatory, she performed Mozart's D minor Concerto with orchestra. The honors ceremony was held in the same Théâtre de Nîmes, one of France's most beautiful eighteenth-century theatres. (It has, unfortunately, since been destroyed by fire.)

> I can still see myself with my pink dress and white shoes, walking on that stage, which was quite vast: I felt I was drawn toward the greatest destiny! And when my beloved sister came to sit next to me, treating me like the little pupil (which I was), I felt deeply humiliated and pushed her away, gently but with willful energy.

Marguerite felt entirely in her element, sitting on the stage by herself, in front of a piano and an orchestra. From that day dates her first review: "This young lady, ahead of whom lies a bright musical future, is gifted with an architectural sense as rich as it is powerful, and with fingers of a rare dexterity" (*Progrès du midi,* August 1, 1886).

Even when she was quite young, Long felt a great sense of pride at being able to perform. Yet she did not perform widely throughout Europe at a tender age, as other child prodigies did; instead she was sheltered by a very protective and conservative French family. But she never let an opportunity to be heard go by. Whenever she visited friends with her family, she expected to be asked to play.

Marguerite Long's parents and sister fueled and guided the child's insatiable appetite for intellectual and artistic life, but at the same time they emphasized the need for hard work and discipline. The parents made a deliberate effort to provide Claire with a sound musical education, and Marguerite always benefited from being included. One of the most striking musical experiences of her childhood occurred when the family went to Paris to hear the Concerts Colonne* at the Théâtre du Châtelet. Marguerite was eight years old; it was the first time she heard an orchestra. She said that it was perhaps on this occasion that she first aspired to perform on that particular stage. Beethoven's Fourth Symphony was on the program. The performance made such a profound impression on her that for the rest of her life she was always deeply moved by that work.

She thrived on strong emotions from an early age, whether they were triggered by the warm scents in the air, the obsessive sound of crickets, music, or the theatre. But also, there were the bullfights. She recalled the *corridas* with passion:

> This exalting spectacle in the Roman arenas of Nîmes, on the burning stones, filled to the highest tier with a packed crowd under the arrows of a dazzling sun; the entrance of the Spanish quadrilles dressed in silver and gold; the Toreador music from *Carmen*—I still shiver at the memory of it.[3]

By the age of ten, she was a real *aficionada* of the sound-filled and bloody drama of the bullfights. The ultimate punishment her father could impose was to keep her from going to the *corrida* on Sunday. "You cannot imagine what that penance represented for me."

The first thirteen years of Marguerite Long's life shaped her temperament forever. She felt like a true *méridionale,* a woman from the south of France. Even though she lived in Paris for the remaining 80 years of her life, her friends and pupils said she always kept a slight *accent du midi,* a delightful sunny streak in her speech that contributed to her charm. She had the warmth and passion typically attributed to southerners, along with a sharp sense of humor and an arresting directness.

From Nîmes to Paris

Less than a year after Marguerite's public debut came a visit from Paris of Théodore Dubois,* composer and National Inspector of Conservatories, disturbing the relative comfort of her life in Nîmes. He heard the young girl and strongly suggested to her family that she pursue her musical vocation in Paris. Pierre Long and his wife were terrified and could not even consider letting their twelve-year-old daughter go to Paris by herself. Marguerite's mother was in poor health and could not have accompanied her daughter to the capital.

*See the Glossary for information about names marked with an asterisk.

The whole idea was rejected. A year later Théodore Dubois was back for a further evaluation of the Nîmes conservatory. The pupil he had heard the previous year had made extraordinary progress, and he was determined. He knocked at the Longs' door and announced: "Madame, one does not have the right to leave this child in Nîmes. She will be a great pianist." Elegant, with a narrow beard which further elongated his face, Théodore Dubois was delicate but persuasive. The Longs were convinced and began to make arrangements.

Marguerite was to travel to Paris with her father. Once there, he would leave her in a convent run by a distant relative, where she would pursue her general education while studying at the Conservatoire. She was thirteen years old. Their first departure, in 1888, was a false start: the Paris Conservatoire had cancelled the entrance examination that year. Marguerite had to go back to Nîmes for another year. Finally, in 1889, the year of the Great Exposition, she entered the Cours Préparatoire at the Paris Conservatoire and earned the Première Médaille at the end of the year. In a touching homage to Long written shortly after her death, the composer Henri Büsser* reminisced:

> It was in 1890 that I met Marguerite Long. She was in the Classe Préparatoire of Mme [Sophie Muller] Chêné. . . . Marguerite Long was already a precocious musical genius. . . . When I met her, I was eighteen and she, sixteen. We became great friends. I had written a piece for the end-of-year sight-reading competition for Mme Chêné's class. Marguerite Long was the only one who read the piece without one mistake . . . and I asked her permission to hug her.[4]

Marguerite was then admitted to the Classe Supérieure under Henri Fissot. Fissot had a beautiful sense of sound, and Long always felt indebted to him for having taught her at a young age to listen for good sound quality. As may be suspected, her austere routine in Paris was a drastic change from life in her sunny Provence. She was always chaperoned, and her only outings were to her classes at the Conservatoire three times a week. This did not give her much of a chance to meet or play with her classmates.

But thanks to her vivacious and independent temperament, Marguerite was able to make good progress, and in one year at the Classe Supérieure level, won her Premier Prix from the Conservatoire on July 24, 1891. The competition consisted of performing a technically brilliant *Allegro de Concert* by Ernest Guiraud and sight-reading a piece by Massenet, two works composed expressly for the occasion. Both composers were in the jury, as was Ambroise Thomas (1811–1896), then Director of the Conservatoire. Marguerite Long recalled this competition with her usual wit:

Marguerite Long around 1890. Bibliothèque Musicale Gustav Mahler, Paris; Marguerite Long Archives.

The "concours" was not as it is today. It was in late July . . . it was very hot and because of the sight-reading exam, we were all locked in a large room so that we could not consult with outsiders. We had to stay in that room from noon until

Marguerite Long as a young girl. Bibliothèque Musicale Gustav Mahler, Paris; Marguerite Long Archives.

the end of the "concours," which ended at God knows what time. So you can imagine what that meant. . . . But they had thought of everything and had put up a large folding screen in a corner of the room (I'll never forget) with the necessary implements behind it so that when the need arose, we could hide back there and pour out whatever overflow was caused by our nerves. Fortunately, the Conservatoire has become more humane today!

Marguerite Long was now sixteen; she had won the highest honors at the Paris Conservatoire in only two years. Yet she felt a great vacuum. On the day of her victory, the Director found her in tears in the courtyard of the Conservatoire. He patted her on the shoulder and tried to comfort her: "Dear, you will get something next year." He was rather confused when he discovered she was a Premier Prix winner. Long felt her time at the almighty Paris Conservatoire had gone by too fast. She suddenly realized that playing the piano was to be her whole life and that if she wanted to be a great pianist, the hard work had not even begun. And yet she had officially graduated from her studies. She felt she did not know anything and that she was now on her own. Her mother's death a few weeks earlier only compounded the complexities of her emotions. It was the overwhelming realization that she was at a turning point in her life: she had to take care of herself, emotionally as well as financially. She also knew she had to continue her general education, which she always believed was of prime importance for any artist worthy of the name.

It is at this point that her old teacher from the Classe Préparatoire, Madame Chêné, intervened and introduced Marguerite to Madame Garnier-Gentilhomme. "I was very fortunate," Long recalled:

> Since I had no family in Paris at all, Madame Garnier-Gentilhomme practically adopted me. She was a remarkable woman, who owned and ran one of the most coveted private schools in Paris, where courses in literature were taught by guest professors from the universities. She was a highly cultured lady, with a powerful organizational talent, and she was for me a marvelous role model.

Marguerite Long lived at the Garnier-Gentilhommes' from 1891 to 1898. To contribute her share, she gave piano lessons to their son in preparation for the Paris Conservatoire entrance competition. Throughout her life Long valued the education she received during her seven years in that home. Madame Garnier-Gentilhomme often entertained, introducing Marguerite to the Parisian milieu of artists, intellectuals, and politicians. She held musical and literary salons, which were always very well attended and gave her young boarder a chance to exhibit her talent among eager and cultured ears. Reviews of the time document not only Long's successful debuts in this milieu but also the prominence that these evenings held in Paris.

Marguerite quickly learned to be at ease in these circles, a skill she used ingeniously all her life. She frequently went out—horseback riding in the Bois de Boulogne, ice skating, dancing at balls—free at last from the rigidity of the convent. She enjoyed having a good time and claimed that she was a very good dancer. While she knew how to have fun, she was also well aware of the demands of the career she envisioned for herself. While completing her secondary studies, she took chamber music and harmony courses at the Conservatoire. She started teaching in order to support herself; she did not enjoy it very much, but she was attracted by its challenge.

What about her own playing? While discovering the joys of Parisian social life and giving lessons to earn her living; taking a few courses to nurture her innate interest in history, literature, and poetry; and expanding and refining her culture, was there time to practice her instrument? "Oh yes!" she exclaimed in one of her interviews, "I did practice, but I must admit that I took advantage of my natural aptitudes." On March 2, 1893, *Le National* praised her recital debut at the Pleyel-Wolff hall, on Rochechouart street: "The young virtuoso, first prize at the Paris Conservatoire . . . deployed all the resources of her quite extraordinary talent. . . . Her success was prodigious . . . and she had a long standing ovation."

Long was heard fairly often in Paris salons and was beginning to make a reputation for herself. She was already interested in the performance of contemporary pieces. Her recital at the Salle Pleyel in April 1898 exemplifies the type of program she would choose: *Carnaval de Vienne* by Schumann, a Scherzo and two Etudes by Chopin, and the Fifteenth Rhapsody by Liszt made up the "standard repertoire" part of the program. For the second half, she played a large selection of contemporary works, some of them written for her: a Capriccio by Francis Thomé (dedicated to her), a Mazurka by Saint-Saëns, *Galatea* by Théodore Dubois (then Director of the Conservatoire), *Promenade d'un Solitaire* by Stephan Heller, *Sérénade de Chérubin* by Pfeiffer, and *Ballet-valse* by Marmontel. The critic for *Le Monde musical* wrote: "Mlle Marguerite Long received her Premier Prix in piano in 1891 . . . and her last concert proved amply that she has not wasted her time since . . ." (April 15, 1898). Other reviewers praised her brilliance and the quality of her sound, as well as her charm, refinement, and ease.

One year later, in March 1899, in the same prestigious hall, Long again divided the program between major piano works of the Romantic period and contemporary pieces. She received high praise from critics and audience alike. In June 1900, in a concert of contemporary works performed by several artists in a variety of media, she participated in the performance of *Fantaisie mélancolique* and *Etude-Valse* by Saint-Saëns. The concert "was again for Mademoiselle Long an occasion for warm ovations . . ." (*Le Monde musical,* June 15, 1900).

Composers began writing pieces for her because she had a facile and brilliant technique, and their pieces glittered under her fingers. She premiered innumerable pieces which were never played again: "I played them and I don't regret it: no piece is useless for a performer," she stated humbly. She strongly believed that a piece that was not performed did not exist, even for its composer. "A musical work must be played, it needs a performer: the performer's role is difficult but fascinating." To get a new score, to read it, to discover it, to polish it was for her a great joy. She considered the responsibility of communicating the new work to her audience a worthy challenge.

Her increasing popularity and easy success in her early twenties did not go to her head. Quite the contrary. She felt unsatisfied and was very much aware of her limitations. Henri Fissot, her teacher at the Conservatoire, had died not long after she had won her Premier Prix, leaving her without a musical guide. So one day she decided to seek out Antonin Marmontel (1850–1907), whom she trusted wholeheartedly and who was the son of the famous Antoine Marmontel. Antoine Marmontel (1816–1898), who was Fissot's mentor, taught at the Conservatoire from 1848 to 1887 and listed among his pupils France's greatest musicians: George Bizet, Claude Debussy, Vincent d'Indy, Francis Planté, and Louis Diémer. He had inherited the class of his teacher, Pierre-Joseph Zimmerman (1785–1853), who was regarded as the ancestor of the so-called French school. Zimmerman was credited with having eased the transition from the Couperin-Rameau harpsichord type of keyboard technique to the modern piano touch.

Antonin Marmontel, the son, embodied for Marguerite Long the great tradition of French masters. He had been Professor of Piano at the Paris Conservatoire since 1901, after having taught solfège there since 1875. He had encouraged Long on several occasions while she was a student at the Conservatoire. She confided in him, in all sincerity: "I feel that I do not know much, I don't play very well. I would like to be able to teach better than I do now. Will you help me and give me lessons?" He accepted, and "this is when the miracle began," she said solemnly. She felt indebted to him, for the rest of her life, for her pedagogical success. For several years, she went to his home every Sunday afternoon for lessons. She admired him for having shared with her the science and wonders of teaching as well as its beauty and rewards. Marmontel helped her discover the joys it brought to one's life, how much one learned from it. For that she revered him. Soon he entrusted her with students.

Long's eagerness to excel, along with her desire to please her new mentor, could only make of her an excellent pedagogue. It was not long before her student recitals were favorably reviewed: "Mlle Marguerite Long gave a recital of her students, which included no fewer than forty-six numbers. We wish we could have heard every one of them, because the teaching is quite remarkable" (*Le Monde musical,* March 15, 1898).

Marguerite Long never met Antonin's father, Antoine Marmontel, then the most coveted teacher in Paris. One day, after she had pleased Antonin with her performance of Schumann's *Carnaval de Vienne,* he said that she should play for his father. The day was chosen and she went, with great anticipation, but at Marmontel's building, the concierge prevented her from getting on the elevator and firmly forbade her to go up. Long was determined to get to her long-awaited appointment, and let the concierge know that, in no uncertain terms. The argument ended when he solemnly informed the young pianist: "You cannot go up. M. Marmontel died this morning." Subsequently, Long frequented his beautiful apartment, which Antonin inherited. It housed an impressive art collection, including pieces that eventually went to the Louvre, such as Delacroix's *Chopin* and Greuse's *Gluck.*

Joseph de Marliave (1873–1914)

During her twenties Marguerite Long spent summers with her sister, Claire, who was now married and living in the southwest, in Castelnaudary. The region was not devoid of musical events: in nearby Béziers a wealthy patron, Fernand Castelbon de Beauxhostes, funded open-air music festivals during the summers. Gabriel Fauré's *Prométhée* was premiered there in the summer of 1900, under the artistic advice of Camille Saint-Saëns. On a hot August day in 1902, Marguerite, her sister, and her sister's husband were invited to a musical gathering at the Château de Mireval, a nearby estate. An elegant crowd was present to hear the host and his friends perform a Brahms string quartet. Marguerite Long had already eyed the piano in the room and was expecting to be asked to play later in the evening. Enthusiastic applause broke out after her performance of Beethoven's C minor Variations and Liszt's E major Polonaise. After covering her with compliments, the host relayed the request of a young officer in the audience that she perform a work by Fauré. She had to decline, having no piece by Fauré in her fingers. He was still an obscure composer to most pianists. In any case, the young officer was very disappointed and is reported to have said, "I do not understand everyone's enthusiasm for this young woman. She plays very well, but she cannot be a musician, she does not play a line of Fauré's music."[5] Marguerite Long promptly remedied this embarrassment: she began learning Fauré's music and married the young officer three and a half years later, becoming Marguerite Long de Marliave on February 26, 1906. She was 31 years old. Fauré and Marmontel were best men at their wedding.

Joseph de Marliave (1873–1914) began his career in the prestigious officer training school of Saint-Cyr. While in Verdun, in his first assignment, he formed a string quartet with his colleagues in order to read through the great literature. During the concert season, he took the train to Paris every week to attend the Colonne or Lamoureux orchestras' Sunday concerts. His passion for arts and letters soon led him to forego his brilliantly begun military career for one in academe. His intellectual gifts were soon recognized. He regularly published critical essays on the music of his time in *Nouvelle revue;* these articles were posthumously collected and published.[6] His numerous writings on Fauré's music revealed his keen sensitivity and understanding of "the most French of French composers."[7] His esteem for Fauré was reciprocated; the two men often met to collaborate on an article or other musical projects.

Marliave was at ease in several languages and undertook the translation of Albeniz's lyrical comedy *Pepita Jimenez.* The translated version was premiered at the Opéra-Comique in 1923, long after the composer's death. Marliave also began work on a French version of *Goyescas* by Granados.

But it was for his extensive work on the Beethoven string quartets that Marliave was highly esteemed as a musicologist.[8] His book, published posthumously in 1925, represents a profound and complete study of the quartets and was considered the authoritative work on the subject for the greater part of the twentieth century. In the Preface Gabriel Fauré praises the achievement of his one-time friend and collaborator:

> Joseph de Marliave gave us this magnificent work . . . glowing with youth, strength and faith. It exhibits two qualities, rarely united: the rigor of a thorough and abundant documentation, and the charm of an emotion which gives music criticism the sparkle of life. Joseph de Marliave knew music very well, and, what is more, he loved it: a singular virtue. . . . He loved before he thought; he felt intuitively before he tried to understand. The acuteness of his critical faculties was subordinate to his joy. . . . How can I hide how delicious it is for a composer to feel understood and, more important, to feel loved?[9]

Marguerite and Joseph de Marliave. Bibliothèque Musicale Gustav Mahler, Paris; Marguerite Long Archives.

Marguerite Long talked about her erudite husband all her life. Her extensive library and lasting interest in the humanities owed a great deal to the life she shared with him. He carried the title of Marquis, which in turn made his wife La Marquise de Marliave, a distinction to which she did not object and which only enhanced her ability to move about in certain circles. Some of Marguerite Long's pupils recalled how handsome the Marquis de Marliave was. When they came for their lessons, as little girls, they would sometimes hide in the hallway, waiting to see him walk by. The Marliaves' marriage, which was built on mutual esteem and mutual passion for music, was to end tragically during the first month of World War I.

2

Marguerite Long and Gabriel Fauré: 1902–1912

As the new century began, important musical encounters and opportunities were to affect the direction of Marguerite Long's career. The most dramatic ones were early hints of future collaborations with both Debussy and Fauré.

The Opéra-Comique in Paris presented the first performances of Debussy's *Pelléas et Mélisande,* directed by André Messager.* The dress rehearsal was held on April 28, 1902, the premiere on April 30. The controversy that had been hovering around this opera emerged on the day of the first performance. But many supporters were also there, intoxicated by the overwhelming atmosphere of this new work. Long was one of them and wrote later of this event:

> Today's young people cannot realize what *Pelléas* represented for those who welcomed it at its birth. You had to be twenty to love the freshness of those unknown thoughts, to listen, worried, enraptured, to those foreign harmonies never heard before. Without analyzing our sensations, we let ourselves be carried by the sinuous charm of this subtle art, which sang the impalpable and carried you to the world of the unconscious and the dream.[1]

Gabriel Fauré, in a photograph inscribed "To Marguerite Long, her most devoted Gabriel Fauré." Bibliothèque Musicale Gustav Mahler, Paris; Marguerite Long Archives.

Debussy's music held Long in awe. She was bewildered by the elusive quality of its harmonies, its atmosphere, its "aura." While many pianists already performed this music, she did not dare play it until much later. She was afraid of it because of the completely new textures and pianistic approach it required.

During the spring of 1902, Long's Debussyan leanings were strengthened. After three performances of *Pelléas*, André Messager was called to Covent Garden, where he was also music director. He chose as his substitute Henri Büsser, then choir master at the Opéra-Comique. Büsser asked Long for help in learning the opera. The two spent many hours playing through the score of *Pelléas* at the piano and got to know this music intimately. Long felt as though she had entered the "enchanted forest." Several years elapsed, however, before she met Debussy and began to work on his piano music with great intensity.

About the same time that Long had been humbled by the Marquis de Marliave for not playing a note of Fauré's music, Antonin Marmontel suggested that she study the composer's Third Valse-Caprice. He promised that as soon as she had learned the piece, he would ask Fauré to hear her. This music was new to Long, and she let its charm and refinement grow on her. In the spring of 1903 she met Fauré for the first time and played for him at his home, at 152 Boulevard Malesherbes in Paris. Long was moved by the gentle and humble disposition of the handsome 58-year-old composer, who did not look his age, in spite of his silvery hair. Saint-Saëns always used to say that Fauré had no age and never would. Fauré was very pleased with her playing of the Valse-Caprice. He liked her temperament, rhythmic spark, and rich bass lines; and he expressed how delighted he was to hear his music played *avec de l'accent,* as opposed to being played *en abat-jour* (under a lampshade, or muted), as was so often the case. Fauré resented just as much "the opinion that a strong voice was not necessary to sing his *mélodies.*"[2]

A new piece, the Sixth Barcarolle, was resting on his music stand, and he asked Long to work on it. Filled with emotion, she left his apartment, the score under her arm, flushed with a new musical passion and the realization that she had entered a realm of piano music still undiscovered by other pianists. Almost single-handedly, she was to bring this music to life for audiences during the first half of the twentieth century; and she transmitted her passion to her pupils.

In early April 1903 Long and Fauré took part in a chamber music concert. Fauré performed his own Second Piano Quartet, with Pierre Monteux* playing the viola part, and accompanied a singer, a Miss Melno, in three of his *mélodies.* Long carried the rest of the program with two solo pieces and two chamber works: César Franck's Violin Sonata, with a Mr. Denayer; and a sonata for cello and piano by Camille Chevillard,* with Louis Hasselmans.*

In the summer of 1903, Long's collaboration with Fauré continued in the mountain town of Aix-les-Bains, beautifully situated in the Alps on Lac du Bourget. Years before music festivals became fashionable, Aix-les-Bains had a summer season whose renown crossed borders. A concert of Fauré's music was planned, and Long was in close association with the composer.

In August, Long was engaged to perform Schumann's A minor Piano Concerto there, as part of a large program conducted by Léon Jehin. She had played this work for the first time in Toulouse the previous March: "While the admirable A minor Concerto was being played, and the superb interpreter was passionately expressing Schumann's passionate soul, a long and delicious shiver ran through the mesmerized hall" (*Midi-Artiste*, March, 7, 1903). Fauré offered to hear her play the Schumann Concerto and his own new Sixth Barcarolle. Long's success with the Schumann work earned her many more engagements with Léon Jehin, then music director at Monte Carlo. At the first one, on January 4, 1904, Long played Beethoven's C minor Concerto and Cécile Chaminade's *Concertstück*, in her usual balance of classical and contemporary repertoire. Chaminade was present to supervise rehearsals.

A Blossoming Career

In 1903 Long's concert appearances became more frequent and professionally more important. Long was heard and noticed by prominent musicians, among them Camille Chevillard, who was very pleased by her interpretation of his sonata at the April chamber music concert with Hasselmans. Chevillard, an important musical figure in France at the turn of the century, was the music director of the Orchestre Lamoureux, one of the three most prestigious orchestras in Paris, the others being Orchestre Colonne and the Société des Concerts du Conservatoire. With his thick, square crew cut and imposing mustache, he was an intimidating presence.

Chevillard's decision to engage Long with the Orchestre Lamoureux fulfilled her long-standing aspiration. The date was set for November 22, 1903, Saint Cecilia's Day, and she hoped that the patron saint of music would sustain her in a twofold challenge. First, it would be her debut on a Paris stage with one of the city's major orchestras; but it was the second part of the challenge that concerned her more.

Soloists were very unpopular at the turn of the century. A very peculiar campaign was led by the Schola Cantorum against virtuosic music and in favor of "pure, serious music." It banned performing by memory as a form of virtuosity, and concertos were outlawed. Pianists appearing with orchestra

Camille Chevillard, in a photograph inscribed in 1918, "To my dear and eminent friend Marguerite de Marliave, affectionate thoughts." Bibliothèque Musicale Gustav Mahler, Paris; Marguerite Long Archives.

were prime targets and were occasionally booed off the stage. This wave had taken on such proportions that a critic was moved to write an article about the damage done by this "sect composed of intolerant adepts," "as well as *intolerable,*" added Long.[3] Vincent d'Indy was leading the charge, and he had a large following, particularly in the provinces. The austerity of the Schola Cantorum championed the "Classics," Baroque music, Bach's Passions, Handel's oratorios, and concert performances of masses, as a reaction against virtuosity for its own sake, the ideals of the Conservatoire, and the highly regarded Prix de Rome. One reason that the provinces were so eager to abide by such strictures, Long believed, was the mediocrity of many orchestras, which could not follow a soloist after having only one or two rehearsals.

In view of this curious situation, Camille Chevillard asked Long to play

Franck's *Variations Symphoniques,* a work in which the piano part blends equally with the orchestra and whose composer, one might add, was the mentor of the "right sect." Long did not have the piece in her repertoire but was eager to learn it by November 22. The concert was a great success and a momentous step in her career. A dozen reviews expressed unanimous enthusiasm for "one of our most distinguished pianists" (*Journal amusant,* November 28, 1903). Gabriel Fauré himself, then music critic for *Le Figaro,* wrote:

> To reach perfection, the interpretation of the piano part of the *Variations Symphoniques* demands the clean, solid, impeccable virtuosity, the musical quality and proper sentiment, that the truly remarkable artist Marguerite Long exhibited yesterday. One could not play with better fingers, with more clarity and good taste, with a more charming and natural simplicity, and, I should add, with greater success. [November 23, 1903.]

On the shadier side, other reviews, juxtaposing praise and passing comments about the anti-concerto crowd, attest to the musical climate of the days: "The young virtuoso honored so brilliantly Marmontel's school that this time the anti-concerto clan behaved, and we did not have the classic scene in the hall" (*Le Siècle,* November 23, 1903). Long's success crossed the Channel. On November 26 the *London Weekly Critical Review* wrote of her temperament, perfect technique, and velvety tone. This and many subsequent collaborations would earn her Chevillard's most faithful and lasting friendship.

On April 30, 1903, Long gave a solo recital in the Salle Erard in Paris. *Le Courrier des Théâtres* called it "one of the most remarkable concerts of the year" (May 3, 1903). The first half consisted of the Chromatic Fantasy and Fugue by Bach, the C minor Variations by Beethoven, the A-flat Sonata by Weber, and the *Carnaval de Vienne* of Schumann; the second half featured contemporary pieces by Marmontel, Thomé, and Lazzari; the Prelude in C-sharp minor by Rachmaninov; and the Polonaise in E major by Liszt.

> She is sensitive, she is intelligent. With her, the piano disappears, the soul sings. [*Guide musical,* May 10, 1903.]

> A virile performance in its breadth and confidence, but always keeping the charm and delicacy of a feminine virtuosity which ranks Mlle Long among our great performers. [*Le Siècle,* May 3, 1903.]

As often happened in those days, a singer participated in the concert with an interlude of sorts. On this occasion, it was Mary Garden, the Mélisande chosen by Debussy, whose voice had enthralled the Opéra-Comique audiences the previous spring.

By the end of 1903, Long's reputation was well established, and her engagements began to multiply. As she always told her pupils: "Engagements do not make a career; re-engagements are what counts."[4] Superlative reviews trace her travels in 1904: she played again in Monte Carlo; Toulouse; Marseille; her home town, Nîmes—which she always included in her tours; and Bordeaux. In Toulouse, Joseph de Marliave, using the pen name Saint-Jean, wrote a most eloquent piece for *Midi-Artiste;* it was dramatic, lyrical, and beautifully composed. He had asked for Long's hand in marriage during the spring of 1904, and this article was more than a review: it was an extraordinarily impassioned statement of admiration, love, and respect.

Back in Paris in May 1904 and now engaged to an ardent lover of Fauré's music, Long planned an all-Fauré program in the salon of Madame Bouglise. She gathered some of the most notable young performers of the time—Lucien Capet* (violin), Henri Casadesus* (viola), and Louis Hasselmans—to play with her in Fauré's First Piano Quartet, in C minor. The composer stood next to her to turn pages: she could hardly contain her emotion, particularly in the *Adagio,* when tears streamed down her cheeks. "We rarely have been given the opportunity to hear such a remarkable and homogeneous performance of the First Quartet," said the *Courrier musical* critic (June 17, 1904). Fauré himself accompanied a Mlle. Challet in three of his *mélodies;* and Long played three solo works for the first time in public: the First Valse-Caprice, and two transcriptions—"Fileuse" from the incidental music from *Pelléas et Mélisande,* transcribed for piano by Alfred Cortot; and a Romance in A-flat for violin. To end this elitist evening, Lucien Capet and Long gave the difficult Fauré Violin Sonata in A major "a performance worthy of pleasing the most choosy music lover" (*Journal musical,* June 1904). This beautiful initiative earned Marguerite Long a warm letter from Fauré:

> Dear Mademoiselle,
>
> Let me thank you for the delicious matinee you arranged with a friendly simplicity that infinitely touched me, and let me also thank you for having played my piece with the most ideal perfection.
>
> You thus created an exquisite memory, which I will keep preciously.
>
> I hope you have not been too tired, but I think you must be sad and lonely since your fiancé left.

> As soon as I return around June 2, we will have to organize something fun with the Hasselmans.[†]
>
> From the bottom of my heart thank you again.
>
> Gabriel Fauré
>
> I am leaving tomorrow and beg you to forgive me if I do not come to tell you in person what I am writing here.[5]

Encouraged by the composer's appreciation for the "most ideal perfection" of her playing, Long continued her mission and played his music again, at the Salle Erard under the auspices of the Société Nationale de Musique (S.N.M.), on January 7, 1905.

The S.N.M. was founded in 1871 by Saint-Saëns and Fauré, along with Massenet, Duparc, Franck, Chabrier, and Bizet. The S.N.M. could be understood as the musical counterpart of the Salon des refusés for painters. Its aims were to cultivate and encourage compositions generally in contradiction to the taste of the French public of the day, and to disseminate published and unpublished works by French composers. It was established precisely because there were few concerts of "serious music" in France; only theatrical music was performed. The S.N.M. was responsible for the great proliferation of chamber music at the turn of the century in France: many of Fauré's works were premiered there, including his A major Violin Sonata (1877), his First Piano Quartet (1880), and much of his piano music (see below, p. 41).

It was prestigious to play at the S.N.M. concerts, since they were attended by true *aficionados* as well as professional musicians. January 7, 1905 was the opening night of the season, and many premières were programmed, including Fauré's Impromptu for Harp in D-flat (later transcribed for piano by Alfred Cortot and entitled Sixth Impromptu).

> This selection of new works was followed in the most delightful manner by three piano pieces by Gabriel Fauré: Sixth Barcarolle, *Fileuse de Pelléas et Mélisande* (transcribed by Cortot), and the First Valse-Caprice, which earned Marguerite Long the greatest success of the evening. [*Le Monde musical,* January 1905.]

All three pieces exhibited the more brilliant and digital aspect of Fauré's music. The Sixth Barcarolle, for instance, is lighter and more extroverted than the Fifth, the most popular of the set today. Long's choice of the Sixth

[†]Louis and his sister, Marguerite. See below, pp. 37–38.

Barcarolle, with its fast-running scales, and the Valse-Caprice was intended to show that Fauré could write very flashy, virtuosic music, contrary to the opinion that he was a composer of understatements. Long recounted, indignantly, the reaction of Fauré's publisher Hamelle, who said: " 'I never realized this music was so effective!' He looked totally astounded and delighted. . . . He simply could not get over it. . . ."[6] Hamelle had been Fauré's publisher for more than 25 years, since 1879. Could this remark have contributed to Fauré's switching to Heugel in 1906?

On February 25, 1905 Long's re-engagement with Chevillard and the Orchestre Lamoureux at the Salle Erard created a sensation in Paris. *Le Monde musical* of February 15 drew the public's attention to this upcoming event with a lengthy column on Long, highlighting her artistic as well as pedagogical achievements. She played two major concertos, Beethoven's C minor and Liszt's E-flat major, separated by a sequence of solo pieces by Bach (Toccata and Fugue in D minor), Scarlatti, Fauré (Sixth Barcarolle), and Chopin (an Etude). Long was perfectly aware of the impression such a weighty program would make, and the challenge fueled her ambition. An astonishing spurt of glowing reviews filled the newspapers and periodicals. *Paris musical* (March 1, 1905) referred to "her grand musical qualities, . . . her irreproachable technique . . . her remarkable finesse, elegance and sobriety."

La Nouvelle revue, a monthly musical journal, devoted a sizable article to Long, tracing her steps from her brilliant Conservatoire Premier Prix to her debut with Chevillard. Referring to the February 25 concert, it rejoiced in the Beethoven Concerto, "played with admirable depth, emotion, and joy"; the Liszt Concerto, "which is not only a prodigious accumulation of difficulties, but also a work full of chivalrous and noble passion, performed with an incomparable ardor and flame"; and "the Sixth Barcarolle, a delicious piece by G. Fauré, of whom Marguerite Long is the incomparable interpreter." The critic concluded:

> Marguerite Long embodies all the graces of feminine genius, united to . . . a power rare among women. . . . Her performance is intelligent and vivid . . . a powerful dynamism makes *every moment* of the performed work very much alive. Her virtuosity, calm, secure, and entirely exempt from mannerisms inspires great quietude in her audience. . . . Marguerite Long is without a doubt one of the greatest pianists of our time. [March 1, 1905.]

Always committed to the music of her time, a few days before her success at Lamoureux, Long played a new Piano Trio by Edouard Lalo at La Trompette, a coveted concert series. Lalo was an exact contemporary of César Franck. A few days later, she premiered a set of pieces by Florent Schmitt entitled *Musique Intime* at a concert of the Société Nationale. Alfred Cortot and Blanche Selva also participated in this concert, the former in a cello and piano sonata by Guy Ropartz, the latter in a violin and piano sonata by Vincent d'Indy.

Marguerite Long reserved a special place in her heart for Florent Schmitt, whom she considered "one of the greatest musicians of our epoch." He was also a friend of Marliave, with whom he corresponded frequently. Long saved many of Schmitt's letters. Some confirmed the time a student was to play one of his works for him, in preparation for a recital. Others discussed interpretative matters pertaining to a new piece Long was about to premiere. With his usual good humor, Schmitt would say, "You will have to live for two hundred years to be able to play all of our music,"[7] referring to all the French composers.

Musique Intime, Op. 16, is a collection of six character pieces, à la Schumann, and Long was very fond of their poetic character. On her score, the autograph dedication by the composer reads:

> A Mademoiselle Long en admiration profonde pour son jeu délicat et ému et sa compréhension si fine des oeuvres de Fauré.
>
> Florent Schmitt, Mars 1905.[8]
>
> [To Miss Long, with profound admiration for her delicate and moving playing, and her very fine understanding of the works of Fauré.]

Marguerite Long and Gabriel Fauré

Barely two years after Long learned the first notes of Fauré's piano music, she was unanimously recognized as the one who best understood his music, whose sensitivity best captured its very distinctive flavor. Gabriel Fauré himself, inspired by her artistry, composed for and dedicated to her his Fourth Impromptu, Op. 90 (1906), in D-flat. Curiously, it was not Long who premiered the work but Edouard Risler,* at the Société Nationale on January 12, 1907.† Risler was also a devoted interpreter of Fauré's music: the composer had dedicated the Sixth Barcarolle to him in 1896.

†It was at that concert that the première of Ravel's *Histoires Naturelles* precipitated riots.

"Life, usually stingy in gifts, brought me undivided happiness in this year of 1906."[9] Long's marriage to the Marquis de Marliave and her first appointment to the Paris Conservatoire occurred almost simultaneously. The former, on February 26, crowned a two-year engagement. The wedding took place in Joseph de Marliave's birthplace, Saint-Jean-de-Lauragais. During the couple's honeymoon Marmontel sent a telegram to Long informing her of an opening at the Conservatoire for a Classe Préparatoire and strongly suggesting that she apply for the position. A few months later she was appointed by Fauré, then Director of the Conservatoire.

> To be Professor at the Paris Conservatoire thrilled me. . . . I began my "apostolate" with enthusiasm. . . . I can still see Fauré . . . announcing to me my pupils' success [at my first end-of-year concours of 1907] and saying: "There is one person who is even happier than you, and it is Marmontel."[10]

On May 15, 1906, at a Fauré festival at the Société Nationale de Musique, the composer accompanied Jane Bathori in *La Bonne Chanson* and Lucien Capet in his First Violin Sonata. The only other pianist on the program was Marguerite Long, who performed Fauré's *Thème et variations,* the Sixth Nocturne, the Third Barcarolle, and the First Piano Quintet.

In spite of her fast-rising fame, officially acknowledged by her appointment to the Conservatoire (the prestige of which only the French can appreciate), Long had to wait till 1907 to give her first concert outside of France. She explained in radio interviews that a career took longer to start at the beginning of the century than it did in the 1950s. There were no international competitions to enable young musicians to travel, be heard, and earn engagements abroad; and traveling was complicated and tiring. Neither recordings nor radio existed to promote and disseminate new artists and performances. Only audiences' memories and the press could promote an artist and prolong her career. But Long did not resent that. She believed that the most important thing was to continue working hard in order to improve one's overall musicianship and knowledge of the piano, and to learn to know oneself, which required a great deal of humility. All that took time but it was terribly necessary: "science, patience, and conscience" formed her doctrine. After years of teaching and launching other people's careers, Long felt that "today, they want to arrive before they have even started!"[11] She liked to collect quotes from authors, and in this instance she would recall Montaigne: "Il n'est science si ardue que de bien savoir vivre sa vie." (There is no science so arduous as that of knowing well how to live one's life.)

In February 1907, at the last Broadwood Concert of the season at Aeolian Hall, Long made her London debut. It was also the British debut of Gabriel Fauré's D minor Quintet, which she and the Capet Quartet played at the end of a long program. The First Piano Quintet, Op. 89, in three movements, had a long gestation period. Fauré began it in 1887, at the time of the first version of his Requiem; he continued working on it from 1890 to 1894 and finally completed it in 1903–1905. The first performance took place in Brussels on March 23, 1906, followed by a second one at the Salle Pleyel in Paris on April 30.[†] Fauré was at the piano, joined by the Ysaÿe Quartet on both occasions. Critics' opinions, although unanimous on the high caliber of the performance, varied with regard to the new work, which often seemed to elude them:

> To appreciate music of this kind adequately demands more than one hearing, and if the Quintet rather conveyed the impression of being more laboured than spontaneous, it is possible that this impression may be modified upon better acquaintance. Certainly the performance by the members of the Capet Quartet, with Marguerite Long at the piano, left nothing to be desired in point of finish. [*The Morning Post,* February 1907.]

Marguerite Long always associated the growth of her career with her increasing involvement with Fauré's music, which was also her husband's passion. This involvement, in turn, earned her the reputation of being Fauré's most sensitive interpreter. During the first decade of the twentieth century, she rarely played a concert that did not include Fauré's music. Her personal ties with the composer were also growing stronger, as her husband's friendship with Fauré was of long standing; Joseph de Marliave, who loved this *musique de fantaisie et de raison,*[12] as he called it, wrote many critical essays about it.

In the summer of 1907, Long and Marliave spent a few days in Lugano, on the border of Switzerland and Italy, with Fauré, who was then Director of the Paris Conservatoire. He looked forward to summers, for they were the only times he had to compose. At this time Fauré was immersed in the first stages of the composition of his lyric drama *Pénélope.* Marliave was with him more often than not, copying parts, and listening as Fauré played excerpts on the piano.

When inspiration sagged, Fauré would take long walks. He usually asked

[†]It is the only Fauré score published by Schirmer (New York, 1907), appearing shortly after its premiére.

Long to go with him. They might be gone for two or three hours. He characteristically walked with his hands behind his back and did not say a word, but when he returned he would resume composition. During that summer Long pursued her work with Fauré and expanded her repertoire of his music. He had recently composed the Ninth Barcarolle (the "Venetian nocturnal lady," as Marliave called it[13]) and wrote the Fifth Impromptu between two scenes of *Pénélope*. Long was to premiere both pieces two years later, in 1909. Surrounded by the encouragement of the composer and her husband's fervent admiration of him, she breathed this music every day.

Soon Fauré's Ballade for Piano and Orchestra made its grand entrance into Long's repertoire. Originally composed as a piano solo in 1879 and dedicated to Saint-Saëns, the Ballade was revised for piano and orchestra in 1881, and premiered with Fauré at the piano on April 23 of that year, at the Société Nationale. (The Ballade and his later Fantaisie, Op. 111, were Fauré's main contributions to concerto literature.) Here again Fauré's music was intimately connected with one of Long's milestones: her debut with the Société des Concerts du Conservatoire, the oldest and most prestigious orchestra in France. (During the nineteenth century it had been led by world-renowned maestros; in the 1960s it became the Orchestre de Paris.)

We cannot overestimate what this date meant to Long. The orchestra's roster of earlier guest soloists was intimidating: Liszt, Saint-Saëns, Sarasate, Planté, Busoni, Paderewski. The function of president of the Société was intimately connected with that of the Director of the Paris Conservatoire—and Fauré had been Director since 1905—thus the choice of soloist was a reflection of this composer's wish. Young artists were not customarily invited; Long reminds us that a date with the Société des Concerts was considered such an honor that no remuneration was provided. The orchestra had the reputation of being very conservative both in its choice of programs and in the taste of its audience, most of whom held inherited season tickets. Fauré's Ballade, for example, was no longer a new work, but it seemed to have been neglected since its première in 1881, except for one performance in 1907, by the Orchestre Lamoureux with Alfred Cortot at the piano.

So, on January 19, 1908, Marguerite Long's challenge was to overcome three handicaps: her relative youth, being a woman, and presenting a little-known piece by a contemporary composer. Long was very nervous before her Ballade debut. She was pacing in her long dress, white with golden flowers, and Fauré, who was with her backstage, exclaimed: "Oh! What a beautiful dress, in F-sharp major, exactly in the tone [key] of the Ballade!"[†] "Thank you, but I still cannot remember how it starts." "Don't worry, you do not start, the orchestra does."[14] In fact the orchestra only plays a low F-sharp as a support for the immediate entrance of the piano solo. There is no doubt that once under the spotlights, Long's memory did not fail:

> At the Conservatoire, the success of the day went to the delicious Ballade for piano and orchestra by Gabriel Fauré, of a mood so delicately poetic, with a sonority so vaporous and airborne that it leads one to dream of Corot's silvery landscapes. Mlle Marguerite Long executed the piano part with ease and perfection, a profound understanding of the spirit of the work, a supple adaptability to the orchestral atmosphere which delighted the audience. [*Eclair*, January 1908.]

Robert Brussel, critic for *Le Figaro,* added: "her technique, as dazzling as it is, disappears in front of the musical sense and the natural poetry which ennoble her playing" (January 20, 1908).

Reviews from around the country attest to the repeated success of the Ballade and its performer. Sometimes Liszt's E-flat Concerto, other times Beethoven's C minor preceded it in the two-concerto programs not uncommon at the time.

The Ballade was to hold a primary place in Long's career. She could not keep count of the number of times she played it. To this day, people speak in glowing terms of the way she played this particular work. In 1954, when she was 80 years old and rarely performed in public, she was asked once again by the Société des Concerts to play the Ballade, to commemorate the 30th anniversary of Fauré's death. Her performance, at the Théatre des Champs-Elysées, was such a success that she had to play the Ballade a second time as an encore. Five years later, in 1959, the Orchestre National asked her to celebrate its own 25th anniversary with the Ballade. She was 85 and was greeted with a standing ovation. She made her farewell to the stage with this work, which she played for over 50 years to ever-enthusiastic audiences.

Long's commitment to Fauré's music was confirmed and reinforced by her success with the Ballade. She believed that his music held a unique place in history; Fauré was the guardian of French tradition. In the 1880s, the period during which the Ballade was composed, in an epoch when most French

[†]The French word for "key" is *ton,* which also means color. Hence Fauré's playful pun: "Voilà une bien jolie robe en Fa-dièze majeur, tout à fait dans le *ton* de la Ballade."

composers were worshiping at the Wagnerian altar, Fauré managed to avoid the Germanic tidal wave altogether. Long was convinced that it was Fauré who opened the gate for the great epoch of French contemporary music in which Debussy and Ravel could make their entrances. Contrary to the experience of Debussy, whose genius and novelty were instantly appreciated, Fauré's influence was subtle and understated, but terribly important. Fauré embodied French art, and created, without ever wavering, a distinctive style, purely his own and purely French in its taste and refinement, and in its precious balance of "fantasy and reason," as Marliave described it: "On the one side a whimsical exterior full of dazzling wit, of the unexpected, of verve; on the other a lucid and strong logic, the result of a firm will."[15] Whereas Debussy revolutionized musical practices and aesthetics, Fauré created a new style within the tradition, which was for him a discipline and not a constraint.

Long described Fauré's piano music as absolutely pianistic. It is admittedly arduous, however. While appearing charming and effortlessly flowing, it requires an extremely well-grounded technique, excellent finger independence, and a thorough knowledge of all the colors one can obtain from the instrument. What is more, it does not show to advantage all the fine qualities required of the performer. But it is pianistic in that it was thought of and composed expressly *for* the piano. Long often said that the two great *lyriques du piano* were Chopin and Fauré. Fauré owed Chopin his poetic atmosphere, the curves of his ornamentation, and his titles: Nocturne, Barcarolle, Impromptu, Ballade. Long deplored pianists' neglect of this large repertoire, which she believed to be one of their richest treasures.

One of those treasures was Fauré's *Thème et Variations,* which she played again at the Salle Gaveau, on May 27, 1908, at a concert "A la gloire de Gabriel Fauré." This concert united the most prominent musicians of the time. Fauré performed his First Violin Sonata with Jacques Thibaud. Cortot, Thibaud, Casals, Boucherit, and Denayer played the First Quintet (which Long had performed in London with the Capet Quartet), and Micheline Kahn, one of the greatest French harpists of the time, played the Impromptu. Fauré also accompanied Jeanne Raunay, who sang *La Bonne Chanson* in its entirety; and Pablo Casals gave a heartrending performance of the *Elégie.* To end the celebration, Cortot and Long gave a superb performance of the two-piano transcription by Isidor Philipp of the Fourth Valse-Caprice. This occasion was one of the very few at which the two pianists were seen together, let alone heard together. They kept their distance and very rarely did their paths cross (see p. 162).

For a few years now, Long had had in mind the idea of giving an all-Fauré recital. Since her marriage to Marliave in 1906, Fauré had been part of her personal life, because of the solid friendship between the two men. By now, she had enough pieces in her fingers, and the idea that no one had ever attempted such a project before appealed to her. She was also motivated by the feeling that Fauré's music was not properly appreciated. Because his name did not trigger scandals and riots, by the same token it did not attract the attention it was due. The date of an all-Fauré recital was set for March 30, 1909 at the Salle Erard. The program was to include *Thème et Variations,* three Nocturnes, five Barcarolles, all five Impromptus, three Valse-caprices, and the Ballade, with Fauré playing the orchestral reduction at the second piano.

None of these pieces had been played in public very often, but only two of them were actual premières: the Fifth Impromptu (a short study in whole tones) and the recently composed Ninth Barcarolle. "My preference goes perhaps to this nostalgic Venetian sketch, the Ninth Barcarolle, one of the most beautiful," wrote Long. She always associated her image of Venice with this piece. She explained that it was particularly difficult, in that "its monotony should not be monotonous."[16] The Fifth Impromptu is much lighter and virtuosic in nature; it is a parody of the whole-tone scale, which was fashionable at the time. It was inspired by a piece by Florent Schmitt based on a whole-tone theme, which was played at a concert of new music. Fauré, irritated by its success, turned to the Marliaves at that concert and said: "I, too, can write a piece in whole tones."[17]

On the night of the all-Fauré concert Long suffered an extreme wave of stage fright. Fauré's anticipation only increased her desire to please him. The Salle Erard had attracted a large audience, curious to hear the new Conservatoire Director's music. Finally, the comments of a colleague or two who were surprised that Long planned to perform all this difficult music by memory only exacerbated the frazzled state of her nerves and cast doubt in her mind. But when she walked on stage, she saw the radiant face of Louis Vierne, the great blind organist, who was sitting in the front row. She knew his deep love for Fauré's art. So she played for him and at once overcame her stage fright.

That night Long succeeded in overturning the idea that Fauré's music was only suitable for intimate settings. But for most pianists, it still remained obscure. Saint-Saëns, Fauré's teacher and a magnificent pianist himself, was not attracted to it. When Busoni visited the Conservatoire, Fauré asked Long to play some of his music for his Italian colleague. The only piece Busoni could grasp was *Thème et Variations;* the rest was apparently beyond him. Long was not too surprised, for Busoni had been trained in Germany and had an innate affinity for German culture and philosophy. Fauré's style unfortunately did not withstand the crossing of the Rhine.

As mentioned above, Long believed Fauré's art to be essentially French: in its effusions, it always kept a sort of patrician decency, an elegance and refinement characteristic of a mastery of style. She had spent so many hours working with Fauré—studying other composers' music as well as his—that she felt she understood his thoughts intimately. He helped her enormously with Franck's *Symphonic Variations,* for example. Unlike Debussy, Fauré did not play the piano very well, but watching him was a remarkable lesson for Long. His hands were heavy and limber, his touch quite personal and sensual. As she described it:

> Gabriel Fauré's playing was characterized by precise accentuation, strength, and delicious tenderness, all qualities required for the performance of his music. He had an altogether personal way of striking the keys, heavy and supple at the same time. His rather heavy hands produced a beautiful sound, a kind of round sound that I associate with the "Fauré style of playing."[18]

His playing was a reflection of the firmness and the tenderness of his music. Both physical and spiritual qualities had to be expressed, "the spirit and the flesh never to be disjointed."[19] And that was why the performance of Fauré's music was so difficult and delicate but at the same time so enriching and thrilling. The piano was his favorite instrument, and he admitted that he found it more challenging to write for it than for any other medium. He wrote to his wife on August 2, 1910: "In piano music there is no way to use fillers. One is held accountable for every note in order to keep the music interesting. It is the most difficult genre if one wants to be completely satisfied . . . and I sure strive for that."[20]

When it came to Classic music, Fauré was very exacting. Long recalled that one day, walking out with her from a rehearsal of Beethoven's Third Piano Concerto with Chevillard, Fauré was obviously annoyed. Suddenly he came out of his sulk: "Why did you play the last run in the *Finale* with both hands? Beethoven's technique is not the same as Liszt's." Marliave agreed. Long, understandably irritated, nevertheless accepted the composer's criticism: "All right, I will play it with one hand the day of the concert." "And you will miss it," retorted Fauré. She practiced it that night and the next day pulled it off perfectly, right hand alone. Chevillard rewarded her efforts: "It seems to me you changed the fingering of the last run. That was much better. What you did before was not worthy of you."[21]

This anecdote is one of several that illustrate Fauré's respect for the printed page and matters of style, particularly with composers of the past. Long learned from him a strong sense of artistic conscience and responsibility. He would not discourage strong personalities or new ideas as long as they did not run counter to taste or musical style and intelligence. For his many pupils, who included most of the French composers of the next generation, he was a liberal, above all passionately dedicated to art. But his profound individuality was repulsed by the kind of lust for success that led some musicians to make concessions. In his own composition, Fauré never took passing fads or audiences' infatuations into account. He always remained true to his artistic conscience. Long was grateful for the way he influenced her as an artist and a pedagogue. The man and his music always remained associated in her heart with the happiest years of her life, her thirties—her youth and her blossoming career.

In 1909, a new musical society, the Société Musicale Independante, known as the S.M.I., was created under Ravel's initiative. In a letter to Nicolas Slonimsky, Charles Koechlin expressed his frustration with the old Société Nationale, which reflected the biases of the Schola Cantorum:

> The Société Nationale has been useful to French art, but since about 1900 it has come under the influence of Vincent d'Indy. While pieces by mediocre students of the Schola Cantorum were being performed in the Société's concerts, they often refused to consider works of real merit by others. Ravel was received with suspicion. In his first performance [of the *Histoires Naturelles]* the entire ring of the Schola was rude to the point of discourtesy.[22]

Even though he had been one of the founding members of the rival Société Nationale, Fauré was asked to be president of the S.M.I. Most of its founders were his pupils, including Ravel, Koechlin, and Florent Schmitt. Paul Dukas, André Caplet, Louis Aubert, and Jean Huré were also active members of the committee, whose aim was to

> make known through performance French or foreign modern music, published or unpublished, without exception of genre or style. . . . Fauré defended the S.M.I. against attack from d'Indy, stressing that his reasons in so doing were purely musical. He had "complete confidence" in the new society, where he was happy to discover men who were both "old pupils and faithful friends."[23]

The inaugural concert of the S.M.I. took place on April 20, 1910. The program consisted of premières of major works by Fauré, Debussy, and Ravel, with all three composers present. Fauré accompanied Jeanne Raunay in the song cycle *La Chanson d'Eve;* Ravel performed Debussy's *D'un cahier d'esquisses;* and two children, Jeanne Leleu (future winner of the Prix de Rome and Professor at the Paris Conservatoire) and Geneviève Durony, both pupils of Long, played Ravel's *Ma Mère l'Oye* (for piano duet). That start augured well for the new S.M.I.

At the Société's next concert, on May 17, 1910, Long premiered three Preludes by Fauré, the only ones he had finished out of the set of nine, Op. 103. In addition, she played the Eighth and Ninth Barcarolles and the Fifth Impromptu, all of which had been heard only once in concert, at her March 1909 all-Fauré recital. The composer and critic Gustave Samazeuilh wrote that the Fauré piano pieces "constituted the main attraction of the evening." He recognized "Marguerite Long's subtle and communicative understanding" of the music of Fauré, particularly in the "exquisite continuity of the rocking rhythm of the Ninth Barcarolle" (*La République,* May 22, 1910).

Twilight of a Friendship

Unfortunately, the friendship between Fauré and the Long-Marliave couple later soured. Some attribute it to Long's jealousy toward Fauré's longtime lady friend and pianist Marguerite Hasselmans. Hasselmans came from a noted family of musicians. Her grandfather Joseph Hasselmans had been Director of the Strasbourg conservatory and a reputable conductor. Her father, Alphonse Hasselmans (1845–1912), was professor of harp at the Conservatoire and harp soloist in the Orchestre de la Société des Concerts and at the Opéra-Comique; he invented the new Erard harp, and his wife was the dedicatee of Fauré's Impromptu for harp, Op. 86, of 1904. And finally her brother, Louis (1878–1957), was a noted cellist. He had earned a Premier Prix at the Paris Conservatoire at the age of fifteen; and Fauré had dedicated his First Cello Sonata, in D minor, Op. 109, to him. Louis was a member of the celebrated Capet Quartet, with whom Long had performed Fauré's C minor Quartet. He was also a conductor, and had founded his own orchestra, the Société des Concerts Hasselmans. The first Paris performances of Fauré's lyric drama *Pénélope,* at the Théatre des Champs-Elysées in May 1913, were under his baton, a decision on which Fauré had undoubtedly much influence.

Marguerite Hasselmans (1876–1947) met Fauré in 1900, around the period of *Prométhée;* she was extremely beautiful by all accounts, highly intelligent and sensitive, and became Fauré's intimate friend, confidante, and mistress. She was also a close friend of Paul Dukas and Isaac Albeniz, who dedicated his third book of *Iberia* to her. Marguerite was 24 when she met Fauré; he was 55 (exactly her father's age). From then on, they were seen together all the time, and there was nothing secret about their intimacy, which lasted until Fauré's death.

> If Fauré never dedicated any works to Marguerite Hasselmans it was because he felt, at least, a duty and respect to his wife and because his mistress shared so fully in all his activities. . . . She also spoke Russian, taught her by her mother, read Nietzsche in the original, and held her own in philosophical conversations with Paul Dukas. She was, moreover, a "modern" young woman, using make-up and daring to smoke in public.[24]

A fine pianist, Marguerite occasionally played with her brother and father. On April 15, 1902, for example, she was the soloist in Mozart's Piano Concerto in C minor, K. 491, with the Société des Concerts Hasselmans under her brother's baton. On that occasion she premiered Fauré's cadenza to the concerto, which had been written especially for her. She also premiered his Fantaisie, Op. 111, in Monte Carlo on April 12, 1919, as she was the composer's chosen interpreter. On his deathbed Fauré confided to her his wishes for his String Quartet, for which final performance markings had yet to be inserted.[25] French philosopher and musicologist Vladimir Jankélévitch wrote about Marguerite Hasselmans with utmost respect:

> Modesty, reflectiveness, delicacy, taste in literature and ideas . . . Marguerite Hasselmans possessed all these qualities from birth. Her conversation was fascinating. By a tactfully probing remark, by a caustic anecdote or a memory she could recreate the atmosphere in which a work came to be written, whether it was *Pénélope* or *Pépita Jimenez,* the Sixth Nocturne or *El Albaicin.* She could make you feel the power of Dukas's formidable intelligence, Albéniz's amazing virtuosity, his kindness and creative flair, Fauré's genius; all these she would bring to life for a few moments, sitting at the modest Erard upright on which lay these composers' annotated scores. In that humble ground-floor apartment on the rue du Bouquet-de-Longchamp, she was able to conjure up the presence of those wonderful years.[26]

The rivalry between the two Marguerites is a plausible reason for the estrangement, although this is only a conjecture. Long was not one to accept anything but first place; and she probably could not help but resent the recognized physical beauty of her rival, as she was aware of her own disadvantage in that regard. If one could read between the lines, Long's bittersweet allusion to Fauré's new companion in her book *Au piano avec Fauré* is telling. She refers to "A young person-pianist and . . . ambitious had just filled an opening in Gabriel Fauré's rather flighty heart."[27] The three dots are strategically placed, and the rest of the paragraph supplies plenty of double entendres. The voice of a strong woman whose pride had been hurt speaks through these lines, in spite of herself.

Another factor that may have contributed to the rift was Long's disappointment at not being promoted to the professorship of a Classe Supérieure at the Conservatoire on two occasions: the first was in 1907, when an opening occurred upon the death of her mentor, Antonin Marmontel, on July 23; the second occurred in 1913, upon the death of Delaborde. In 1907 Long felt strongly that she should be Marmontel's successor, that she would most naturally continue his tradition, since he had opened the doors for her to a rewarding career of teaching piano. Instead, Fauré chose to appoint Alfred Cortot, a decision he justified in a letter to his wife on July 31, 1907: "It would be the most brilliant addition possible to the list Chevillard, Risler, Lucien Capet. It would serve the Conservatoire's needs admirably and be an honor for me too."[28]

To add to this illustrious list, in March 1907 Isidor Philipp had been appointed to replace the late Alphonse Duvernoy. In the summer of 1907, Fauré explained firmly to Long the motives behind his choice in a letter she alluded to in her book:

> You know how much I dislike being dogmatic . . . but if it is true that during Dubois's tenure I did not worry about what could happen to the Conservatoire, now that I am in charge and realize how much good one can do here, the interest of this school overrides all other considerations. Hence, I believe it is crucial for the Conservatoire that Cortot be appointed at this time and contribute, along with Risler, Chevillard, Capet and yourself to the rejuvenation and strengthening of our teaching. . . . It is touching, but you are deluding yourself to think that no one could perpetuate Marmontel's principles as well as you could. I loved the man and admired the devotion and passion he brought to his teaching, two qualities we will never find again; but I was far from approving all his methods; and I am sure you would not have continued his way, judging from the quality of your young pupils. You know how interested I am in your career, you know how I wish to provide you with opportunities that highlight your

> talent, but you also know—and I believe my life as an artist is a good example—how I prefer things to happen in due time.[29]

The tone is friendly but unequivocal. It reveals Fauré's clairvoyance and strength in leading the Paris Conservatoire.

Long respected his choice, assured that the next opening would be hers: "You will find me resolutely in favor of your appointment next time," he had written.[30] Long admitted in her book: "I resigned myself all the more easily that I enjoyed the work with my young pupils very much. . . . I did not regret having to prolong my present position, as I had Fauré's promise that it would not last forever."[31] It did not last forever but it did last longer than she had hoped.

In 1913 Elie Delaborde died and left vacant a Classe Supérieure for women. To Long's utter disappointment, Fauré chose Victor Staub as his successor. Long blamed Fauré's decision on his advisors, who had, in her view, led him astray. French musicologist Jean-Michel Nectoux concluded:

> Unfortunately Fauré was unwise in his letter to promise her, for some future occasion, his "warm, devoted, enthusiastic" support. He must soon have wished that unwritten because, from 1913 to 1919, the question of a woman taking over a senior class at the Conservatoire (in the end it was indeed Mme Long) was to become a real bone of contention in an establishment which was certainly not short of such things.[32]

Another "real bone of contention" was that even though the Conservatoire admitted both men and women, the two sexes did not attend the same classes. There were men's classes, and there were women's classes, a factor which contributed to the controversy surrounding Long's promotion. It was not until the middle of World War I, around 1916–17, that piano classes at the Paris Conservatoire became co-ed. When Louis Diémer died, Fauré finally granted Long the long-awaited promotion: it was February 1920, Long was 45, and Fauré was to retire as Director of the Conservatoire on October 1 of that year. Nevertheless, it is clear that after 1913, Long's intense involvement with Fauré declined.

> For my part, I got used to (not without difficulty) separating my admiration from my resentment. . . . Between Fauré and us [Long and Marliave], never a word of explanation came. From one day to the next, he ceased to come and sit at our dinner table, where his place was always set.[33]

From 1903, the year that Long played for the composer for the first time, through 1910 or so, their collaboration grew steadily. Her marriage to Joseph de Marliave in 1906 added a personal dimension to that collaboration, enhanced by the several summers the three spent in Lugano, during which Fauré was absorbed by the composition of *Pénélope* (1907–1912). Long was learning much of his piano music, and Fauré was inspired to write the Fourth Impromptu for her. Between 1904 and 1910 her public performances of this repertoire were increasingly frequent, culminating in her all-Fauré recital of March 1909. It is disconcerting to see the sudden absence of Fauré performances by Long in the Société Nationale de Musique (S.N.M.), Société Musicale Indépendante (S.N.I.), and other concerts in the years preceding World War I, as well as immediately following the war.

Alfred Cortot, who premiered the Seventh Nocturne, was often featured instead, particularly in the premières of chamber works: The Second Violin Sonata played with Lucien Capet (S.N.M., November 10, 1917), First Cello Sonata with André Hekking (S.N.M., January 19, 1918), Second Cello Sonata with Gerard Hekking (S.N.M., May 13, 1922), Piano Trio with Pablo Casals and Jacques Thibaud (second performance, June 29, 1923). Cortot was also the dedicatee of Fauré's Fantaisie for piano and orchestra (1918). There were other pianists who began showing an increasing interest in Fauré's music: Edouard Risler premiered the Sixth (S.N.M., April 3, 1897) and Eighth Barcarolles (S.N.M., January 12, 1907), the Fourth Impromptu (S.N.M., January 12, 1907), and the suite *Dolly* for piano duet, with the collaboration of Alfred Cortot (S.N.M., April 30, 1898); Blanche Selva premiered the Thirteenth Barcarolle and the Thirteenth Nocturne (S.N.M., April 28, 1923); Ricardo Viñes* premiered four of the Eight Pièces Brèves, Op. 84 (S.N.M., April 18, 1903); Louis Diémer premiered the Twelfth Nocturne and the Twelfth Barcarolle (Concerts Durand, November 23, 1916); and Raoul Pugno.

In discussing her falling out of favor with Fauré, Long is evasive and yet quite lengthy: one gets the impression that she is unwilling to tell the whole story or that she is hiding something. Her tone tends to confirm that jealousy toward a rival is not a far-fetched explanation. Finally, the death of her husband in August 1914 only widened the gap, since he had been a close friend of Fauré. It took many years for Marguerite Long to play his music again, but in the end, the music survived the human differences. One of the last lines in her book *Au piano avec Fauré* reads: "The music of Fauré was one of my reasons for being and, because it remained connected to all that my musical youth had been, I keep an irreversible fidelity toward it."[34]

3

Other Musical Collaborations

In addition to her teaching at the Conservatoire and her frequent concerto and recital appearances in Paris and throughout the country, Long was also a noted chamber musician. "The best chamber music pianist I have ever had the chance of hearing and applauding to date," wrote *Le Monde musical* in November 1911, on the occasion of a Brahms festival at which Long had played the G minor Quartet. During the first two decades of the twentieth century, she learned contemporary as well as eighteenth- and nineteenth-century chamber works with equal dedication. On March 16, 1908, shortly after her debut with the Orchestre de la Société des Concerts du Conservatoire, where she had played Fauré's Ballade, Long gave a highly acclaimed concert with violinist Maurice Hayot.* The program included three of the great sonatas of the repertoire: Fauré's A major, Franck's A major, and Beethoven's "Kreutzer." The press admired their perfectly coordinated performance and beautiful artistry: "In the Kreutzer Sonata, the *Andante con Variazioni* was a genuine triumph. . . . One could not better understand or perform Beethoven's great work along with the two other sonatas, which figure among the best ones of our modern era . . ." (*Le Ménestrel,* March 21, 1908).

Long's contemporary repertoire in chamber music included sonatas by Franck, Fauré, and Chevillard; Fauré's First Piano Quartet and First Piano Quintet; and Lalo's Trio. In 1912, at the Société Nationale, Long performed Ernest Chausson's Piano Quartet and "put tears in every eye, an enthusiasm in every heart" (*Le Feu,* January 1912); and a few weeks later, also at the Société

Marguerite Long, image of an epoch. Bibliothèque Musicale Gustav Mahler, Paris; Marguerite Long Archives.

Nationale, she premiered Louis Vierne's Cello Sonata, a "very beautiful work, which provoked a profound impression" (*Action Française,* March 10, 1912). She accompanied Philippe Gaubert* in his own Flute Sonata at the March 22, 1919 Société Nationale concert: "Mme. Long identifies so well with the music she plays . . . that she never lets herself get in the way," wrote Bertelin, whose Nocturne Long performed at the same concert (*Le Courrier musical,* May 15, 1919). At a special concert in 1920, at the Ecole Normale, honoring Camille Saint-Saëns, she played his F major Trio, joined by the violinist Hayot and the cellist Feuillard. Chamber music always held an important place in Long's career: her very last recording, made in 1956, when she was 81, was of Fauré's First Piano Quartet.

During the years leading up to World War I, Long added contemporary concertos to her repertoire, namely those of d'Indy, Saint-Saëns, and Louis Aubert. At this time she also sealed old and new friendships with such figures as Albeniz, Granados, Roger-Ducasse, Déodat de Séverac, d'Indy, and Saint-Saëns. Her meeting and initial work with Claude Debussy in 1914, long overdue, marked the climax of this period. It coincided with the beginning of the war and the most tragic and painful period of Long's life.

Isaac Albeniz (1860–1909)

Long was very fond of Isaac Albeniz, as he was of her. In interviews, she recalled his exceptional temperament, enthusiastic, always inflamed. "You see, I must show that I am a Spaniard,"[1] he would exclaim, concerning the impassioned dedications he wrote. Albeniz was a friend of both Long and her husband. Marliave had written a French translation of Albeniz's *comédie lyrique, Pepita Jimenez.* Certain problems arose before its French première, so after the deaths of Albeniz (1909) and Marliave (1914), Long found herself the mediator between the publishing house of Max Eschig and Albeniz's widow. An extensive correspondence between Albeniz's family and Long documents the controversy surrounding *Pepita.* The family counted on Long's influence and prominence to resolve those problems; on the other side, the publisher chose to communicate through Long rather than directly with the Albenizes. Even after this issue was resolved, the correspondence continued, particularly between Albeniz's daughter, Laura, and Long. *Pepita Jimenez* was finally performed in Paris, at the Opéra-Comique, in 1923.

Albeniz composed a major work for Long: *Navarra.* Unfortunately, he never finished it, and it was completed by Déodat de Séverac, with great respect and taste. *Navarra* was intended to be a suite for piano not unlike *Iberia,* which consists of several volumes. Albeniz would tell Long, "You will have to eat lots of steak if you want to play all of it!" She regretted never having played it, even though she taught it to a number of students. Another big regret was her failure to keep the promise she made to Albeniz shortly before his death to play *La Vega.* She felt it was a magnificent work but that it was too lengthy to perform. She gave it to Déodat de Séverac and to Paul Dukas, to attempt a shorter version, but neither dared touch it in spite of the consent of Albeniz's widow.

What solidified the friendship between Long and Albeniz was their common love for Fauré. During the last years of his life, Albeniz organized concerts of Fauré's music in Barcelona. In 1909, as part of a celebration of the city's musical association, Long played a recital, and Fauré conducted his own orchestral concert, in which the two joined forces for the Ballade. Long wrote that "like many great composers he was an appalling conductor. . . ."[2] That night, Fauré was particularly distracted because he was awaiting news of his election to L'Institut de France. Even though in Saint-Saëns, the sculptor Frémiet, and Massenet he had strong supporters at L'Institut, Fauré also had detractors, who were in favor of electing the organist Charles Marie Widor. As Long reported,

> The rehearsal started at eight o'clock in the evening. My husband waited in his hotel room for the telegram, which he was supposed to bring to us immediately. Gabriel Fauré, on the podium, kept looking at me, not so much to follow the music, but more in nervous anticipation of the news. In this huge hall of the Liceo, which seated 7,000 people, my eyes were riveted on the door. At the end of the rehearsal, past midnight, we still had no news. Fauré wanted to go and find out what was going on. At the post office he learned that a mail strike had stalled everything.
>
> Very agitated, Fauré told us that if he did not hear anything by morning, he would cancel the lunch given in his honor. We urged him to be patient. . . . At dawn . . . Fauré knocked on our door, waving the telegram at us . . . he was elected . . . and naturally, the banquet took place.[3]

Albeniz believed that Fauré was France's "purest" composer. In 1908 he had arranged for him to receive Spain's highest honor, the Order of Isabella the Catholic. Long suggested that Albeniz had as much veneration for Fauré as

Liszt had had for Wagner, particularly at the end of his life. This admiration was reciprocal. In the early years of his tenure as Director of the Conservatoire, Fauré often asked Albeniz to be on the jury for piano examinations and competitions. In a postscript to a letter written at a time when Albeniz was not on the juries, Fauré complained, "And all these examinations, without Albeniz and those amusing luncheons, are wretched."[4] In the same letter, concerned about his friend's health, Fauré expressed his deep affection:

> You are having a dreadful year, and I can imagine that your health is suffering and that you are feeling quite shattered. . . . Dear friend, it has often occurred to me that in the future you ought to live HERE all the time, among us who are so fond of you. One can SHUT ONE'S DOOR in Paris . . . and work in as much peace as anywhere else. We . . . need to communicate with one another, to talk, to discuss things, and to tell one another that we appreciate and are deeply fond of one another. . . . So this is the place, dear Albeniz, where you must pitch your tent in earnest. And even as regards your health, you will be better off here than anywhere else . . . surrounded by affection, and you know quite well you have won us all over completely . . . and we love you dearly.[5]

Albeniz spent the last months of his life in Paris, with his health deteriorating quickly. Long cherished her last visit to him. It was on a Sunday afternoon, and the composer was leaving the next day for Cambo. Fauré and Paul Dukas were also present, as they visited him regularly at that time. Albeniz asked Long if she would play Fauré's Second Valse-Caprice one last time: "One can only guess with what fervor I went to the piano. . . ."[6] Albeniz died in Cambo a few days later; Fauré's Requiem was played at his funeral. Long admired him tremendously:

> He was an extraordinary person, trusting his impulses wholeheartedly as when, in his youth, he gave up his scholarship in Brussels to follow Liszt throughout Europe. He was above all a man capable of great affection. He showed it in the way he cared for his wife and in his music, which is grand, full of sun and intensity. I loved Albeniz dearly.

Albeniz returned this great respect; he wrote on Long's score of *Iberia,* Vol. IV: "A l'incomparable Madame de Marliave son admirateur le plus *admirateur*!!! I. Albeniz, Paris 25 October 1908"[7] (To the incomparable Madame de Marliave, her admirer the most *admiring*!!!).

Enrique Granados (1867–1916)

"Enrique Granados was very kind, but of a completely different nature from Albeniz." Long and her husband knew Granados well. When he was in Paris to perform in concert, he would come to their house for meals. He always followed complicated diets because of his fragile health. He would also practice in their home. According to Long, he played very well, but he performed his own music in a surprisingly dry manner, with very precise and unrelenting rhythm, which was marvelous in "El Fandango del Candil." Long played the piano suite *Goyescas* often and had a special place in her heart for "El Fandango del Candil" and "La Maya y el Ruiseñor": "This music is simply ravishing!" Joseph de Marliave undertook a French translation of Granados' opera *Goyescas,* an expansion of the suite, but it is not known whether that version was ever performed.

Long's last token of Granados was a postcard he sent her from the United States in 1916, just before he embarked on an ocean liner that was to bring him back to Spain. The ship was torpedoed by the Germans, and Granados lost his life. The card read: "My health is a lot better, I am still taking good care of it. If only it could always be this way." Long called it "a touching and cruel memory."

Jean Roger-Ducasse (1873–1954)

Long's efforts to promote young composers never slackened, and in 1911 she began learning Roger-Ducasse's piano music and making it known to the public. At the first concert of 1912 at the Société Nationale, where Long performed Ernest Chausson's Piano Quartet, she also gave the première of Six Preludes by Roger-Ducasse. (Debussy's String Quartet was on the program as well.) It was an exceptional concert for the "old" Société Nationale, whose programs had suffered and which had been referred to as "painful sessions devoted to sub-d'Indys or pseudo Ravels!" (*Le Feu,* January 1912). The situation was described in the *Musical Courier* of January 31, 1912:

> For two years or more the National Society of French Composers has been waging war against the Independent Society of French Composers [S.M.I.] by simply pretending that the latter society, the recessionists, did not exist.

> Meanwhile the new Society got all the new men, while the old Society . . . found itself . . . very much deserted. They had no one to depend upon for their concerts except men of little talent and less genius. Result: a very brilliant concert last week made up entirely of compositions by members of the rival Society. The first rendition of a work by Roger-Ducasse, three pieces for piano by Gabriel Fauré . . . and a quartet by Debussy.

The relationship between Long and Roger-Ducasse went back many years. Born in 1873, Roger-Ducasse (whose full name was Jean Jules Amable Roger Ducasse) was a year older than Long and exactly Marliave's contemporary. He was Fauré's favored pupil, but also his intimate friend and disciple. Roger-Ducasse met Marliave through Fauré, for the two had been friends since the early days of the century.[†] It was through their shared admiration for Fauré that the friendship between Marliave and Roger-Ducasse developed. The following cheerful invitation was addressed to Marliave on June 21, 1913:

> My dear friend, Lambinet[‡] is coming for lunch on Sunday. Why don't you come as well? Then there would be nothing missing in such a friendly day. You could play *Pénélope* [Fauré's opera] with him from 2 P.M. to 2 A.M. The countryside is beautiful and my house is beginning to take a turn for the best.
>
> R.D.[8]

In 1912 Roger-Ducasse published a symphonic poem for orchestra and choir entitled *Au Jardin de Marguerite,* which he dedicated to Joseph de Marliave. Long met Roger-Ducasse through Marliave; unfortunately it was only after Marliave's death (in 1914) that their affection grew. Their extensive correspondence vividly documents their faithful friendship.

In 1915, when Long started to compile Marliave's writings from the *Nouvelle revue* into a single volume,[9] Roger-Ducasse contributed significantly to the project by editing some of the manuscripts. One of the letters he wrote

---

[†]It was indirectly through Fauré as well that Roger-Ducasse came to know Debussy, whose second wife, Emma Bardac, was part of Fauré's entourage. That Roger-Ducasse was present at Debussy's death, joined only by two doctors, Emma, and her daughter, Chouchou, attests to the two composers' very strong personal ties. (Letter from Chouchou to Raoul Bardac, her step-brother, of April 8, 1918, in *Claude Debussy: Lettres,* edited by François Lesure [Paris: Hermann, 1980], pp. 286–87. See also below, chapter 4.)

[‡]Lambinet was a mutual friend of Roger-Ducasse, Marliave, and Fauré. He was a Professor of Literature in Bordeaux and a fervent music lover.

to Long while working on this project ends with a moving memory of Marliave:

> I was reading his card again this morning, where he told me of your courage when he left from Toulouse, and which ends with "All is well." It is the most cherished memory I have of him, for there he is, whole, with his two beautiful loves, that of life and that which he had for you. . . . I embrace you with all my heart,
>
> R.D.[10]

"His card" refers to one Marliave sent shortly after he left for the front in August 1914.

Reciprocally, whenever Roger-Ducasse had difficulties with his publishers, usually Durand, he would call on Long, not only for sympathetic ears but in many cases personal intervention as well. Their abundant correspondence from the winter of 1915 is indicative of Roger-Ducasse's frustration with these matters and his reliance on Long. One letter ends with a hopeful "Anyhow do what you can . . ."; another specifies "I would just rather that you remain our intermediary: it will be safer."[11] It is interesting that Long came to the rescue of both Albeniz's family and Roger-Ducasse when they had squabbles with their publishers. She may have had entrée into the publishers' world through her husband; or perhaps her reputation as a champion of contemporary music gave her credibility, and the publishers relied on her good judgment.

After the mysterious schism between Fauré and Long, Roger-Ducasse became a mediator between them, particularly toward the end of Fauré's life. It was he who transmitted to Fauré Long's wish that he write a preface to Marliave's book on the Beethoven Quartets when it was submitted for publication in 1920. And Fauré accepted (see above, p. 17). Roger-Ducasse was well aware that Long was very hurt by Fauré's indifference after their former close friendship. Long wrote: "In March 1924, Roger-Ducasse transmitted to me the stirring message from Fauré, which said 'I would like to die without leaving a dark cloud and thus I wish to see Marguerite Long again.' "[12] Roger-Ducasse insisted that Fauré expected her visit. Long continued: "It was on a Tuesday, I never forgot it. . . . When I arrived at his home, my heart beating, I was told that earlier that day, at five in the morning, Gabriel Fauré had ceased to live."

In turn, Long had a strong admiration for Roger-Ducasse's music: she believed that it never became popular because it was too complex for the listener. She learned all of it, which was no small task, and performed it in small parts. The Six Preludes she premiered at the Société Nationale concert of 1912 did not prove as successful as later works: they had been composed several years earlier, in 1907, and were judged a little monotonous, in spite of the pianist's "marvelous rendition," wrote *Le Monde musical.* No matter, a solid friendship had begun between the two musicians, and Roger-Ducasse asked Long if she would play his Barcarolle and join him in a two-piano transcription of his *Joli Jeu de Furet* at one of the Concerts Durand in March 1913. In later years, Roger-Ducasse was very often Long's chosen second piano (in place of an orchestra) when she performed Fauré's Ballade.

Curiously, this friendship of close to twenty years was dissolved sometime in the 1930s. Without any specific references to either one's actions, letters from Roger-Ducasse written to other parties in the 1940s make extremely disparaging allusions to Long. His bitterness and the imaginative cruelty of his remarks about his one-time friend are astonishing.[13]

Joseph Déodat de Séverac (1873–1921)

Déodat de Séverac was a man of great charm. He sought to fight musical conformism, and to this end, he spent most of his life in his home region, near Toulouse, avoiding Paris and its musical feuds and intrigues. After he completed his studies at the Schola Cantorum in Paris, he published a deliciously provocative article denouncing France's centralization of the arts, and in particular, of music.[14] He deplored the polarization of composers in the capital and wished that musicians would not only cherish their regional identities but also use them in developing their art. He condemned centralized national institutions such as the Prix de Rome and the Conservatoire for standardizing music composition and creating rigid formulas, which forced all aspiring French composers into one mold. Déodat de Séverac wished to see flourish in each French composer's music this *je ne sais quoi* which would highlight regional differences. Indeed, Déodat de Séverac's music was inspired, colored, and nurtured by the rich flavor of his homeland. Though he did not denigrate his friends, his mentors, and his training, he ran back to the southwest of France, the Lauragais, as soon as he completed his studies in Paris.

Long knew Déodat de Séverac intimately because her husband's family was native to the same area. The Château de Saint-Félix, which belonged to the Séverac family, was only eight miles from the Marliaves' estate, the

Château de Saint-Jean. Occasionally, Déodat would walk there to invite the Marliaves to dinner. Long remembered fondly those happy years, filled with the atmosphere of a bygone epoch, when there were lively musical evenings at Déodat de Séverac's château. The Spanish pianist Ricardo Viñes (a childhood friend of Ravel) was often part of the group, and everyone would play music until the early morning hours. And since they did not have automobiles, they would often stay the night.

Long said that Déodat was a troubadour at heart and a creator of songs. That was his aesthetic. Inspired by his native folklore, his oeuvre was "pure music: it conveyed the soul of the land, and amidst the sonorous atmosphere created by the composer in his work, a pure melody always seemed to rise above it."[15] His letters to Marliave reveal that he too needed help in dealing with his publishers. On Marliave's recommendation, Déodat de Séverac was hoping to change publishers; he wrote to his friend: "You would do me a *great* service if you could test the water with Durand, and I would be infinitely grateful to you."[16]

Déodat de Séverac dedicated one of his most important works for piano to Marguerite Long, "Le retour des muletiers." "I have a tiny hand, and he gave me a left-hand part full of tenths! But I played it quite often, with love." "Le retour des muletiers" is the last movement of *Cerdaña,* a very large and difficult work in five movements, composed between 1908 and 1910. On a new year's postcard sent to Joseph de Marliave, dated "St Félix, 3 January, 1911," Déodat de Séverac wrote: "Would you tell me if Madame de Marliave would allow me to dedicate to her a piano piece from my new suite *Cerdaña?*"[17]

Vincent d'Indy (1851–1931)

"Après la Mer, la Montagne" (After the Sea, the Mountains) was the clever headline of a review of a concert conducted by Camille Chevillard at the Salle Gaveau in December 1911. Three major works by French composers made up the program: *La Mer* by Debussy, *L'Apprenti sorcier* by Paul Dukas, and *Symphonie Cévenole* (also known as *Symphonie sur un chant montagnard*) by Vincent d'Indy. The last has such a prominent piano part that it is essentially a piano concerto. Alfred Bruneau, composer and critic, congratulated Chevillard for his "praiseworthy effort to broaden and modernize the all too narrow and conservative repertory of the illustrious Société des Concerts." Regarding the *Symphonie sur un chant montagnard,* Bruneau continued: "Marguerite Long, highly acclaimed, performed the piano part with utmost simplicity and style, with deep poetry and musicality" (*Le Matin,* December 18, 1911). An avalanche of reviews enthusiastically described the evening, extolling the soloist in glowing terms. The *Excelsior* claimed that "d'Indy's Symphony had never been played with such talent."

The piece itself has great audience appeal. Although it has fallen out of fashion today, it is an effective work, full of panache and one of d'Indy's best. Written in 1886, it was based on a folk song from the mountain region of Ardèche, where d'Indy had a summer residence. Long played the work for him as she did whenever she learned a piece by a contemporary composer. D'Indy, as might be expected, was not an admirer of Fauré since the two men headed rival institutions, the Schola Cantorum and the Paris Conservatoire. And the existence of the recently created Société Musicale Indépendante (presided over by Fauré) as a splinter group of the Société Nationale (presided over by d'Indy) gave a barbed meaning to d'Indy's comment: "I am so happy, Madame, to hear you play a major work. I have only heard you play little things," evidently referring to Fauré's piano music. To which Long replied, indignant: "As if there were not as much music in a *lied,* in a sublime piano quartet, in a barcarolle or a nocturne as in a large symphony of which only its self-importance and duration supposedly impress its audience!"

Fauré was quite capable of rising above these musical rivalries. While Director of the Conservatoire, he was eager to bring new blood to the old institution and to hire anyone whose talent he respected, regardless of "clan" affiliation. Hence d'Indy's appointment to the Conservatoire as Professor of Orchestration in 1912 and Professor of Conducting in 1914. To satisfy the "antisoloist" climate, Long added Louis Aubert's Fantaisie to her contemporary repertoire and performed it several times in 1913. She always paired it with d'Indy's work, thus presenting two modern compositions in which the piano was not treated as a solo instrument but as part of the orchestra.

> Mme Marguerite Long proved with d'Indy's Symphony and Louis Aubert's Fantasy for piano and orchestra that a genuine artist can triumph without the slightest concession to virtuosity and in fact can even honor not only great masters such as d'Indy, but also promising young composers such as Louis Aubert. [*Revue française de musique,* March 1913.]

Camille Saint-Saëns, in a photograph inscribed in 1909, "To Madame Marguerite Long, her grateful admirer." Bibliothèque Musicale Gustav Mahler, Paris; Marguerite Long Archives.

Camille Saint-Saëns (1835–1921)

In the same year, 1913, Long was frequently heard in Saint-Saëns' Third Piano Concerto (written in 1869). It was a new piece for her and one that was rarely performed. She claimed it had not been played for 30 years. Although Liszt's influence is clearly felt, it is a mature work, quite original in character. It is the longest of Saint-Saëns' five piano concertos and is excessively virtuosic. Long worked on it with the composer accompanying her on the second piano. She believed that Saint-Saëns was a master pianist. When she heard him play his transcription of Gluck's *Désir d'Alceste,* she was overwhelmed: "His problem though was that he tended to play too fast!" Rehearsing his concerto with him was a "wild chase." She tried to follow him up to a point and then she had to stop: "Maître, I cannot keep up with you!" He would candidly reply, "Oh! I may have rushed a bit, no?"

Long had known Saint-Saëns for years, as he was a close friend and mentor of Fauré. She did not play many of his works, but she did perform his *Etude en forme de Valse* and now this concerto, which earned her the composer's gratitude: "I could never thank you enough for devoting yourself to this extremely difficult work. You give me here one of those extreme pleasures that are too seldom in the life of an artist and console many an unhappiness."[18] In Monte Carlo, under the baton of Léon Jehin, to whom Long owed most of her first engagements, Saint-Saëns' concerto, followed by Fauré's Ballade, brought Long renewed acclaim:

> Aroused by the power and the charm of this artist of rare musical qualities, the audience acclaimed her frenetically. Mme Long played as an encore a brilliant *Finale* of a Mozart Sonata with exquisite delicacy and limpidity. [*Courrier de Nice,* January 20, 1913.]

Opposite qualities, such as "power and charm," "strength and grace," and "dash and sensitivity," were recurring themes in Long's press book.

Many years later Long recounted her last remembrance of Saint-Saëns. In 1920, at a concert given in his honor at the Ecole Normale, Long performed in his F major Trio, and he played the piano part in one of his violin sonatas. After the concert, while many people waited to congratulate him backstage, he did not care to acknowledge anyone. He was sitting at a table dunking cookies in hot chocolate (a typical French habit, such as dipping a croissant in one's coffee). When Long was ready to leave and went to greet him, he got up, and with his mustache full of chocolate, gave her a big kiss on both cheeks. He was 85 years old.

Emmanuel Chabrier (1841–1894)

Long was too young to have known Chabrier very well. He had become quite popular, particularly after the première of his *España* (1883). As a little girl she played two of his *Pièces pittoresques* for him. "I only have a vague memory of it," she recalled, "but what I remember is that he looked like an old man to me. When I realized later that he was 52 when he died, I was horrified to have taken him for a grandpa!"[19] Long made these remarks on the radio when she was 80. No wonder she was horrified.

Women and Music

That the musical world in which Long lived was dominated by men was nothing unusual for the period. Only the most outstanding women, such as Clara Schumann, had been able to make their mark in the history of music. While their artistry had not been challenged, they still had to overcome certain hurdles and fight against prejudices at crucial moments in their careers. For Long it was at the Paris Conservatoire.

Long was not afraid to encourage competent female initiatives such as the orchestra of the Union des Femmes Professeurs et Compositeurs de musique. The U.F.P.C., an active group of professional women musicians, decided to enlarge its efforts by forming an almost-all-woman orchestra. Fifty-two female string players were joined by the wind section of the Société des Concerts Hasselmans, Louis Hasselmans' orchestra. The opening concert at the Salle Gaveau in December 1911 offered a long, diverse, and interesting program. It included Schubert's First Symphony, Ravel's *Pavane pour une infante défunte,* a Corelli concerto grosso, a Saint-Saëns overture, and Borodin's "Polovtsian Dances" from *Prince Igor*. Long was proud of this undertaking and participated in the event by performing Liszt's E-flat Concerto.

What is most revealing is not that the concert was a resounding success but that critics consistently expressed their surprise at the high level of the performance:

> I confess with humility that I was not going without some apprehension. . . . This distrust proved unjustified. First, the U.F.P.C. proves with utmost simplicity how easy it is to compose a delightfully new program simply by using old

> works that other orchestras neglect to perform. Second, these ladies . . . form the best string section in Paris, except for the Société des Concerts du Conservatoire. [*Liberté*, December 19, 1911.]

This critic reveals the deep-seated bias in the music world at that time. For centuries, and particularly in the Romantic period, all women of a certain class received a musical education, usually in the form of piano lessons. This fact perpetuated the idea that women were only amateur musicians and not professionals, and explains the reaction to this U.F.P.C. concert. *Le Figaro* even spoke of "a revelation. This orchestra is simply one of the most remarkable one can hear today . . . and the concert was a great deal more significant than was originally anticipated" (December 19, 1911).

4

Marguerite Long and Claude Debussy: 1914–1919

The Eve of World War I

The year 1914 began a new and very important chapter in the life of Marguerite Long. Debussy's *Pelléas et Mélisande* had made a formidable impression on her in 1902 (see pp. 19–20): "It was the biggest bewilderment of my life," she said at the end of her career.[1] Twelve years had elapsed since *Pelléas*, and Long could still not play Debussy's piano music. She thought it too difficult, and she did not feel that she could understand it from a pianistic point of view. It moved her deeply, yet she was repeatedly disappointed when she heard it played by other pianists, even very good ones. Between May 1910 and March 1913, Debussy himself gave the first performance of eleven of his Preludes; he played on four separate dates, some of which Long might have attended. During the same period, Fauré appointed Debussy as a judge for some of the Conservatoire examinations, providing another chance for Long's and Debussy's paths to cross. They might have met at concerts of the Société

Nationale or the Société de Musique Indépendante, as performer, composer, or listener. Watching this young pianist play so much *other* French contemporary repertoire, Debussy confronted her: "So, I guess you have made up your mind and you simply do not like my music, is that right?"[2] Taken aback, Long expressed her infinite adoration for *Pelléas et Mélisande,* but added that she believed his piano music was too difficult. "Too difficult! Not for you, considering all that you play," answered Debussy. "The notes are not difficult but the realization puzzles me, it escapes me."[3] Long was intimidated by the completely new sounds, the impalpable atmosphere, the sensuality of Debussy's pianism. She used Massenet's expression: "Debussy is the enigma."[4] She tried to convey her feelings to the composer, who then suggested: "And what if you worked with me?" She accepted immediately.

Although Long may have overstated her connections with Debussy in her book *Au piano avec Debussy,* many musicians have down-played them. A letter written by Long's husband to her sister, Claire, confirms the situation. The story seen through his eyes gives a helpful perspective. The letter, dated May 5, 1914, is long and newsy. Marliave describes to his sister-in-law Long's latest worries about student examinations and recitals, about her heavy upcoming concert schedule, about woes with her cook, and so on. Then:

> The Ducasses, who often see the Debussys, told Marguerite that they [the Debussys] were delighted to have found an interpreter. The fact is that Debussy's piano music is very seldom performed: it is very difficult technically and in interpretation, and it demands a very accurate and refined musical sensitivity. Actually, I believe Marguerite will play it admirably, after she receives the composer's coaching. And it will be an excellent thing for her to be Debussy's assigned artist—not to mention that it will enrage Fauré and Boutroux. For now it has brought the composer's participation in her concert, which is nothing to laugh at, since he gets a full house everywhere he plays.[5]

The dart aimed at Fauré is evidence of Long's recent estrangement from him. The concert Marliave alluded to was an ambitious project: Long singlehandedly organized a benefit concert for a charity group known as L'Entraide Artistique; it took place on May 27, 1914, with Debussy participating. She got permission from the administration of the Conservatoire to use the large hall where the Société des Concerts du Conservatoire performed, and she asked her dear friend and supporter Camille Chevillard to conduct the Orchestre Lamoureux. The program was composed entirely of French music: three concertos (Saint-Saëns, Fauré, d'Indy), a piece by her friend Alfred Bruneau, and two *mélodies* by Debussy—"Chansons de Bilitis" and "Le promenoir des deux amants," with the composer at the piano. In the same letter, Marliave wrote to Claire:

> It is, as you can see, a "chic" program. You will notice that Debussy himself will come to accompany his music. It will have all the more impact in that he has refused the same favor to a number of people and musical organizations for the same period. He has been his absolute kindest toward Marguerite; but in all fairness, one must say that he is not acting completely without self-interest. Of course, keep this to yourself, even though it is quite flattering to Marguerite. It was Madame Debussy who asked Debussy to participate in this concert; when she had his consent, she called Marguerite and, after giving her the good news, told her bluntly: "Now, you know, you will have to play his piano music. . . . He has no performers with whom he is happy; male pianists do not understand a thing about his music. We went to hear you recently: you are the only one who could play it well."

Madame Debussy (Emma Bardac) was always very close to her husband's thoughts, and her statements can always be trusted. In view of the intimate family context of Marliave's report, its sincerity is beyond question. His letter continued:

> Marguerite, very flattered . . . thanked her profusely: "I would love to. . . . I have wanted to play his music for a long time, but after working on it, and having heard M. Debussy himself play these pieces, I felt quite discouraged. . . ." Which is the truth: Debussy plays his own music *marvelously*. Then Mme. Debussy said: "Well, you will come and work with him: you are too great an artist and too intelligent not to accept all the observations he will make about his music: just come over, without timidity or false modesty."

It is obvious that Debussy's collaboration at this concert meant a great deal to the Long-Marliave couple. Neither did it go unnoticed by the numerous critics in attendance.

> With the collaboration of M. Camille Chevillard conducting the Orchestre Lamoureux, of Mlle. Féart from the Opéra, and of M. Claude Debussy, this evening took on the importance of a momentous artistic event. [*Le Monde musical*, June 15, 1914.]

Long's achievement that night was prodigious, playing three concertos in a row. Programming two concertos was not unusual for her, but three was quite an undertaking, by any standard; and they exhibited very different styles: Saint-Saëns' E-flat opened the program, and d'Indy's *Symphonie sur un chant montagnard* closed it. The Ballade by Fauré came between Debussy's *mélodies* and the Prelude to the fourth act of *Messidor* by Alfred Bruneau. The *Guide Musical* of June 7, 1914 concluded: "Sold-out hall and handsome receipts for an interesting evidence of artistic solidarity."

One may say that this concert officially opened the Debussy chapter in Long's life. Unfortunately, it was to be cruelly interrupted by rising international tension, which culminated on June 28 with the assassination of Archduke Franz Ferdinand in Sarajevo. Debussy and Long had nevertheless agreed on a program, and their work together began on a hot Sunday in July, on the eve of World War I. How excited she must have been when she started to play *L'Isle joyeuse,* with Debussy sitting next to her! "Do not expect a performance!" she said. "You will stop me at the second measure!"[6] *L'Isle joyeuse* held a special place in the composer's heart. He had written it during the summer of 1904, during his first idyllic trip to Jersey with Emma Bardac, shortly after he had left his first wife, Lilly. Long worked on the piece with Debussy on many occasions.

Long had vivid memories of Debussy's beautiful home, at 24 Square du Bois-de-Boulogne. Since his marriage to Emma Bardac in 1905, his financial situation had improved, and Debussy could enjoy the comfort and luxury of which he had always been so fond. He loved flowers, and his living room was always filled with red roses. He would say: "How can one write an ample, great work if the mediocrity of your everyday life constrains you at every movement?"[7] Most important of all was his relationship with the resourceful Emma Bardac. During the last years of his life, she was everything to him. Long described her as "a woman of genius, who had a musical intuition to the most extraordinary degree and was the ideal woman for the artist he was. She had always lived around great musicians."[8] For Fauré, whose greatest song cycle, *La Bonne Chanson,* was dedicated to Emma Bardac, "she remained its most moving interpreter."[9]

Emma Bardac bore Debussy's only child, Chouchou, whom he adored and who brought him relief, optimism, and inspiration during the painful war years. In a letter to Jacques Durand dated August 30, 1913, Debussy wrote:

> You cannot imagine the hours filled with anguish I am enduring these days! I can assure you that if I did not have my little Chouchou I would just blow my brains out in spite of the cowardice and ridiculousness of this gesture.[10]

Long had a special affection for the little girl, who was extremely musical and bright. Long found her playing of *The Little Shepherd* "quite moving." Chouchou complained to her: "Papa wants me to practice but he wants complete silence in the house for his work. So how can I?"[11] A few months after Debussy died Alfred Cortot played several of Debussy's Preludes for Emma. When he asked Chouchou whether his performance was anything close to the way her father played, she hesitated and then said, "Yes, but Papa listened more carefully."[12]

Chouchou was an unusually perceptive, sensitive, and mature child. She was only twelve years old when she wrote to her stepbrother, Raoul Bardac, about her father's death:

> My dear Raoul,
>
> Have you received my last telegram? . . . It was I who first thought of sending it to you. I wrote it out and then, thinking that identification papers, which I don't possess because I am a little girl, would have to be produced at the post office, I asked Dolly to have it sent to you. She came here because I asked her to, on account of the completely anguished expression of my poor mother. As soon as she left, Maman was asked to see Papa, for the nurse said he was "very bad." . . . As you may well believe, I understood what was happening. Roger-Ducasse, who was there, said to me: "Come Chouchou, kiss your father." So I immediately thought it was all over. When I went into the room, Papa was sleeping and breathing regularly but in short breaths. He went on sleeping in this way until ten o'clock in the evening, and at this time, sweetly, angelically, he went to sleep forever. What happened afterwards, I cannot tell you. I wanted to burst into a torrent of tears, but I repressed them because of Maman. Alone throughout the night in the big bed with Maman, I was unable to sleep one minute. I developed a temperature, my dry eyes questioned the walls, I could not believe what had happened.
>
> The next day far too many people came to see Maman. . . . Thursday came, Thursday when he was going to be taken away forever! I saw him for the last time in that horrible box—on the ground. He looked happy, oh so happy, and this time I did not have the courage to repress my tears and, as I almost fell over, I couldn't kiss him. At the cemetery, Maman could not have controlled her feelings any better. As for myself, I could think of nothing but one thing: "You must not cry because of Maman." And so I gathered all my courage, which came from where? I do not know. I did not shed one tear. . . . And now it is night forever. Papa is dead. Those three words, I do not understand them, or rather I understand them only too well. And to be here all alone, struggling against the indescribable grief of Maman is frightful. For a few days it made me forget my own grief but now, I feel it all the more poignantly. You, who are so far away, think a little of your poor little sister who would like to hug you so

Joseph de Marliave, Marguerite Long's husband. Bibliothèque Musicale Gustav Mahler, Paris; Marguerite Long Archives.

much and tell you how much she loves you. Can you understand all that I feel and cannot be written? A thousand kisses and all my love from your little sister.

Chouchou

It is unbelievable. I do not know how I go on living, and I cannot believe in the horrible reality.[13]

The Death of Joseph de Marliave

In the summer of 1914, Long's work with Debussy was interrupted after their second meeting. "It was on the last Sunday of July that, sitting next to Madame Debussy, my husband heard me play for the last time."[14] A few days later France's armed forces were mobilized, and on August 3 Germany declared war.

Marliave was called to the army on August 12 and was killed on August 24. But his body was not immediately identified, and his loved ones lived in fear of the worst for weeks. The following correspondence from Alfred Bruneau, composer and friend of the Marliaves, dramatizes their suffering, which lasted well into October. Bruneau wrote to Long on September 18, 1914:

> My dearest friend,
>
> Your moving and painful letter fills us with horrible anguish. Nevertheless, as long as we do not have the absolute certainty of a tragedy, we must keep hope. . . . Who knows if he is not, at this time, prisoner in some German town and unable to get in touch with you? We suffer, we weep with you but we simply cannot believe in the reality of the awful thing. . . . It has not even been two months since the fighting began; and no one can predict when the war will end. We beg you not to lose courage . . . we think of you and of him with all our heart and we hug you sadly and affectionately.
>
> Alfred Bruneau[15]

And again on October 10:

> Dear friend,
>
> We spent the whole day Sunday in the country at Monsieur G.'s, our old *Ministre,* and we asked him if he could get information on the fate of our dear Jo. Here is what he sent me. It does not add anything to what you already know but it does not take anything away either, and our hopes remain strong. . . .
>
> How happy we would be to see a happy ending to your horrible anguish, which we share so vividly.

It was not until October 13, 1914 that the official announcement from Lieutenant Colonel Lallemand was sent to Claire's husband, the Commandant Marquier:

> My dear Commandant,
>
> I have just completed an investigation, at the request of your poor sister-in-law. Alas! I have precise information and there can be no doubt left concerning the fate of Capitaine de Marliave.
>
> I am sending you the report of the Colonel heading the 166th regiment to which Dr. Touraine belonged. With good intentions—although susceptible to criticism—the Doctor picked up the [identification] papers of poor Jo. . . . The colonel of the 166th regiment added that the body of Marliave had been found in a wood and that the doctor did not have time to bury it. The burial took place later. I am giving these details and I write to you directly. . . . It would be too painful for me to give her [Marguerite] this sad and awful information myself.
>
> Lallemand[16]

Lallemand, an avid amateur musician, remained a loyal friend of Long and followed her career.

The news reached Long a month before her 40th birthday, and her husband was only a year older when he was killed. She had lived in fear of his death from August to the middle of October. Bruneau wrote to Long on October 20:

> Dear friend,
>
> We just learned the horrible news. For days and days we could not believe in this tragedy. Poor Jo, so lively, so kind and so brave! We are mourning him with you. If something could soften your suffering, which we share, it would be the idea that he died gloriously to defend us all and save his country. . . . We express to you our profound pain, and we embrace you with the strongest affection of our torn hearts.

It was not only the tremendous loss that devastated Long; it was the lack of a tangible way to come to terms with his passing, and with it, the unsettling hope that a miracle could occur. She was left facing a wide vacuum, without a grave to visit or a last image to recollect. Thus ended eight years of a very happy marriage. Long lived another 52 years, but she never remarried; and those who knew her intimately attested to her everlasting loving memory, devotion, and admiration for Joseph de Marliave. Gabriel Fauré wrote to her on October 24:

> I knew, Madame, the extent of your fears; I learned with great emotion that they were cruelly realized. I pity you quite sincerely in the great sorrow that

strikes you and I beg you to believe in my sentiments of profound compassion and affliction.

Gabriel Fauré

Nadia Boulanger, thirteen years younger than Long, joined those who expressed their sympathy to Long. Writing from Nice on October 27, Boulanger reminds us of the strength of the Long-Marliave union:

> I cannot tell you, Dear Madam, how much I share your pain, and I do not know what words to write to you, feeling how useless they all are in the face of such mourning. . . . Today I have only heartfelt thoughts for you.
>
> There is no consolation, and if the glorious death of your husband will forever surround his memory with pride, the fact remains that from now on his place in your home is left empty, and that nothing can make it less terrible.
>
> I was often told of the profound admiration your missing one had toward you and also what love united the two of you—Alas! You were perhaps not even able to see him one last time.
>
> Nadia Boulanger[17]

The friendship of Roger-Ducasse was also of great moral support to the young widow. He and his sisters† offered her comfort and hospitality in their country home, in Le Taillan, near Bordeaux. In November, shortly after her visit there, Roger-Ducasse wrote to her:

> My dear friend,
>
> Your letter . . . arrived this morning . . . and we were happy to hear from you, even though your news was sad, and distressful. . . . I could picture you returning home and seeing each object as a new source of despair. And how, after two lives as united as yours were, could things bring any consolation? They could only revive your sorrow in reminding you of a memory attached to it. . . . However, I always said to you: you must live, not for yourself, but for the memory of those who have left us. Courage, then, and God knows how much we need it. This is what was written to me by your brother-in-law, François [Marliave's brother], whose touching letter gave me the illusion for a moment that I had received a letter from Jo. How deeply he thinks of you, and what support he will be for you. . . .
>
> What else dear friend? I tried to distract you for a moment. I would much rather announce to you our visit to Paris. . . . I am impatient at the thought that we could help you with our affection and push you, if I may say so, to resume life. . . . We embrace you, all three of us,
>
> Affectionately, R.D.[18]

†Roger-Ducasse lived with his sisters, Yvonne and Marguerite; none of them ever married.

October was the beginning of the academic year at the Paris Conservatoire, and Long had to resume her responsibilities there, as well as her private teaching. But she could not be consoled for the loss of her life's companion. A few months later, Roger-Ducasse expressed growing concern for his friend:

> My dear Marguerite,
>
> We were beginning to despair having not received a word from you. I liked to think that you were reacting a little, that, even if sad, your visit to Belfort and the few moments spent near Jo's brothers would provide comfort and appeasement. I see, alas, that there is nothing of the sort. To blame you? To scold you? It is impossible in the memory of what you have lost. Nevertheless, it is impossible for you to remain in this state and for us to leave you there. Could you come back here for a few days? You were feeling better when you last left. I do not know what to advise you anymore. . . . How can you let yourself drift along. . . . Good bye, my dear Marguerite, all three of us embrace you tenderly,
>
> R.D.

By the end of 1915, more than a year after Marliave's death, Roger-Ducasse seemed a little more optimistic about Long's emotional state:

> My dear friend,
>
> I hope this note will reach you in the morning of this new year, not merely carrying useless wishes but rather, filled with my affection. Although the countryside where you are staying [the Lauragais] is full of painful memories for you, I imagine it was better for you to spend these days far from Paris. I strongly feel the hope that, while keeping his memory intact, life however resumes little by little for you, this life which was altogether his, which he had practically assimilated into yours. . . .
>
> See you soon, dear friend, I kiss you with all my heart.
>
> R.D.

The warmth of Roger-Ducasse's affection for Long grew with the years; and it was Roger-Ducasse, along with Chevillard, who was largely responsible for her eventual return to the stage in 1917.

The uncertainty of Marliave's death followed by the confirmation of this loss seemed to magnify her grief. Long could not find the emotional strength to play the piano in public; she left the concert stage for a few years and retired into a maturing solitude. This abrupt halt in her flourishing career marked the end of what Long herself considered her youth and the happier years of her life. The loss of her husband and the afflictions of the war endured by so many of her musician friends transformed her life and hardened her already well-forged spirit.

Long entered a self-teaching period, during which she read a great deal and filled numerous notebooks on musical subjects. Among these observations, which later fueled many a lecture, one stands out as a symbol of her strength: "What is important is not to spoil your life but to be able to say to yourself: I did all I could. It is the only thing that can bring a little happiness."[19] She believed that sincerely, and her life is an illustration of this statement. She tried to communicate this belief to her disciples. Her three years of relative reclusion prepared her for the scope her career was to take in the 1920s and 30s, and the climax it was to reach in the late 1940s and the 1950s. "Faire face," became her guiding motto: to brave a challenge, to confront a situation with determination.

Return to the Stage

Thanks to the friendly and professional support of her colleagues, Long returned to the stage in April 1917 after a 32-month silence. As her career resumed, her activity increased. The following three years witnessed important new premières, among them Ravel's *Tombeau de Couperin* and Debussy's Fantaisie for piano and orchestra, which brought Long close to Debussy and his wife again. For several months, they pursued the work started in the summer of 1914. Finally, in 1920, Long's now-universally recognized artistry led to her promotion from a Classe Préparatoire to a Classe Supérieure at the Conservatoire.

The musicians we have to thank for encouraging Long to return to the stage in the spring of 1917 are Gabriel Pierné,* Camille Chevillard, and Roger-Ducasse.

Pierné and Chevillard were directors of the Colonne and Lamoureux orchestras respectively. During the war, while many of the players were mobilized, the two orchestras were merged, providing Paris with a full ensemble which could play regularly during the dark years. Pierné and Chevillard alternated in conducting Sunday concerts. They persuaded Long to play at one of their benefit concerts for prisoners of war, which was scheduled at the Salle Gaveau on April 8, 1917. Chevillard confirmed the engagement in his characteristic playful manner:

Tuesday the Third
My dear friend,

You have quite a recalcitrant telephone!!!!! Do not forget that you are to play under my skillful direction (as the critics say) next Sunday. We will rehearse Saturday at 10:30. . . .

Affectionately, your Camille Chevillard[20]

Long, who held him in high regard, remembered with joy one of his many colorful remarks: "I am so afraid of thunderstorms that when I conduct the Pastoral Symphony [by Beethoven] I feel rather uneasy."[21]

This time the two conductors shared the program; Pierné led the all-Russian first half, consisting of works by Stravinsky, Rimsky-Korsakov, and Mussorgsky; and Chevillard conducted the all-French second half, which included Debussy's *La Mer* (premiered by Chevillard in 1905) and a piece by Braunstein, a composer who had died at the front. As a grand finale, Long was the soloist in d'Indy's *Symphonie Cévenole:* "I do not believe it is possible to interpret the *Symphonie Cévenole* by V. d'Indy with a more complete understanding of the work than did Long . . . her personal success was great" (*Le Courrier musical*, May 1917).

One can only imagine with what emotions Long walked onstage again, to play a benefit for prisoners of war while still mourning the loss of her husband. The next year Chevillard invited her again, this time to play Beethoven's "Emperor" Concerto with the still-combined Colonne-Lamoureux orchestra. This concerto was new to Long's repertoire, and her first public performance of it on February 3, 1918 proved a success. She would play this work many times throughout her career, and she later recorded it with Charles Münch* and the Société des Concerts.

During the war years, Roger-Ducasse corresponded regularly with Long. His letters were lengthy, cheerful, conversational, and intended to break the pianist's solitude. At the same time, he hoped strongly that Long would recover from her tragedy, and to that end, he never missed a chance to encourage her to resume her flourishing career.

My dear friend,

Suzanne tells us that you started practicing a little again. That makes me very happy, for nowhere will you find such a desire to live again; I say live again, for the months you have just been through have been for you as if you did not exist anymore, or rather, as if nothing in you existed anymore. That was neither fairness nor reason, and this is why I am so thrilled to see you return to what may save you.

R.D.[22]

To encourage his friend further, Roger-Ducasse composed two Etudes for her, and asked her to give their first performance at the Société Musicale Indépendante concert of May 1917. Many prominent composers would be present, not only because the S.M.I.'s activity had slowed down during the war but also because the program was promising: Debussy's two-piano suite *En blanc et noir;* Ravel's *Trois Chansons* for unaccompanied choir; and the two very difficult Etudes by Roger-Ducasse, *Sur les sixtes* and *Notes répétées.* The last were so successfully performed by Long, and so much appreciated, that she had to encore the *Notes répétées.* On May 9, 1917, Debussy wrote to Roger-Ducasse, who could not be present at the concert:

Dear friend,

You already know that your two Etudes had a success that one should qualify as considerable, particularly the "Etude for Repeated Notes," which was encored. For my humble part, I have rarely heard such a fulgurant handling of sonorities. . . . Madame Long's fingers seemed to have multiplied, and you owe her an enthusiastic "encore."

Your old friend, very happy C.D.[23]

At that concert Long renewed relations with Debussy. He went up to her afterwards and said: "I would like to feel these arms and find out of what they are made to play and master all this difficult music." To which Emma Debussy added: "And we will expect you for lunch tomorrow."[24]

Resumed Collaboration between Debussy and Long

Debussy and his wife were planning to spend the summer of 1917 in Saint-Jean-de-Luz, in the south of France, near the Spanish border. Long was to join them there to pursue her work with Debussy. Even though Debussy was already very ill, his artistic faculties were not diminished in any way. When Long talked about him and his physical appearance, she could almost feel his strong presence in the room:

He had fuzzy hair, burning eyes and a reserved gaze, an almost feline demeanor. His voice was contained, his speech slow with an occasional sudden dash in his

> voice, full of resonance. He loved nature with ardent sensuality: "Listen to the sea, it is the most musical of things," he would exclaim.[25]

The sea *(la mer)* was a lifelong fascination for Debussy. He talked or wrote about it quite often, particularly in his abundant correspondence with Jacques Durand, his friend and publisher.

The summer of 1917 was a painful time for Long and Debussy, and both found relief and consolation in their work and in music. The war devastated Debussy. On August 8, 1914 he wrote to Durand:

> My dear Jacques,
>
> . . . All that makes my life intensely troubled. . . . I am nothing but a poor atom rolled by this horrible cataclysm; what I do seems miserably small to me! . . . It even brings me to envy Satie, who will seriously take care of defending Paris in the role of Corporal.[26]

Debussy was also fighting his own war with cancer. Long, however, was regaining her strength, and it was during that summer that she learned a great deal of Debussy's music: *Images* Book I, *Estampes,* several *Preludes,* his recent *Etudes,* and *Pour le Piano.* Debussy wrote with scrupulous accuracy. He carefully marked his scores in great detail and expected interpreters to respect his directions faithfully. He often said, each time with equal outrage: "There are people who write music, people who edit it, and some pianists who do what they feel like!"[27] He made another of his famous statements after an "artist of genius" was suggested for the role of Mélisande: "A faithful interpreter is all I need."[28]

During the summer months, Long tried to learn Debussy's way, *his* piano technique. She believed he had revolutionized piano music: "We never listened to or played the piano after Debussy in the same way as we did before him. . . . He was an incomparable pianist."[29] His hands were deep into the keys, but always very gentle, creating a wide range of colors. Without any harshness ever ("one must forget that a piano has hammers" was his well-known remark), his sound was always full and intense, yet keeping to the dynamic range between *pianississimo* and *forte.* Within that range, he never lost the subtleties of his harmonic palette. His ideal was Chopin's art, and like his Polish predecessor, whom he revered infinitely, Debussy believed in the importance of the pedal: "The pedal is a sort of respiration."[30] Long insisted that to understand Debussy's piano music fully, she had to learn his own technique, by observing and listening to his playing and by receiving his demanding coaching. Debussy was intransigent: "Pianists' fifth fingers are such an 'ear-sore.' " What he meant was that he disliked melodies emphasized at the expense of harmony. Harmony was for him the essence, and melody should be part of it, blending in but never dominating.

Debussy abhorred the label "Impressionist" when it referred to him. Not particularly fond of the Impressionist painters, he revered most Turner and Whistler. For Debussy, music was never intended to depict a scene but to express man's intimate emotional response to a particular environment. Titles were important to him, but he forbade one to take them literally: that was not their object, and he usually chose them after the pieces were composed. Titles, like the music, evoked an impression, a mood, or a sensual perception. After hearing a pianist play one of his Preludes, *Les collines d'Anacapri,* he remarked: "It's not bad, but it is too gypsy and not Neapolitan enough."[31] When Long played *Jardins sous la pluie* for him, he would demand: "More sun, please! It is about children dancing a round in the Luxembourg gardens [in Paris]. The rain stopped. Now there is beautiful sunshine."[32] Clearly, he meant to suggest a mood different from that of a grayish, drizzly garden in the rain. But more important, it explains the character of the piece, which certainly sparkles more than it drizzles. Indeed, Long's recording of *Jardins sous la pluie* reflects this "sparkle," particularly in her choice of tempo. *Bruyère* (Heather), as another example, evoked for him the strong fragrance of tall pine trees and forests. "*That* is Bruyère! And not those tiny little flowers . . . that I hate!" he said.[33] These flowers were associated in his mind with the depth and smells of forests.

During her Saint-Jean-de-Luz sojourn, Long was preparing for a concert of the Société Nationale on November 10, 1917. The concert celebrated the resumption of the Société's activity, which had stopped for three years, because of the war. It was an occasion to gather many composers, regardless of "clan": d'Indy, George Hüe, Pierre de Bréville, Roger-Ducasse, Debussy, Alfred Bruneau, Henri Duparc, and Fauré. Included in a large program of chamber music was the première of Fauré's Second Violin Sonata, performed by Lucien Capet and Alfred Cortot. The piece was highly acclaimed, as were its interpreters. Long gave the première of Roger-Ducasse's *Variations sur un Choral* and also played two Etudes by Debussy: *Pour les arpèges composés* and *Pour les cinq doigts.*[34] Impressed by the technical difficulty of the Etudes, *Le Courrier musical* wrote:

Pour les arpèges composés and *Pour les cinq doigts*, of a prodigious difficulty, are curiously wrought and interestingly colored . . . it is impossible to play them with more lightness . . . more charm and clarity than did Mme. Long, who also performed the *Variations* by Ducasse with a thorough knowledge of sonorities. [November 15, 1917.]

On the eve of the concert, Long went to play for Debussy one last time. He was very ill by then, his condition having worsened since the summer. He tried to dedicate his photo to her that night, but he could merely write her name faintly. He could not attend the concert the next day. His wife tried to go, but she missed the performance for reasons that are not clear:

Dear Madame,

I just got back from the Conservatoire with the huge disappointment of not having been able to hear you. . . . In spite of the bad weather, the distance, my bronchitis, and above all the bad health of the master [Debussy], who has been bedridden for two days, I really wanted to go to this concert and here I am empty handed!

I am sure you played deliciously . . . and you can guess all my regrets. . . . These two Etudes that I love, these Variations I would have liked so much to hear. . . . Well, you will forgive me, I hope. But I am still not consoled from this mishap. I am doing all I can to fight the bad cold which wants to take hold of my poor husband—but I fear not being able to succeed.

All my faithfully admiring thoughts to you.

Emma Claude Debussy[35]

Emma Debussy's letter confirms her husband's bad health; Debussy died on March 25, 1918, four and a half months later. Long did not see him very often after that concert, but her friendship with Emma Debussy outlived the composer. Numerous letters from Emma to Marguerite bespeak their mutual admiration and growing affection. Emma could not be consoled on the death of Debussy but she found a sympathetic soul in Long:

I looked for this little intimate photograph for you—taken by me (very badly) "at our home." . . . You leave me so many things. Memories add up one by one and the chain will become all the more precious. I have lost too much to be consoled—and you think like me—I will tell you almost nothing, for this permanent anguish crushes me too hard. You will feel, I hope, all the affectionate recognition I owe you for what you allow me to listen to so marvelously. I will give you roses. Who would deserve them more than he (except you), and he loved them so much!

Claude Debussy, in a photograph inscribed to Long on November 9, 1917, the last time she played for him. Bibliothèque Musicale Gustav Mahler, Paris; Marguerite Long Archives.

I keep preciously all that you entrusted to me. And now we must "smile" even on this day doubly sad. See you soon!
Profoundly yours,

Emma Claude Debussy.

In the absence of Debussy, Emma advised Long in matters concerning her husband's music. In a letter written late in 1918, Emma made suggestions for the program of a concert at the Philarmonique:

> Certainly, dear friend, you are doing too much. . . . Try to fit a little rest in between your work or you will not survive! Forgive me for telling you all this but it is only because of my affection for you that I take the liberty of giving you advice.
>
> At the Philarmonique why don't you play *Mouvement* and a Prelude if the *Hommage* [à Rameau] is lost on these people. But do not give them the Etudes, which you play like an angel because they will not understand a thing! Don't you think? Chevillard asks me to please go hear him. I will see how that can be arranged. If you like, I will keep you posted. . . . A thousand tender thoughts and hope to see you soon.
>
> Emma C.D.

At the end of the summer of 1918, Long was back in Saint-Jean-de-Luz to play several concerts under the auspices of the Société Charles Bordes. *Le Courrier musical* of November 1, 1918 summarized the wealth of events, including recitals by Francis Planté, Paul Loyonnet, Ricardo Viñes, and Long. There were several chamber music sessions, and Long's performance of the Franck Piano Quintet and the Fauré First Sonata for Violin and Piano received renewed acclaim: "Truly, audience and artists were as one, savoring the rapture of such music" (*Courrier de Bayonne et du Pays Basque,* September 20, 1918). The Schumann A minor Sonata for Violin and Piano and Gustave Samazeuilh's *Fantaisie Elégiaque* for the same duo were also heard. But Long's recital at the Golf-Hotel for the benefit of prisoners of war earned the warmest reception:

> We can consider peerless Marguerite Long's performance of works by Gabriel Fauré, of whom she remains the unrivaled interpreter. . . . It is the master's very genius which palpitates under her fingers. . . . Her rendition of *L'Isle joyeuse* is a genuine sonorous feast, a sort of apotheosis of an elegant orgy. . . . One must mention the real success of the concert: the two-piano arrangement of Liszt's *Mephisto Waltz* with her brilliant pupil, Denise Haas. [*Courrier de Bayonne et du Pays Basque,* September 20, 1918.]

About a year later, Emma alluded to those wonderful concerts, reassuring Long, who could not be there this time:

> Do not regret the Golf-Hotel, or even Saint-Jean [-de-Luz], neither one of which is what it was last year judging from what knowledgeable people have been saying. Your friends, saddened by your absence, will see you soon. . . . Your poor friend ECD—and I keep calling Chouchou. . . . She does not hear me anymore. . . .

The last line of the letter refers to another tragedy that struck the Debussy home. On July 16, 1919, the fourteen-year-old Chouchou died suddenly from diphtheria. It was just over a year since her father's death. Long always felt thankful that this agonizing pain was spared Debussy, who was unhappy if he did not see the daughter he adored every day: "Your poor Papa . . . is quite sad for being deprived for so many days from seeing your pretty little Chouchou face, from hearing your songs, your laughter."[36] For Emma Chouchou's death was a devastating blow:

> Your thoughtfulness is sweet to me, dear friend, and I thank you. But the horrible nightmare in which I live is so deep in me that I do not quite know where I am—it does not matter—nothing matters anymore. She does not live, my only reason to live. So why do I have to stay. She, gone! All her dear projects, all her future, all is dead! How in the world can my damned health endure such suffering? To have lost her, my pretty little girl, whose only wish was to blossom like a beautiful little flower!
>
> It is too, too cruel, too unfair. Forgive me, dear friend, I am in such pain . . . but you loved her and will be able to understand my dreadful agony.
>
> Yours, ECD

Only a month earlier, the Société Nationale had organized a concert in honor of Debussy. The program was designed to review his different styles: the String Quartet, the Cello and Piano Sonata, many songs, and piano music. Ricardo Viñes played *Pour le piano,*† and Long *L'Isle joyeuse, Hommage à Rameau,* and *Mouvement.* In the numerous reviews of this concert, the opinion that Long's style was closest to Debussy's was reiterated many times: "Debussy, minus her [Marguerite Long's] impeccable virtuosity, did not play any differently and there is no other way to execute this music" (*L'Avenir,* June 2, 1919). Since Debussy often played his own music in concert, critics had had a first-hand opportunity to experience his very personal style.[37] The composer Georges Migot wrote: "We believe that, perhaps, in this line of thought, Mme. Long at the piano, and Mme. Croiza for the voice . . . gave the interpretations most faithful to the composer's intentions" (*Le Monde musical,* June 1919). *Le Courrier musical* added:

> Finally, I wish to mention in a special way *Hommage à Rameau, Mouvement* and *L'Isle joyeuse* . . . because they found in Mme. Marguerite Long the interpreter

†Ricardo Viñes had premiered *Pour le piano* in January 1902. He went on to premiere many more of Debussy's works, including both books of *Images, Estampes, Masques, L'Isle joyeuse,* and several Preludes.

> who, thanks to her intuitive understanding of the mind and sensitivity of the composer, was the most capable of performing these pieces in the way he would have done it himself. [June 15, 1919.]

The praise of the one who was truly closest to Debussy's soul and sensitivity certainly meant the most to Long:

> In spite of the hour and my exhaustion I must tell you, my dear, all my affectionate admiration, all my true emotion in hearing you perform so marvelously this adorable music which you knew how to penetrate. The rest of the program was also wonderful. . . . Thank you from my aching heart which you know how to cradle so well! I kiss you tenderly,
>
> Emma

Debussy's posthumous *Fantaisie* for Piano and Orchestra had a tormented history. Written during his tenure at the Villa Medici in 1889, it was supposed to be performed under d'Indy's direction on April 20, 1890 at the Société Nationale. Unhappy with the orchestration, the composer removed the parts from the music stands after the dress rehearsal and cancelled the performance as well as subsequent publication. The work remained dormant for the rest of Debussy's life. The decision in 1919 to publish and give the work its first performance was perceived as an important event, for most musicians had known of the work since its aborted debut 30 years earlier.

Emma Debussy chose the two artists who would bring this new "old work" to the public according to what she believed her husband's wishes would have been. The pianist was to be Long; and the conductor André Messager, to whom Debussy dedicated *Pelléas et Mélisande.* The two had intimately collaborated for the first performances of the opera at the Opéra-Comique in April 1902, and Debussy was deeply grateful to Messager for his fine understanding of such a novel work. A letter from Emma Debussy to Long confirms her choice, which excluded any other conductors for this important première:

> I find myself obliged . . . to correspond with Pierné and [Gustave] Samazeuilh, for both wrote to me this morning and the matter was taken care of by itself since the direction of the *Fantaisie* has been promised to Messager since *last year.*

The work's 30-year history created great curiosity. On December 7, 1919, the day of the première, the Salle Gaveau was sold out, and practically all the major French composers were present. (On the same night, Alfred Cortot performed this *Fantaisie* in Lyon under Witkowski at the Grands Concerts). Dozens of articles were published following the performance; many were not simply reviews but essays written by composers, evaluating the significance of the piece in Debussy's development. The work was very well received; many heard in it premonitions of the composer's *Nocturnes,* in particular *Sirènes,* as well as his String Quartet. Roland Manuel even wrote that "the harmonic color and the melodic shape set the atmosphere of *L'Après-midi d'un Faune* . . . and occasionally *Pelléas*" (*L'Eclair,* December 8, 1919). Many appreciated the role of the soloist, as it blended with the orchestral texture: "the piano *Fantaisie,* contemporary disguise for the old and objectionable concerto, enjoys in our times an unexpected vogue" (*Comoedia,* December 8, 1919). Henri Büsser, although positive about Debussy's piece, was much more opinionated in his review and reminds us of the anticoncerto clan: "There the piano is not the 'barbaric' instrument of ordinary 'concertos,' where most of the time the various pieces are only pretext to the most insipid virtuosity." Others compared it to d'Indy's *Symphonie Cévenole,* in that the piano was treated as an orchestral instrument.

Florent Schmitt expressed many of these opinions in his extensive article of January 1920 in the *Le Courrier musical:*

> The *Fantaisie,* which contains more than brilliant promises, inaugurates, one might say, the mature and definitive Debussy of *L'après-midi d'un Faune, Fêtes, Jeux de Vagues,* of which the orchestra already forecasts the sumptuous color, the transparency, the exquisite *grisaille.* The piano part is treated in a very unusual way, being an integral part of the orchestra in a manner anticipating *Petroushka,* with nothing in common with the aggressive virtuosity of the usual concerto. Mme. Marguerite Long brings to it . . . a remarkable refinement in sonorities which would have thrilled Debussy.

All the reviews praised Long for her sense of color, her search for a wide sound palette, and her sensitivity to Debussy's wish. Composer Gustave Samazeuilh elaborated on the choice of interpreters for this important musical event:

> It was only fair that the honor to present it [the *Fantaisie*] for the first time in public be reserved for the one whose intimate collaboration with the author of *Pelléas* enabled the same author to see his work beautifully realized at the Opéra-Comique. . . . And those who remember how much, in the last years of his life, Debussy appreciated the way she could translate the unique fantasy of

> his music, will not doubt for a moment that the choice of Mme. Marguerite Long . . . would have answered his wish. [*Le Ménestrel*, December 12, 1919.]

Emma Debussy attended the performance, since the choice of artists was hers. Still grieving for both her husband and Chouchou, she could not stay after the performance to greet the musicians. Instead she wrote to Long:

> Forgive me, my dear friend, for having left without coming to see you backstage . . . but I was too distressed to stay any longer. There are no more words to express all that you know how to render with those flying fingers . . . and my emotion was doubled with such a cruel sorrow. Without him—without her—both would have been so completely happy to hear you because I am so *sure* that the beloved Master would have approved of your interpretation and lauded once again your incomparable and fairylike virtuosity. She [Chouchou] admired you so much. And myself, poor "all alone," I thank you from the deepest part of my heart, so harmoniously sore.
>
> Emma Claude Debussy
>
> (Where is the manuscript? I would like to give it to you.)

Long confirms in *Au piano avec Debussy* that Emma Debussy gave her the manuscript of the orchestral score of the *Fantaisie*. (It was probably sold at the auction following Long's death, for it is no longer in the Long Archives.)

Long played this work very often in the early 1920s, throughout France and abroad, where she was recognized as the ambassador of French music. She would typically pair it with Fauré's Ballade. She gave the second and third performances of the *Fantaisie* in Paris, on November 13 and 14, 1920, with Orchestre Colonne conducted by Henri Rabaud,* who was replacing Gabriel Pierné, the orchestra's music director. In the fall of 1920 Rabaud began his tenure as Director of the Paris Conservatoire, succeeding Fauré. A letter from Pierné to Long, dated June 30, 1919, shows how coveted the first performance of the *Fantaisie* was:

> May I ask for your valuable collaboration at one of our concerts in giving the *Fantaisie* of our dear Debussy its first performance? I would like this work to be played by you the first time. . . . If you are willing to answer my wish we can pick dates—I say dates because I am trying out popular concerts on Saturdays between 5 P.M. and 7 P.M. and we should perform this work twice.[38]

Apparently Gabriel Pierné did not realize that Emma Debussy had already decided that André Messager would conduct the première. Pierné therefore programmed the *Fantaisie* during the following season, fall 1920, keeping his original idea of two consecutive performances, on Saturday and Sunday.

A few years later, before one of her tours, Long received the following letter from Emma Debussy:

> I hear, dear friend, that the *Fantaisie* by our poor dear Master will be performed by you in the fall in Geneva. Do not doubt for a minute all the joy and all the confidence that this news brings me. I remember the unique way you had of interpreting the innermost thoughts of the one who appreciated your art so much. . . .
>
> I hope to see you Sunday and tell you again all my faithful admiration.
>
> Emma Claude Debussy

After Debussy's death, Long was respected for her "unique way of interpreting" Debussy's art not only by the musical world but, most important, by the one who was closest to Debussy, who intimately knew the man and his music, and who could genuinely appreciate the faithful rendition of his art.

5

The Postwar Years and the 1920s

The year 1919 symbolized the culmination of Long's collaboration with Debussy in her presentation of the *Fantaisie* for piano and orchestra, but it also marked the beginning of another historical association: that of Marguerite Long and Maurice Ravel.

Le Tombeau de Couperin

On April 11, 1919, Long gave the world première of Ravel's *Le Tombeau de Couperin* at a concert of the Société Musicale Indépendante. The work had been composed mostly during the war and was completed and published in 1917. Ravel had asked Long to attempt a first performance while she was in Saint-Jean-de-Luz, in his native Basque country, in 1918, but as the war was still going on, the idea was abandoned.

To Ravel, *Le Tombeau de Couperin* represented an homage to French music of the eighteenth century, not specifically Couperin. Like Debussy, Ravel was so deeply disturbed by the war that he felt the need to look back to more glorious days. At the same time, the work's apparent freshness and optimism conceals his personal grief, for each movement is dedicated to a friend killed in battle. One of the friends was Joseph de Marliave, Marguerite's husband, who is the dedicatee of the "Toccata," the last movement of the suite. Long remarked that the only hint of tragedy in the piece was a brief moment in the middle of the "Menuet's" Musette, in a powerful crescendo of chords over a G pedal. Long had known and admired Ravel for a long time but had not played his music. *Le Tombeau de Couperin* was her entrance into a new realm (and she later became the dedicatee of Ravel's G major Concerto; see below, pp. 92–94).

The new work and its composer were acclaimed at the S.M.I. and instantly appreciated by the press. In May 1919, *Le Monde musical* wrote:

> The long-awaited *Tombeau de Couperin* was finally performed and acclaimed in a truly triumphant manner, and how well deserved! I tasted with an intense pleasure this recent work by M. Ravel: his art, so delicately French . . . measured in taste and balance like a tragedy by Racine, a fable by La Fontaine or *L'Embarquement pour Cythère* by Watteau, *Le Tombeau de Couperin* will be a classic before long. The audience, delirious, celebrated the composer and his admirable interpreter, Marguerite Long, in a manner that M. Ravel will certainly never forget. . . . One hears a lot about the "Forlane," which was encored the other night. . . . It is so beautiful in its harmonic impertinence, so savory and so refined, with its initial alteration and later its descending tritones highlighted by little appoggiaturas.

In *Liberté,* Gaston Carraud chose to highlight other movements: "*Le Tombeau de Couperin* . . . a fine line between sensitivity and irony, a flavor both old-fashioned and ultramodern which sometimes characterizes M. Ravel. . . . I enjoyed most the 'Prelude,' the 'Fugue,' and 'Menuet.' Another critic picked the "Fugue," "Forlane," and "Toccata" as the three most striking movements. When one adds up all the reviews, each of the six movements was somebody's favorite; and the audience unanimously requested an encore of the "Forlane." It is worth noting the immediate success of the "Fugue," which tends to be less appreciated and even frequently omitted in performance nowadays. Ravel was enthusiastically applauded when he appeared onstage after the performance.

To ensure that this newest gem by Ravel would be known to her neighbors abroad, Long often programmed *Le Tombeau de Couperin* on tour. In 1921, for example, at the Exposition de l'Art Français in Wiesbaden, she gave the first performance in Germany of *Le Tombeau de Couperin,* along with works by Debussy and Roger-Ducasse. Long never recorded this work, which was always associated with her, especially since her performance had the composer's stamp of approval. She played the "Prelude" quite fast, and Ravel used to tell other pianists, "not as fast as Marguerite Long." When she asked him whether that meant she played it too fast, he answered: "No, because with you we can hear all the notes!" But she thought, "How can we ever be sure of that when playing Ravel's music!"[1]

Ravel insisted that the "Forlane" be played in strict tempo, "with a metronome." He complained that the middle section of the "Rigaudon" was always too fast, while the two outer sections needed to be played with very marked rhythm. The tempo of the "Menuet" was tricky. One always has to search for the right tempo for a Ravel minuet, be it the *Menuet Antique,* the "Menuet" from his Sonatine, or this one. Ravel believed that the true minuet form and tempo were those of Beethoven's E-flat major Sonata, Op. 31, No. 3, and that to find the pace for his Minuets, one should refer to Beethoven's. Long felt that even though the "Toccata" presented some technical difficulties, it was the easiest movement of the suite, for its effect was produced simply by playing evenly and strictly in tempo from beginning to end. It did not have all the subtle and delicate pitfalls of the preceding movements.

When Ravel went from his home in Monfort-L'Amaury to the hospital, from which he never returned, everything was left on the piano as he had last seen it. On the music stand was one score, *Le Tombeau de Couperin,* with its naive drawing on the cover in the composer's hand. Why this piece? Was it one that held a special place in Ravel's heart?

The Nineteen-Twenties

The death of Louis Diémer, on December 22, 1919, left an opening for a teacher of a Classe Supérieure at the Conservatoire. This time Long was determined to get the coveted promotion she had been denied eight years earlier. She had the strong support of a whole generation of composers, as well as good results with the pupils of her Classe Préparatoire, who, for the past fourteen years, had been living proof of her pedagogical competence. In spite of some controversy and political difficulties, her promotion was confirmed by the Ministre de l'Instruction Publique et des Beaux-Arts in February 1920, and Long thus became the first woman to be granted a Classe Supérieure at the

Paris Conservatoire (see above, p. 39–40).[†] She was also the first woman to have men in her class, since until the middle of the war, around 1916–17, piano classes were not co-ed, and women professors were not allowed to teach the men's classes!

One has to be French to grasp the significance of such an appointment in France's musical world. It is the supreme form of official recognition: in this case it was even more, since she had overcome her biggest handicap, that of being a woman. And the Conservatoire was hardly receptive to change: the Director, Théodore Dubois, had warned Gabriel Fauré, his all-too-liberal successor, that the Conservatoire was intended to *conserve.*

Long was now 45, and this promotion celebrated the scope of her dual career, that of concert artist and pedagogue. Now that her reputation was solidly established, she undertook new projects. She began organizing and delivering lectures on the music of Fauré and Debussy, as well as other contemporaries, an activity she pursued throughout her life. In 1925, her public master classes were inaugurated at the Salle Erard. They gained an ever-growing reputation for the next 35 years and were an occasion for Long to present her best pupils to the Paris public. The climax of the decade of the twenties was the pressing of her first recording in 1929.

While her concert schedule and teaching responsibilities steadily increased, Long's resolute commitment to contemporary music never flagged. In 1921, Long gave a lecture on Florent Schmitt, Maurice Ravel, and Roger-Ducasse at the newly founded Ecole Normale. She opened her session with an apologia on modern music:

> How many foolish things, empty words have been said about modern music, and how much misunderstanding! For some it is "mathematics," which means absolutely nothing; for others, it is only dissonance, meaning wrong chords, which is even worse.[2]

[†]In all fairness, it must be pointed out that two women had taught advanced classes at the Paris Conservatoire before Long: Louise Farrenc (1804–1875), who was appointed in 1842 and retired on January 1, 1873, had an illustrious career as pianist and composer; and Louise Aglaé Massart (1827–1887), who succeeded Henri Hertz in 1874 and taught at the Conservatoire until her death. However, at that time classes were not designated "Préparatoire" or "Supérieure," but were simply called "Classe de Piano," and women could teach only "Women's Classes." Terminology therefore grants Long the honor of being the first woman to hold that specific title, *and* to have men in her class.

After describing the laws of harmony which govern Classic and Romantic music and which differ with those of contemporary music, Long fervently emphasized the importance of discovering the music of the present:

> Don't today's musicians have thoughts, ideas, themes? Don't they enjoy the pleasure of finding chords, or as one might say today, sound effects? Certainly they do. Our contemporaries think, suffer, love just as much as their most distant ancestors did. . . . Let us look at what their works may contain. And this is what may be the most arduous task because . . . one needs a certain courage and a profound love for music to dare venture into this maze of sharps, flats and naturals, of superposed chords requiring occasionally a third or fourth staff . . . obviously discouraging the most willing from reading their works. But do not despair! Others have discovered virgin forest . . . and they returned all the stronger, proud and mature. . . . Let us study this music and, solidly armed, we will be able to defend it.[3]

She continued to defend modern music, and to appear regularly at concerts of the Société Nationale and the Société Musicale Indépendante.

In March 1920, the Société Nationale programmed Fauré's Second Violin Sonata, played by Georges Enesco and Marcel Ciampi, and Ravel's *Histoires Naturelles,* accompanied by Alfredo Casella. Long gave the first performance of *Le chant de la Mer,* a large piano piece in three parts by Gustave Samazeuilh. The three movements—"Prélude," "Clair de lune au large," and "Tempête et lever du soleil sur les flots,"—were dedicated to Francis Planté, Long, and Alfred Cortot respectively. Planté, who had been given the score at the same time as Long, was said to have exclaimed: "How can she be already performing this piece when I am still putting in the fingerings!"[4] The concert attracted a large audience, "all that are of note among Parisian composers, critics, virtuosos and enlightened amateur musicians."[5] *Le chant de la Mer,* a rather complex work, was well received by critics; and the composer expressed his gratitude for Long's extreme musicality, technical mastery, and profound understanding of the work in *La République* (March 23, 1920).

At the S.M.I., several weeks later, Long presented two new works by Roger-Ducasse, *Seconde Arabesque* and *Sonorités,* and four Preludes by Leo Sachs. Roger-Ducasse was still close to Long and the memory of her late husband, whose strong presence was still felt six years after his death. In April 1920 he wrote:

> Durand told me that you agreed to play *Le Tombeau [de Couperin]* at his house on the 4th, along with my Quartet. I am thrilled, and I remember that the last time you heard it, which was the première, I believe, Jo was there and heard it too. I remember his emotion during the Adagio, and this Adagio means a great deal to me, for it had found the way to his heart. There are a few such works, which bring back to us the memory of loved ones, and isn't that what gives them . . . a special meaning?
>
> R.D.[6]

Roger-Ducasse's Quartet for piano and strings was dedicated to Long and had been premiered on March 26, 1912 at the Concerts Durand. The composer had played the piano part.

The anniversary of Marliave's death, August 24, was faithfully remembered by her friends, especially Roger-Ducasse, who sent her a thoughtful letter every year. On August 22, 1921 he wrote

> My dear friend,
>
> I would like my wishes to reach you today, and you to know how much my thoughts are surrounding you; I relive with you the tragic hours spent in Bordeaux, inquiring in vain and without much hope. For a very long time my heart refused to admit that Jo had left us. . . . Every time I finish any composition, I immediately ask myself: would he have liked it?[7]

Her new promotion at the Conservatoire not only put Long in the spotlight but triggered renewed confidence and a desire for challenge. She decided to schedule two consecutive solo recitals in April 1921. In spite of her frequent concert appearances with orchestras or at new music programs, she had not given a full solo recital in Paris since her all-Fauré program at the Salle Erard in 1909. In a lengthy article-review, Roger-Ducasse praised her absence from the solo recital:

> In a time when every little pianist out of the Conservatoire feels obliged to climb onto a stage . . . the true artists work in a long silence which, thanks to the collaboration with great masters, strengthens and matures their understanding, their technique and their talents. [*Le Monde musical,* May 1921.]

The two programs were carefully chosen, saving a place of honor for the two composers with whom Long was most closely associated: Fauré and Debussy. On April 23, 1921, she opened with Beethoven's Op. 53, the

"Waldstein" Sonata, followed by a group of Chopin pieces: the Barcarolle, three Etudes, and the Fantaisie. Debussy's *Images,* Book I; two Preludes; *Masques;* and *L'Isle joyeuse* ended the evening. The second concert on April 30, opened with Mozart's D major Sonata, K. 576, followed by Shumann's *Kreisleriana.* The second half was all Fauré: *Thème et Variations,* the Sixth and Seventh Nocturnes, and the Third Valse-Caprice, which closed the program on a lighter note. Long was asked to repeat Chopin's Fantaisie, as an encore.

By any standard, these two programs were both musically and pianistically very demanding. Long's success was complete, and the reviews were ecstatic. Detailed essays on the performance of each work attempted to emphasize her aesthetic sense and deep understanding of each composer. Her technique was so strong that it was not even discussed; instead one was enraptured by her control of sound, of dynamics, of line, and of harmonic color. Her remarkable skill in using the pedal contributed in large part to the clarity and warmth of her sound.

Long's hard work and strong commitment in all aspects of her life led to many national decorations. The first, which was announced on October 12, 1921, six months after her triumph at the Salle Erard, was Chevalier de la Légion d'Honneur.

> This distinction, while honoring one of the greatest pianists of our time, crowns the beautiful and persevering effort of an artist, dedicated as much to the cause of Classical music as she is to the propagation of the young French school. . . . Through her teaching as well as her concert tours, she has never ceased to be the most ardent promoter of our music. [*Comoedia,* October 17, 1921.]

Throughout the 1920s Long regularly appeared with all three orchestras: Lamoureux under Chevillard, Colonne under Pierné, and the Société des Concerts du Conservatoire under Philippe Gaubert. Schumann's A minor Concerto, Franck's *Symphonic Variations,* Beethoven's C minor and "Emperor" Concertos, Fauré's Ballade, and Debussy's *Fantaisie* formed the core of her repertoire. At this time she also added Chopin's F minor Concerto, which was to become one of "her" pieces. Many of her pupils, now mature pianists themselves, told me with emotion about the magic of her Larghetto: "No one has been able to replace her in the second movement of Chopin's F minor Concerto," claimed several of them. Another distinction about "her" Chopin Concerto was that she played a version that had been re-orchestrated for her by André Messager, who conducted the first performance of it in 1925. The second performance, a few weeks later, was conducted by Gabriel Pierné: "In the Larghetto, performed by Marguerite Long with admirable and moving control in the most serene simplicity, there was a minute of absolute beauty which sent a little shudder of ecstacy through the hall."[8] Apparently, this concerto was not popular in pianists' repertoires in the first decades of the twentieth century, for Long's revival with Messager's orchestration—qualified as "a *tour de force* of tact and elegance" by Vuillermoz*—was welcomed with enthusiasm. So much so that during the year 1927 alone, Long performed the work three times in Paris, once with each of its orchestras.

In 1922, a new collaboration began between Long and the great singer Jeanne Raunay. Raunay was the dedicatee of Fauré's *Chanson d'Eve,* which she sang many times, beginning with its première in 1910, when she was accompanied by the composer. She and Fauré gave many performances together of his music, including the sublime *La Bonne Chanson.* She was definitely part of Fauré's chosen inner circle of musicians. Long and Raunay, both renowned for their dedication to French contemporary music, gave a joint recital in January 1923 at the Salle Erard honoring Fauré, Debussy, Ravel, and Caplet. In addition to assisting Raunay in several songs—Debussy's *Il pleure dans mon coeur* and *Recueillement,* Caplet's *Notre Chaumière,* Fauré's *Le Parfum Impérissable,* and Ravel's *Mélodies Populaires Grecques*—Long played two Etudes by Debussy, Ravel's recently premiered *Le Tombeau de Couperin,* and Fauré's Second Nocturne, Fifth Barcarolle, and Fifth Impromptu. The press enthusiastically remarked on the subtle musical affinity between the two musicians.

Sharing the same musical fervor, Long and Raunay gave another recital in June 1924, also in the Salle Erard. The entire program was dedicated to Schumann and Fauré: Fauré was often referred to as the "French Schumann" for his prolific and inspired song production. Raunay sang "her" cycle, *La Chanson d'Eve,* and six Schumann *Lieder.* Long played Fauré's Second Barcarolle, Fourth Nocturne, and Third Valse-Caprice and Schumann's *Kreisleriana.* "The two artists knew how to catch the moment where intelligence meets the heart," wrote Georges Migot (*Le Monde musical,* June 1924). He praised Long's sense of phrasing and sound in *Kreisleriana,* which gave an architectural balance to these spontaneous and impassioned pages.

The music of Fauré and Debussy continued to hold a place of honor in Long's career. Her work with the composers not only authenticated her interpretations but also added another dimension to her teaching. She never missed a chance to play their music, whether at an anniversary concert or on some other occasion. Her personal estrangement from Fauré in the last decade of the composer's life in no way diminished Long's wholehearted dedication to his oeuvre. In January 1925, two months after his death, Long gave a performance of the Second Piano Quartet, in G minor, at the Société Nationale. This work held a special place in her heart. She was to play and record it with Jacques Thibaud in 1940, during World War II (see below, pp. 126–27). She always performed as much music of Fauré as possible, in addition to teaching it to her students, in the hope that he would gain the same recognition that Debussy and Ravel had. She believed Fauré's timing had hurt him: squeezed between the French fascination for the powerful Wagnerian phenomenon in the late nineteenth century and the magic spell cast by Debussy and Ravel, Fauré's highly refined and original art had been eclipsed. In addition to her frequent appearances with the Ballade, in chamber groups, or in new music concerts (S.N.M. and S.M.I.) where single or small groups of pieces were played, Long set out to program all-Fauré recitals periodically.

The first one, on May 19, 1925, half a year after the composer's death, exhibited many facets of Fauré's music. Paul Landormy* wrote:

> There is not only the pretty, the graceful and the elegant Fauré. There is the Fauré impassioned, ardent, dramatic, somber, with strange visions. It is this Fauré that Marguerite Long intended to have us discover the other night. . . . She tried to express certain exalted moments of the Master's soul with a warmth and intensity which she had never manifested to this degree before. . . . Under her fingers, the Barcarolles took on a grandeur one would never have suspected. [*La Victoire,* May 26, 1925.]

The program included the Second, Fourth, and Sixth Nocturnes, the Second and Fifth Impromptus, the Third Valse-Caprice, and the Ballade, for which Roger-Ducasse played the orchestra part on a second piano. It was indeed a cross-section of Fauré's stylistic periods. "Let us hope that Fauré's beauty will be so revealed to us every year by her in whom he lives again," wrote *Le Temps,* May 31, 1927.

Two years later, on May 18, 1927, Long repeated the program, making a few changes and adding Cortot's transcription for two hands of the *Dolly* Suite. Many critics deplored the scarcity of Fauré's works in pianists' repertoires. As one of them put it:

> What place do Fauré's piano pieces occupy on concert programs? None, or almost none. . . . Marguerite Long, in evoking those magnificent pages, as only she can do, gives us both exquisite pleasure and an example which should prove fecund. [*L'Intransigeant,* May 24, 1927.]

Can one say that Long's efforts paid off? Certainly, in France today, certain works by Fauré are considered part of the standard piano repertoire. They figure regularly on recital programs and as competition requirements. Long's dedication to this cause was publicly recognized: "In the long run, the role Marguerite Long has chosen for herself will acquire a historical significance" (*Chantecler,* May 28, 1927).

In the decade following Debussy's death, Long was often solicited to give all-Debussy recitals as well. In May 1925, at the Salle Erard—"this hall which alone stands as a living vestige of the grand epoch of romantic virtuosos" (*Le National,* May 27, 1925)—the program was representative of Debussy's stylistic periods, from the early suite *Pour le piano* to the Etudes of 1915. In between, Long played Book I of *Images, L'Isle joyeuse, Masques,* and four Preludes:

> The elite crowded into this temple of music to receive the quintessence of an exemplary interpretation. . . . The art and playing of Mme. Long is not unrelated to the marvelous art of Frederic Chopin: elegant phrasing, runs deliciously *legato,* airy, extremely velvety, notes subtly brought out and clearly heard. . . . These minutes of genuine music and of remarkable piano playing . . . will remain forever engraved in our memory. In the midst of a wave of concerts for the "Grande Saison de Paris," the recital given by Marguerite Long and devoted to Debussy stands out as a gem. [*Le National,* May 27, 1925.]

A similar program was announced for May 14, 1928, in the same hall, in observance of the tenth anniversary of Debussy's death. To the eyes and ears of the musical world, Long embodied the Debussyan tradition. The aging Francis Planté responded to this concert from a distance, since he could not be there in person. His youthful spirit sparkled through these lines, dated May 29, 1928, from his home in Saint-Avit par Mont-de-Marsan:

> Dear wonderful artist and so perfect friend,
>
> How much I was *touched* by your good letter and how happy I would have been to applaud you in person at your *Debussy Festival!*
>
> Thank you for the interesting program: I did not know the four Preludes at all. . . . *L'Isle joyeuse,* I know it well . . . on the other hand I threw myself on the two Etudes, which I did not know either. . . .

> Your energy is remarkable. . . . It is with all my heart that I think of you with tenderness and admiration.
> Your very old friend who has just entered his ninetieth year,
>
> Francis Planté.[9]

It would seem that Planté, retired in his southern home, discovered some of Debussy's late piano music through Long.

On November 10, 1928 she made her debut with Ernest Ansermet, then in his 40s, playing Debussy's *Fantaisie* at the Théâtre des Champs-Elysées. Roger-Ducasse (who was a close friend of Debussy) reminded his readers of a comment the composer had made after one of Long's concerts: "How fortunate to have at last found an interpreter who will not betray us and who, when I am no longer here, will play my music according to my intentions and my wishes."[10]

Long's First Recordings

Long thought of the phonograph as a musical stimulant and an ideal means of musical propaganda. She also valued its use by students and professionals, for it enabled them to hear their masters and learn a great deal from other artists' performances. She often wished she could have heard Clara Schumann's playing.

Long made her first recording in 1929; the piece was Chopin's F minor Concerto in André Messager's orchestration, with Philippe Gaubert conducting the Orchestre de la Société des Concerts. It proved to be a tremendous success: "And finally, we have Chopin's Concerto in F minor by Marguerite Long, who has made a triumphant entrance into the studio with an exceptional recording" (*Le Progrès civique,* March 15, 1930). In an age when recording the piano was still an engineering puzzle—it was difficult to reproduce the sound faithfully and minimize distortion—critics made the claim that "Mme. Marguerite Long is certainly the artist whose piano playing records the best" (*Paris-Midi,* August 16, 1930). Vuillermoz described her first recording as

> a milestone in the history of piano recording. . . . It is admirable for its clarity, its cleanness, its contrasting sonorities and its life. . . . At the first attack, the fidelity to the actual piano sound and its brilliance . . . simply astonish you. [*Le Progrès civique,* March 15, 1930.]

Within the year this recording was awarded the newly instituted Grand Prix du Disque, making Marguerite Long, Chopin, and Columbia its first recipients.[11] Another, the equally successful, engraving of Chopin's music soon followed: "Still moved by the Chopin Concerto, we are now blessed with the F minor Fantasy" (*L'Echo d'Alger,* April 23, 1930).

It comes as no surprise that the next work to be recorded by Long was Fauré's Ballade for piano and orchestra, conducted by Philippe Gaubert. "Fauré's Ballade: two splendid records that recall by their perfection the celebrated Chopin F minor Concerto, which remains the most genuine jewel of our pianistic discography" (*Edition musicale vivante,* July 1930). Close to thirty reviews welcomed the initiative. "Not only is the acoustical quality of this record first class, but its style and interpretation make it a collector's item," wrote Vuillermoz in *Excelsior* on July 20, 1930. In addition to praising the recording itself, critics described at length the pianist's unique gift for this music: "How many pianists exist on this planet who can give us such a penetrating and faithful page of Fauré's music?" (*Edition musicale vivante,* July 1930).

Most of Long's discography was recorded by Columbia in the following decade. Among the highlights are the Ravel G major Concerto, which was pressed immediately after its first performance on January 14, 1932, and Milhaud's First Piano Concerto. Beethoven's C minor and "Emperor" Concertos were recorded with the Orchestre de la Société des Concerts, conducted by Felix Weingartner and Charles Münch respectively. Later, Long made a stunning recording of d'Indy's *Symphonie sur un chant montagnard,* with the Orchestre Colonne conducted by Paul Paray.

Nine concertos and a number of solo and chamber works (mainly by Fauré) constitute a respectable list of recordings for an artist of her epoch, but Long did not record two crucial pieces that were always associated with her and which she premiered: Debussy's *Fantaisie* for Piano and Orchestra and Ravel's *Le Tombeau de Couperin.* The reasons for these regretable omissions are not clear. The scarcity of recordings of her Classic and Romantic repertoire, as well as of Debussy's solo piano music, is equally regretable.

6

The 1930s: Marguerite Long and Maurice Ravel

In 1930, Long was 55, and her career was still on an ascending curve. She had made her first recordings, and her prominence in France's musical life was unchallenged. The decade of the 1930s was to be rich in every aspect.

The year 1932 sealed the Long-Ravel collaboration, with the creation of the G major Concerto, followed by a tour throughout Europe, where the new work was presented with Long at the piano and Ravel on the podium. In the same year she embarked for Brazil under the auspices of the French government. Shortly afterward came her collaboration with Darius Milhaud, who dedicated his First Piano Concerto to her, entrusting her also with its first performance, in 1934.

Long's career was punctuated with national honors in the form of promotions within the order of Légion d'Honneur. It was also celebrated at the Universal Exhibition of 1937, where seventeen composers contributed to two collections of pieces to be played by her pupils during the Exhibition. Finally, her influence as a pedagogue was now clear, as she was reaching the end of her third decade at the Paris Conservatoire and launching Premier Prix laureates into the world. The audience at her annual series of public master classes was steadily growing, as was the popularity of her lectures; and her student recitals attracted conductors, composers, and critics alike.

Maurice Ravel and Long in Saint-Jean-du-Luz, 1935. Bibliothèque Gustav Musicale Mahler, Paris; Marguerite Long Archives.

Ravel's G Major Piano Concerto

The 1931–32 season and the première of Ravel's G major Piano Concerto was a milestone in Long's life and career. At a musical gathering in the home of Madame de Saint-Marceau, Ravel told Long: "I am writing a concerto for you. Do you mind if it ends pianissimo and with trills?" "Of course not!" she replied.[1] But when he brought her the manuscript on November 11, 1931, she saw to her great surprise that it ended *fortissimo* and in ninths!

Long had known Ravel for many years, for he too was a friend of her husband, Joseph de Marliave. Their musical association went back to 1910, when Ravel had asked her to select two young students from her school to give the première of *Ma Mère l'Oye* at the inaugural concert of the Société Musicale Indépendante on April 20, 1910 (see above, p. 37). The two little girls were Jeanne Leleu and Geneviève Durony. Long remembered the way Ravel worked with them: "He loved children, and he was so kind to them. It was for them a memorable experience."[2] Nine years later the première of *Le Tombeau de Couperin* took place at the S.M.I. And on March 17, 1927, at a benefit concert at the Conservatoire, Long and Ravel played *Ma Mère l'Oye* together.

Ravel originally planned to give the first performance of the G major Concerto himself. He thought he was a better pianist than he really was. Long said laughingly: "If he were told that *Daphnis and Chloé* was worthless but that he was a great pianist, he would have been content!"[3] But as the Concerto was taking its final shape, Ravel realized that he could not do it justice, and he asked Long to perform it instead. The day he brought over the manuscript remained for her one of the most moving moments of her life: "When I read through this concerto, little by little and reached the subline 'Andante,' at the entrance of the English horn, which plays the opening phrase above the piano's thirty-second-note accompaniment, it was so extraordinary that tears streamed down my cheeks."[4] It must have been an extraordinary feeling to be the first to discover this work, particularly that magic moment. A short time later, Long told Ravel of the divine beauty of the "Andante," of hearing the melody, particularly after the excitement of the first movement, of playing "this long phrase, which simply flows." "Simply flows!" exclaimed Ravel, "I wrote it measure by measure and nearly died from it!"[5]

The "Andante" exemplifies Ravel's supreme craftmanship. His music never sounds overwrought; it always breathes inspiration and freshness. Stravinsky, among others, has compared his music to the work of a "Swiss clockmaker" (Ravel's father was a Swiss engineer), because of the perfection of his art and the precision with which he prepared his manuscripts. Long attested to the fact that Ravel hated this comparison. He could not bear the reference to clocklike precision in his music. While he was indeed an extremely meticulous composer, Ravel's music is sensual and voluptuous, lyrical and sensitive above all.

The première of the G major Concerto took place on January 14, 1932 at the Salle Pleyel. The program was composed of Ravel works exclusively, performed by the Orchestre Lamoureux. Ravel conducted the new Concerto, *Pavane pour une Infante Défunte,* and *Boléro*—a piece he grew so tired of that when Long would hum the tune in his presence he would snap: "Quit singing that." She would retort: "Oh! my friend, you shouldn't have composed it, then!"[6] The rest of the program, consisting of *Daphnis et Chloé* (second suite), *La Valse,* and *Rapsodie Espagnole,* was led by a young Portuguese conductor, Pedro de Freitas-Branco. Long was uneasy before the concert, for she had had the manuscript for scarcely two months, during which she had to maintain her concert schecule as well as teach her class at the Conservatoire, and she had not seen the orchestral score until close to the performance. But the hall was sold out, and the new work was highly acclaimed. Important musical personalities came from near and far for this sensational concert. Ravel, usually quite private and discreet, was exuberant as he witnessed his own triumph. Personal interviews with members of the audience contained ecstatic reports of the grandeur of the event.

Ravel and Long left almost immediately to tour throughout Europe with the new work. The first stop was Brussels a week later, on January 21, 1932; then Holland, Austria, Germany, Rumania, Hungary, and Poland.[7]

Long worried about each performance, for Ravel was not a good conductor. He followed the piano part rather than the orchestral score; and for this piece, such a practice could be particularly dangerous. All the instrumental parts are very difficult, the ensemble is tricky, and Ravel did not know how to rehearse the orchestra. According to Long, "There were a few scary moments, but overall we had a good time."[8] Ravel was always cheerful, no matter what happened. Everywhere, his reception was grand, and some audiences simply adored him as the greatest living composer. In Holland (Amsterdam, Rotterdam, Haarlem, The Hague), the minute he appeared on stage, he was given a standing ovation. Austria, in an effort to distinguish itself from Germany, had a great fondness for French music, in particular Debussy and Ravel. The fondness was reciprocated by Ravel, who thoroughly enjoyed his visits to Vienna. When he went shopping in a department store for a new wallet, the saleswoman recognized him and insisted that he accept the wallet as her gift. Ravel thought, "Where else in the world would you find a shop clerk who not only plays *Jeux d'eau,* but recognizes its composer, and offers him her merchandise as a present?"[9] Thanks to the Ravel Concerto, Long met Richard Strauss, who conducted the work with the Vienna

Philharmonic. Strauss later became president of the jury for the Gabriel Fauré competition, which Long created in 1937 but which did not survive the outbreak of war.

On tour Ravel was extremely absent-minded. He was constantly losing his luggage, watch, wallet, train tickets. He would put letters in his pocket and forget about them. Twice his neglecting to read or pass on mail caused unhappy situations, one when he did not acknowledge (let alone attend!) an important invitation by a prime minister. In Berlin, Ravel forgot to get off the train, leaving Long stranded, alone, on the platform without German money and not speaking the language. A few hours later, after she had managed to change some money and find her way to the hotel, Long found him in the lobby. All smiles, Ravel claimed he had just enjoyed a ride around the city to the last stop on the train. In the process, however, he had lost his train ticket to Holland. But what caused the most disruption was that he almost always forgot to pack his black patent leather shoes, "as if a maleficent Scarbo hid them from his attention."[10] His feet were so small that he had to have his shoes custom-made; and he cared so much about his elegant attire that he could not bear the thought of buying just any shoes for the concert. In one case, his shoes were entrusted to the conductor of the next train from Paris.

When in difficult or embarrassing situations, Long would simply laugh and say, with her characteristic sense of humor, "We are gathering memories!"[11] A charming token of these memories is the photograph Ravel inscribed to her: "A Marguerite Long, record woman du Concerto." For her they were significant memories, for the G major Concerto was one of Ravel's last compositions. Only the three *Don Quixote* songs[12] were written later, about the time the Concerto was premiered. Ravel's already fragile health was seriously impaired when he suffered a head injury in a taxi accident in October 1932. The last years of his life were tragic, and yet he loved life so much that he would say to Long during their travels: "I cannot spend one hour without thinking of my parents: I pity them so much for not being alive."[13] He was terrified of death. When he fell ill he was forbidden to drink alcohol. He, who loved the good life, good meals, and fine wines, never had a sip of wine after that for fear of endangering his life. His health never recovered, and he was tortured by his incapacity to compose. He believed that his best compositions had not yet been written. In his despondent moments Long would suggest that even if he did not write another note, what he had already written was of sublime beauty and perfection. Ravel, lost in despair, would answer: "How can you say such a thing? I have not written anything, I am not leaving anything and I have not said or composed anything yet of what I wanted to say."[14]

Even though Ravel was a private and secret person, he enjoyed the company of others and was faithful in his friendships to a rare degree. Many friends followed him through the years from 1934 to his death in 1937. Some accused him of being insensitive; they were wrong. Inside this lover of perfection (in dress, in manner, in house interiors) hid a soul easily hurt. He used to say: "One does not prove he has a heart by simply opening up his chest."[15] His extreme sensitivity manifested itself in his music, in spite of himself.

Even though Ravel was not a virtuoso at the piano, his writing for the instrument shows the pianistic genius of a Liszt or a Chopin. Long said he had "le génie du doigté" (fingering): when he would suggest a fingering, she would argue at first, but on second thought and practice, it invariably proved to be the best one. Long insisted that one should always follow Ravel's indications and fingerings in his scores, for they had strong musical reasons. The same concept, put in a larger context, applies to the Concerto for the Left Hand. Ravel did not tolerate under any circumstance that this piece be rearranged for two hands. He told Long, "Even after I die, no one should dare transcribe it for two hands."[16] Not unlike Debussy, who said "a faithful interpreter is all I need," Ravel had an aversion to artists who did not follow exactly his precisely notated scores. His pupils Vlado Perlemuter and Gaby Casadesus strongly confirmed this aversion. He resented the fact that most conductors played his *Boléro* too fast; this led to a historic confrontation with Toscanini. "That was not my tempo," said Ravel, backstage after a concert. Toscanini replied, "When I play it at your tempo it is not effective." Ravel retorted, "Then do not play it."[17] Ravel's version of Debussy's credo was "I do not ask to be interpreted, but simply to be played."[18] When students asked how to play *Jeux d'eau,* Ravel would answer, "Just as you would play Liszt."[19] Long remarked that, like Liszt, Ravel treated every instrument in the orchestra in a virtuosic manner; he was fascinated by virtuosity.

According to Long, the relationship between Debussy and Ravel had its ups and downs, but the two men admired each other, though distantly. Ravel's sense of humor was always present, however, no matter what the musical world made of his rivalry with Debussy. During a concert performance of *Shéhérazade,* Ravel turned to Long and said: "Oh! my dear! How Debussyan!"[20] *Shéhérazade* contains a great deal of whole-tone harmonies, one of Debussy's most identifiable trademarks. Ravel was not particularly fond of the whole-tone scale and rarely used it in his music after *Shéhérazade*. Actually, Ravel was deeply moved by Debussy's music, in particular by his *Prelude to the Afternoon of a Faun*: "On hearing this work I really understood what music was."[21] He confessed one day to Long: "There is nothing in the world more perfect than Debussy's *Prelude to the Afternoon of a Faun;* I would like to die listening to it."[22] In 1922 Ravel dedicated his Sonata for Violin and Cello to the memory of Claude Debussy.

The story behind the composition of the Concerto for the Left Hand is well known, but what may not be common knowledge is how displeased Ravel was with the performance of its dedicatee, Paul Wittgenstein.* Ravel was livid when he heard Wittgenstein for the first time in a private home in Vienna. The pianist had taken so many liberties with the piece that Ravel tried to prevent the first performance in Paris from taking place altogether. Long witnessed this difficult controversy, for it was contemporary with the genesis of the G major Concerto. The Paris première eventually took place in 1933, but Ravel ignored the event. Later he entrusted the Concerto to Jacques Février, one of Long's earliest Premier Prix winners (1921) at the Conservatoire. But Février had to wait until 1937, when Wittgenstein's six-year exclusive right to perform the piece ended.

Long herself never played the Concerto for the Left Hand because, as she admitted, her hands were too small. Nevertheless, she felt a deep bond with the piece through her disciple Jacques Février, whose first performance of the piece in Paris reflected the composer's meticulous wishes and earned his complete approval. In the same year, Février played the new Concerto in Boston, under Koussevitzky, to an enthusiastic audience (Koussevitzky had commissioned Ravel's famous orchestration of Mussorgsky's *Pictures at an Exhibition*). Février's recording of the Concerto for the Left Hand remains the standard interpretation, just as Long's first recording is the standard for the G major Concerto.

Long made two recordings of the G major Concerto. The first one was recorded by Columbia on three 78 rpm records shortly after the January 1932 première. René Dumesnil* reviewed it in *Eve*:

> The recording of the *Concerto pour piano* by Maurice Ravel . . . is quite worthy of the new work, whose success this winter in Paris, and later in all of Europe's capitals, was resounding. It is Mme. Marguerite Long, dedicatee of the Concerto, whom we hear again at the piano with the same delight as we did at the

> work's première. Her interpretation can be regarded as a model of intelligence, of finesse and of technical perfection. . . . And one must praise equally the orchestra under the direction of the composer. [August 28, 1932.]

The recording was advertised as being conducted by Ravel, but that was not quite the truth. It was actually under the baton of Pedro de Freitas-Branco, who had conducted most of the program on January 14, 1932. But, Long insisted, Ravel was present in the recording booth during the whole session, which lasted well into the night. He attentively followed every minute, voicing his opinion over the smallest details, and demanding that the performers start over until he was completely satisfied. And in the early morning hours he finally was.

Twenty years later, in 1954, with the advent of long-playing records, Long recorded the G major Concerto again, with the Orchestre de la Société du Conservatoire under Georges Tzipine. On the flip-side was a new performance of Fauré's Ballade, conducted by André Cluytens. The 1954 Ravel recording was criticized by many for its stylistic looseness, particularly in the slow movement. At 80, Long chose a more sentimental rendition, as opposed to the classical sobriety of her earlier version. Whether a matter of taste or not, the later performance contradicted Ravel's intentions, as Long herself described them.

The year of the Ravel Concerto's triumphant debut was also the year of Long's first significant journey overseas, to South America. It was her first major official mission, for she was sent to Brazil under the auspices of the Ministère des Affaires Etrangères and the Association Française d'Expansion et d'Echanges Artistiques. Although strong ties were formed, and in spite of the fact that Long kept regular epistolary contacts with Brazil, it was not until 1954 that she returned to Rio de Janeiro. The 1932 sojourn remained a crucial step in her career, however, for it was the first official trip where her role as ambassador of French music was so clearly established, and where her performance as an artist, pedagogue, lecturer, *and* representative of her country was so all-encompassing. She obviously had an innate ease for what might have seemed challenging to another pianist. In the years to come, when Long was in her late sixties, particularly after World War II, she increasingly assumed this role.

Marguerite Long and Darius Milhaud

The composer Darius Milhaud (1892–1974) was a generation younger than Long, but both had strong ties to Brazil (Long visited that country three times; see below, pp. 000–00). Milhaud spent two years in Rio de Janeiro during World War I, as secretary to Paul Claudel, then Minister to Brazil. As with Fauré, Long's personal connection with Milhaud originated with her husband. At a concert of the S.M.I. at the Salle Pleyel, Marliave had heard the First String Quartet by Milhaud, who was then a student at the Conservatoire. Marliave came home from the concert and exclaimed: "I just heard the work of a very young composer. This one is a man of genius."[23] Long met Milhaud shortly thereafter, some time between 1912, when the Quartet was composed, and 1914, the year Marliave died.

In 1920 Long was nominated to teach a Classe Supérieure at the Conservatoire, after Diémer's death had left the post vacant. In France such a position was (and still is) decided by high-ranking ministers and, as a result, was often a political appointment. Long wanted the position badly but feared opposition, for no woman had ever filled this job, and she had been denied it twice. Milhaud wrote to her about this time (unfortunately his letter is not dated):

> Dear Madame Friend,
>
> Coincidence served us well! Last night I was invited to Mme. Alphonse Daudet and I met there Bérard, the Ministre des Beaux Arts. I talked to him at length about Mme Long, telling him that all young French musicians would applaud her appointment, considering the admiration we all feel toward her. He told me that the Conseil Sup[érieur] du Cons[ervatoire] must present *two candidates* to the [Ministrère des] B[eaux] A[rts], that we still don't know who, but they will probably be [Armand] Ferté and Mme Long. He asked me what I thought of Ferté and I told him in no uncertain terms that there was no possible comparison to be made between a great artist such as Mme. Long and a Mr. like Mr. F[erté]. He told me that "she had a chance." Mme Daudet, very nice, to whom I talked about it again told me she would send a note to Bérard on the subject. . . . I would be very happy if this could have a small influence. But ministers remain mysterious things. . . . I will keep you scrupulously informed.
>
> Milhaud[24]

It so happened that, as a little girl, Milhaud's wife, Madeleine, had been a private pupil of Long. She too related to me, with a sparkle in her eyes, how extremely handsome Marliave was.

As in several other cases, Long began playing Milhaud's music long after she knew the man. She had always liked his music, finding it simple, robust, and of a rich harmonic palette. Milhaud composed with great facility (for which some critics reproached him), and his output is astonishing. His versatility enabled him to assimilate Brazilian folk music as easily as American jazz or contemporary music, and he had a gift for juxtaposing tenderness and poetic charm with grandiose music. Most remarkable of all, Long thought, was that he lived in an extremely noisy neighborhood (Place Clichy in Paris), where in addition to the daily commotion there was a fair twice a year. His apartment was on the first floor, and he would work there, with all the windows open, to the sound of merry-go-rounds and street organs. What a contrast to Debussy, who demanded complete silence and made his wife and daughter tiptoe around the house!

In 1933, Milhaud set out to write his First Piano Concerto and asked Long to give its first performance and to be its dedicatee. His inscription on her score is typical of his tongue-in-cheek-wit: "Je dépose à vos pieds chère et sublime amie cette oeuvre que vous ferez vivre par vos mains admirables" (I leave at your feet, dear and sublime friend, this work, which you will bring alive with your admirable hands).[25] Still in the heat of the success of Ravel's G major Concerto, Long accepted wholeheartedly. The première took place on November 25, 1934, with the Orchestre Pasdeloup under the direction of Albert Wolff. The November issue of *Le Monde musical* acknowledged the event with some reserve:

> The concert of Sunday, [November] 25, was a beautiful festival of French contemporary music. It opened with the *Saudades do Brasil* by Darius Milhaud, strongly perfumed with smells of the Brazilian forest, and continued with the first audition of a new Concerto for piano by the same author, dedicated in 1933 to Marguerite Long. Of rather small dimension, it gives the piano a place of honor. It is the piano which leads, plays with the themes, discreetly emphasized by the orchestra soloists. . . . It pales, of course, next to the prodigious Concerto by Ravel, which, under Long's magic fingers met another triumph, but it is a valuable asset to the modern pianist's repertoire.

A second performance took place on January 19, 1935 at the Salle Rameau with Long as soloist. The program consisted of music by French composers, each conducting his own work: Milhaud, Ibert, Gaubert, Siohan, and Honegger. In 1938 the Milhaud Concerto was recorded by Columbia, this time under the direction of the composer. Two pieces for piano, "Paysandu" (from *Saudades do Brasil*) and "Alfama" (from *l'Automne*), complete the record.

Other, smaller works by Milhaud were dedicated to Long. Among them was "Tour de l'Exposition," his contribution to the collection *A l'Exposition* (see below, p. 000). For Long's younger pupils, Milhaud composed *L'Enfantine,* for piano four-hands. It is a set of three very short pieces—"Fumée," "Fête de Bordeaux," and "Fête de Montmarte"—each 25 to 30 measures long, with an easy upper part for the pupil and a lower part for the teacher. And finally, Milhaud's *Album de Madame Bovary* was premiered by Long's pupils in 1934, the same year as his Concerto appeared.

In the spring of 1934, impressed by Long's wide range of activities, Milhaud published an article in *Jour* praising two of her recent lectures: one on Fauré, the other on Debussy. Far from conventional, her talks were illustrated and included performances, sometimes by her students and sometimes by colleagues. This format, which Long frequently adopted, was a clever way to exhibit her many-faceted musicianship and personality, and at the same time, it was a great opportunity for her students, young as well as old (depending on the demands of the repertoire), to be heard by a large Paris audience. The Debussy evening, for example, was held in the Salons du Palais Royal before an elite company: President Herriot, Paul Léon, Robert Brussel, and Ida Rubinstein, among others. As Milhaud wrote: "What a wealth of details and precious memories did Mme Long evoke for us! What her modesty kept her from telling us was how much Debussy admired her and relied on her to maintain the precision which his piano writing demanded." He went on to describe the program: *Children's Corner,* several songs, Preludes, and, to conclude, the Sonata for Flute, Viola and Harp:

> This Sonata brings back a precious memory every time I hear it . . . it is thanks to it that I met Debussy. When the piece was published, M. Jacques Durand presented its première at his home. He told Debussy that he would send him a young violist to talk about tempi and other musical directions [before the première]. I played viola at the time, and it was for me a great emotion to study this Sonata with the Master and a great honor to have played it for the first time.[26]

National Honors

In 1930, her first recordings were being issued, Long became the recipient of the Rosette de la Légion d'Honneur. It was awarded to her by Paul Léon, Director of the Académie des Beaux-Arts, in the name of the French government. The Rosette is the insignia for the title of Officier de la Légion d'Honneur. "Modern music has found in her the most active and the most lucid propagandist. It is to a genuine messenger of music, in the noblest sense of the word, that the *Croix d'Officier de la Légion d'Honneur* was awarded this time" (*Chantecler,* August 30, 1930).

Since the Rosette d'Officier followed the Ruban de Chevalier by nine years, it was almost expected that the next level within the order of the Légion d'Honneur would be awarded to Long before the decade was over. In 1938, the French government was inspired to decorate her with the Cravate Rouge (Red Tie), and promote her to the rank of Commandeur de la Légion d'Honneur. This honor was rarely bestowed on a performer and even more rarely on a woman; Long had the double honor of being the first woman performer to hold this title. When her friends congratulated her and hoped that she would soon receive the next and ultimate grade of the Légion d'Honneur, the Grand Croix, as the writer Colette had done, Long retorted with her characteristic shrewdness: "I sure hope so, for all Colette is about, is stories of cats."[27] The fact that women were only exceptionally recognized in this fashion is blatantly revealed by the ministry's stationery, which uses only masculine forms and is headed by an uncompromising "Monsieur," over which a clerk had to ink in "Madame."[28]

One year earlier, in 1937, Long had been the object of another type of national celebration. Paris was the host of the World Exhibition, in which each country had a chance to display its strongest artistic and technological assets. Music was well represented through numerous concerts. To honor their faithful champion, a group of French composers joined forces and wrote a collection of pieces dedicated to Long, specifically for the occasion. The collection, entitled *A l'Exposition,* included one work each by Georges Auric, Marcel Delannoy, Jacques Ibert, Darius Milhaud, Francis Poulenc, Henri Sauguet, Florent Schmitt, and Germaine Tailleferre. The complete set was premiered by two of Long's younger pupils for the inauguration of the Pavillon de la femme et de l'enfant, and it was subsequently published.

At the same time, nine foreign composers, wishing to express their own gratitude to Long, gathered their work in another volume entitled *Parc d'Attraction* (Amusement Park), which was later published as well. The composers represented were Ernesto Halffter, Bohuslav Martinů, Vittorio Rieti, Tibor Harsanyi, Arthur Honegger, Federico Mompou, Alexandre Tansman, Alexander Tcherepnin, and Marcel Mihalovici. The French collection was intended for children, but this one required an accomplished pianist. Nicole

Henriot, one of Long's pupils in her current class at the Conservatoire, was chosen for the première of this entire collection, to be given at the Exhibition.

The death of Ravel in December 1937 ended a 35-year period in which Marguerite Long had been successively close to Fauré, Debussy, and Ravel. At the age of 63 she still had 30 full and active years ahead of her, but the decades characterized by her collaboration with each of the three greatest French composers of her time formed and matured her musical personality, and confirmed her national and international image. Long's own words best express what each collaboration represented for her. The way she looked back on them was intimately connected with the emotional climates of her personal life:

> Gabriel Fauré, Claude Debussy, Maurice Ravel . . . each one personally represents for me an *epoch:*
>
> The first one, my youth, my happy life; the second one, my grief and the saving return to music; and the third one, through the famous Concerto he wrote for me . . . the climax of a career partly devoted to the proliferation of French music.[29]

With the outbreak of war in 1939 came the end of an era. In Europe, World War II created a gap between the first and second halves of the century. After 1945, life had to start over again, cities had to be rebuilt and families reunited; major political and military changes meant that the world after 1945 was a different one from that before 1939. Marguerite Long was 65 in 1939: both her own timing and that of international events were to steer her life toward new horizons.

PART TWO

Pedagogue and Ambassador of French Music

Vous aimiez les courses de toros à la folie; aujourd'hui, vous ne manquez pas un match de catch sur votre écran de télévision. Il faut y voir, bien plus qu'un caprice, un goût inné pour la lutte et le sens de la victoire.

—*Pierre Barbizet (1959)*

You used to love bullfights with a passion; today you never miss a wrestling match on your television screen. Much more than a whim, one sees in this an innate affinity for the fight and for the reward of victory.

Long at the piano at home, with Sargent's portrait of Fauré, 1953. Photo Roger-Viollet, Paris.

7

Portrait of a Pedagogue

Throughout her multi-faceted career of over 40 years, Marguerite Long had been a well-known pedagogue and certainly a strong champion of French contemporary music. Yet, she seemed to feel that she had not done enough. In 1940, at the age of 65, after 34 years of teaching at the Paris Conservatoire, she resigned. Now her career was ready for a second wind. Armed with the wisdom of age and the experience of a rich and fulfilling career, Long was to concentrate her efforts on the younger generation, on helping the careers of her former and present students and of pianists from around the world. This ambition inspired her to found the Concours Marguerite Long–Jacques Thibaud in 1943, during the grim war years. Her enormous effort radiated throughout the world. After the war ended, her international master classes, her home, and the Concours all became centers of piano playing and music making. Perceived as the vibrant living legacy of three great French composers, Long was approached by foreign governments and institutions to receive national honors, inaugurate competitions, preside over juries, and participate in national celebrations of music.

She performed in public occasionally but preferred to yield the stage to her disciples. Until her death in 1966, at the age of 91, she continued to learn, to discover, to travel, and to love life: "Old age may take away a few things, but it brings many more!"[1]

As a child, Long had a taste for teaching and leading others. Armed with a pile of books she could not yet read, she would gather her dolls around her and lecture to them. But at fifteen, fresh out of the Conservatoire, when she had to give piano lessons to earn a living, "I hated it, it bored me."[2] Among her first pupils were a young boy, who lived at the corner of Place de la

Madeleine and Rue Royale, and an old woman, who lived on Rue du Quatre Septembre. Interestingly enough, at both houses, from the piano, one could see a large clock in the street. Both pupil and teacher kept glancing furtively at the clock, to be sure that the ordeal would not run overtime.

How things were to change! The revelation came to her when she began to study with Antonin Marmontel, and he allowed her to teach. Her skills developed rapidly, and she was rewarded as early as 1898, when she was 23, with reviews praising the first recitals by her students (see above, p. 16). Later, she was appointed to the Conservatoire, but she was also running her own private piano school, the Ecole Marguerite Long.

The school was started in 1906, at 18 Rue Fourcroy, where Long and her husband moved right after they were married. The young couple lived on the third floor, and in the early days Long gave lessons in their apartment. She had several *répétitrices,* who would also teach there. *Répétitrices* were assistants to great teachers, and they were as devoted to the artists under whom they taught as they were to their students. They were usually the ones who did all the work and got intimately involved in their pupils' lives. Long soon acquired a larger space on the first floor of the building and could expand her operations: she had a large classroom with two grand pianos and a smaller room with one upright piano, separated by an entrance hallway. By this time, she had many *répétitrices,* some of whom had obtained their Premier Prix in Long's class at the Conservatoire. Typically, lessons were organized in groups of three or four students, taught by the *répétitrices* and supervised once a month by Long. Solfège classes were given for a few hours a week by a reputable teacher (who had a permanent appointment at the Conservatoire) for those who needed it. These classes were a training ground for children who hoped to attend the Paris Conservatoire. By enrolling in Long's school, they were increasing their chances not only to succeed in the entrance competition, or *concours,* but also to be admitted to her class at the Conservatoire. Those who attended the school felt that they had acquired a very strong foundation, thanks to Long's strict discipline and regimen, and that they were well prepared to explore all kinds of music, technically and intellectually. They also remembered her gift for making students come out of themselves, for making a piece blossom instantly, particularly on the eve of an examination or a competition.

By the 1930s, Long's private school had expanded extensively. Some called it a veritable factory of piano playing, where Long employed and supervised her army of *répétitrices.* The school taught everyone from the youngest beginners to those preparing for the Conservatoire's entrance *con-*

cours; and for those who were not successful at the Conservatoire it provided a fairly prestigious teaching diploma. Many collaborators and disciples claimed that at any one time, Long had more than 500 students in her school and could not follow all of them closely. But every one marveled at her ability to choose first-rate *répétitrices,* who taught extremely well and perpetuated the reputation of the school.

Asked about the secret of her students' success, Long consistently answered: "My method is to have no single method."[3] She realized early on that there are as many methods as there are students. People have different physical conformations and varying intelligences and gifts. One cannot expect the same amount of work from students with different temperaments. There are small flexible hands and large stiff ones, and everything in between, so that even technical exercises must be tailored individually.

Her other secret, one she would not divulge as publicly, was her choice of *répétitrices.* "She was a genius when it came to selecting first-class *répétitrices.* Just as Louis XIV chose his ministers admirably, Long handpicked her assistants," but she also mistreated them, said several of her former pupils.[4] The demands Long put on her pupils she inflicted to an even greater degree on her *répétitrices,* often without acknowledging their dedication. Even though they were treated harshly, they performed with utter devotion. Of the many who served Long's Ecole, the following names were remembered with fondness: Lucie Léon, who was the official Conservatoire *répétitrice;* Hélène François; Mademoiselle Herbault; and Rose Aye Lejour. Lucette Descaves, who eventually taught her own Classe Supérieure at the Conservatoire, was a *répétitrice* in Long's school for a short time, immediately after receiving her Premier Prix at the Conservatoire in 1923. Jacques Février also taught many of Long's students, but he would not be considered a *répétitrice,* for he did not satisfy the first criterion, that of being a woman. He also had his own performing career and did not submit to Long's tyranny with the same humility; in fact, he had his own strong temperament and, in turn, terrorized *his* students.

Interviews with some of the *répétitrices* revealed some less-attractive features of Long's personality. Long delegated a great deal of the teaching responsibility to them and expected an unlimited time commitment on their part, with very little, if any, compensation. When a pupil was having a private lesson with Long or performing in the Conservatoire class, the assigned *répétitrice* was expected to be present. A *répétitrice* could not complain about a student, for Long would retort that there were no bad students, only inadequate teachers. When Long's students prepared contemporary pieces, the *répétitrice* took them to the composers' homes for coaching. Composers came to recitals and occasionally to dress rehearsals, but not to the lessons or to the class (except for Ravel, who visited Long's Conservatoire class occasionally during the period of the Concerto première). Long discouraged her *répétitrices* from becoming attached to their students and the students' families; if that occurred, she might change the *répétitrice*. One of the things that hurt the *répétitrices* the most was that they were never invited to Long's aristocratic friends' musical salons when their students performed there; Long probably did not consider the *répétitrices* part of that social milieu. If they wanted a picture autographed by their mentor, Long expected them to purchase it. These are some of the painful testimonies collected from interviews with Long's *répétitrices*.

As resentful and hurt as they may have been, they still admitted to having learned a great deal about their profession through Long, who had been their teacher and with whom they could take occasional lessons. Long communicated a strong sense of discipline and rigor and firmly believed that gifted pupils should always be pushed ahead rather than held back, even if sometimes they had to slow down later. The *répétitrices* recognized her acute musical intuition and intelligence as well as her ability in detecting notable pedagogical talent in the women she chose to surround her. Long's monthly inspections of the programs of music she assigned kept everyone on their toes: there was never a dull moment in those two rooms on the ground floor of the Rue Fourcroy, which were teeming with activity from morning until night.

Public Master Classes and Student Recitals

In 1921, Long made a brief escapade to the Ecole Normale, a rival institution to the Conservatoire, where she was invited to give a series of master classes. The context was a so-called *Ecole de maîtres,* modeled after what the Germans called the *Meisterschule.* The Ecole Normale hoped to offer a wide range of master classes by the greatest artists residing in France; the participants would be young artists, French and foreign, who had graduated from their respective institutions and wanted to receive further training. It was a rather progressive idea in France at that time, for once a student was attached to a teacher it was considered a betrayal to seek another's guidance. By its very design this *Ecole de maîtres* encouraged independence in a young artist who sought more than one master. In 1921, the Ecole Normale invited

Alfred Cortot, Marguerite Long, Isidor Philipp, Blanche Selva, Wanda Landowska, Jacques Thibaud, Pablo Casals, André Hekking, Marcel Dupré, and Reynaldo Hahn to institute this *Ecole de maîtres.* Everyone on this distinguished roster accepted, and the idea was a success.[5] Unfortunately, the initiative was not repeated in subsequent years.

Through her pedagogical activity, Long sought to reach beyond her students: her goal was to touch the public at large. With both Conservatoire and private students, she saw her responsibility as going further than mere lessons. To achieve this goal she regularly organized her own student recitals and public master classes in prestigious halls, such as the Salle Gaveau or Salle Erard. The Conservatoire did not provide such performing opportunities for its students. There, students only took classes and played at their end-of-year *concours.* Thus it was not uncommon for teachers at the Conservatoire to organize student recitals on their own. But Long's *auditions d'élèves* (student recitals) were quite a popular event among the elite:

> According to tradition, Mme. Marguerite Long staged, on March 28 at the Salle Erard, the annual recital by students of her Conservatoire class. A very elite audience had filled the hall to capacity; so much so that many interested souls could not find a seat and had to . . . retrace their steps. Numerous personalities came to attend this interesting event, notably Mme. Claude Debussy, M. and Mme. Gabriel Faure,† . . . Georges Migot, Francis Poulenc, Armand Ferté . . . M. and Mme. Robert Casadesus. . . . The impression this recital left was excellent. [*Chantecler,* April 2, 1927.]

Part of what made these concerts the "talk of the town" was Long's effort in programming modern music, mostly French, but occasionally Russian and Spanish as well. As early as 1920, a few months after her promotion to a Classe Supérieure, the Salle Gaveau hosted the first of many student recitals. Louis Vuillemin, a critic and composer, strongly expressed his approval of her project:

> Marguerite Long gave us the chance to hear at Salle Gaveau a substantial group of her students in a program of French contemporary music. Such an initiative fills a great gap: that which is created by the official teaching going on at the Conservatoire in matters of modern education. Premier Prix winners come out

†Not the composer, but the author; note the lack of an accent on the *e.*

> . . . and remain quite ignorant about the marvelous art of Fauré, Debussy or Ravel. And that is wrong! . . . Let us properly celebrate, then, a daring initiative, successful as much in its concept as in its realization. [*La Lanterne*, June 22, 1920.]

Le Figaro also pointed out:

> The recital given by Marguerite Long's Premier Prix laureates of 1922 was a genuine festival of contemporary music. It emphasized once more the teaching, always keenly intent on serving the music of today, practiced by one of our best interpreters of contemporary music. [March 15, 1923.]

The opportunity to play at the Salle Erard or the Salle Gaveau once a year was not restricted to Long's Conservatoire class. Several programs and reviews document recitals featuring very young students:

> Mme. Marguerite Long . . . is constantly preoccupied with making sure that her pupils become as familiar with today's masters as they are with classic composers. . . . This was *one* of the student recitals Mme. Long organizes yearly. . . . In this case, we were witnessing a real concert given exclusively by the "eleven-year-olds and under." And the program included no fewer than seven premières! [*Chantecler*, March 22, 1930.]

In the 1930s, Long began combining student recitals in small series, thereby presenting more students from both her school and the Conservatoire. In 1931, "Three sessions of contemporary music given by several students of her school and of her Conservatoire class" took place in the traditional Salle Erard on March 14, 17, and 24. One of the critics described these marathon sessions as "judiciously planned programs . . . exclusively composed of modern pieces, many of which were premières, did not call on fewer than thirty-six living composers, who were all interpreted with magnificent brio" (*Liberté*, April 16, 1931). More than 60 students performed.

In March 1937, six of Long's students were given the coveted opportunity to play with orchestra. Thanks to her clout, Long recruited an ensemble from the members of the Pasdeloup Orchestra (one of the four main orchestras in Paris), and had obtained the participation of Darius Milhaud, who would conduct one of his own pieces, and Armand Ferté, a Conservatoire colleague. The whole event was a benefit concert for the Association des anciens élèves du Conservatoire. All six performers were under fifteen years of age,[6] and the program included Mozart's two-piano Concerto in E-flat, Poulenc's *Concert*

Champêtre, Milhaud's *Le Carnaval d'Aix,* Liszt's *Fantaisie Hongroise,* and Ravel's *Ma Mère L'Oye* arranged for piano, four-hands by the composer. The Salle Erard was filled again. Long's correspondence with conductors, notably with Pierné at the Orchestre Colonne, is further evidence of her way of setting up auditions for her pupils. The conductor would respond by engaging the student, by advising repertoire, or by suggesting a second audition at a later date. In a letter to Long, dated Paris, December 13, 1926, Pierné reacted to three young pianists' auditions:

> My Dear Friend,
>
> . . . I heard three of your pupils . . . who each have their qualities but did not seem to be mature enough to be able to take on, as soloist, our audience of Chaillot [name of the hall]. But since all three do not deserve to be dismissed, do you think they would play J. S. Bach's Three-Piano Concerto together, assuming they will practice it under your supervision?
>
> Your friend,
>
> Gabriel Pierné[7]

Above and beyond these recitals were Long's master classes, known as *Cours de virtuosité et d'interprétation*, which were also held in the Salle Erard or the Salle Gaveau. A meticulously kept notebook that recorded programs, attendance, and finances reveals that they started in 1926. Every year, during February and March, Long gave a series of six master classes that were open to the public; people could purchase tickets for the whole series at a reduced rate, or pay the full price for individual sessions. The press commended not only Long's musicianship but also her breadth of knowledge and her capacity to express herself articulately. According to Paul Landormy,

> How Mme. Marguerite Long knows how to find the right word . . . and how everything she says reveals her vast and sophisticated culture. One wonders how a virtuoso . . . entirely absorbed by her concert preparation and her teaching still finds the time to have read so much and thought so carefully about her art [*Victoire,* March 25, 1930.]

As the master classes gained in popularity, their scope also broadened. Long devoted each class to a different composer and preceded the class with a lecture. The year 1931 saw a series of three such classes, on May 18 and 28 and June 1, on Chopin, Fauré, and Debussy respectively. Only her best students played, all Premier Prix laureates. The idea proved successful, and Long continued this pedagogical format for years.

Later, she opened up the master classes to pianists other than her own students. A 1937 flier advertised "Ten classes of high pianistic teaching by Marguerite Long." They met in the Salons Gaveau on Mondays at 5:00 P.M., from February 15 to March 15 and from April 26 to June 7, 1937. They were open to "Pianists with Premier Prix of the Conservatoire, to those who have a *diplôme supérieur* from the Marguerite Long school and to all French and foreign virtuosos regardless of age."[8] Long's many pages of autograph notes in preparation for this sequence of classes give an insight into her thought and erudition. She had a gift for drawing long historical lines through the centuries, as well as recounting personal experiences in the case of modern composers. Her style was fluent, elegant, and well crafted. In the many interviews I conducted, I was constantly reminded of the ease and distinctiveness of her language, articulate yet always graceful.

Long confessed that her master classes at the Salle Erard and the Salle Gaveau represented the "crowning of my teaching."[9] They were the battleground for Conservatoire laureates. The idea of instituting the *Cours de virtuosité et d'interprétation* came to Long when she realized how young her pupils were when they graduated from the Conservatoire and what little guidance was available to them at this critical point. They still needed a mentor as well as a competitive climate to continue to mature. She wanted to show her disciples how much more lay ahead after the Premier Prix, after one already played very well. As she was solicited more and more to give lectures on the music of various composers, she often used those opportunities to have one or several of her students perform pieces illustrating the subject at hand. Since her name always drew large crowds, these were ideal occasions for students to be heard, to be reviewed, to be noticed.

Emil Sauer

Never running short of ways to broaden her students' experiences, Long invited Emil Sauer, one of Liszt's last pupils, to give three classes in January 1934. Many of her former pupils still treasure their memory of those sessions in the Salle Erard. All three evenings took on grand artistic proportions. They were devoted to the performance of Liszt's piano music and were preceded by talks by Sauer. He reminisced about the 1880s in Weimar, where "around the patriarch of romanticism would gather the pianists who were to become famous in preaching Liszt's teaching . . . d'Albert, Rosenthal, Siloti" (*Marianne,* February 7, 1934). Sauer also insisted that

> Liszt did not give piano lessons in the way it has been done from Czerny to the present; rather, he would wax eloquent on the high forms of art . . . similar to the way that Greek philosophers passed their ideas on to their disciples without being teachers. [*Candide,* February 8, 1934.]

Tall and svelte, with intense, vivacious eyes and silvery hair, Sauer stood in the front of the stage, sharing with his attentive audience memories of half a century earlier. The Paris public was already familiar with Sauer, who had made his debut in the capital in the first decade of the century and had always been warmly received there. Sauer, in turn, remarked that he was deeply grateful to France, which always showed him the most sincere artistic appreciation. "If I feel very small next to my revered mentor [Liszt], there is one point where I dare compare myself to him, and that is our common love for France" (*Comoedia,* January 17, 1934). Although Sauer was very impressed with Long's students, he talked about the universal tendency to play Liszt's music too fast:

> You should have heard how he played the *Campanella:* with what generosity he attacked the octave passages . . . and with what refinement he played the bell. . . . How different appear to me the *Campanellas* that I hear today, which always seem to aim at breaking speed records. [*Comoedia,* January 17, 1934.]

Sauer reiterated this point strongly with regard to *Feux Follets* and *La Leggierezza;* the latter, he insisted, should be *Allegretto.*

During the three evenings, a formidable amount of Liszt repertoire was performed by Long's best students: both concertos, the B minor Sonata, the "Dante" Sonata, *Mephisto Waltz, Campanella, Feux Follets, Mazeppa, La Leggierezza,* Concert Etudes, Sonnets, Legends, and Rhapsodies. At the end of this abundant Liszt festival, Sauer expressed his respect for the pianists he heard. From his vast experience in music centers around the world, he could assert that the teaching at the Paris Conservatoire was the strongest.[10]

Long must have been pleased, for what Sauer heard was exclusively her "product." The press gave ample coverage of the initiative, each article devoting generous space to Sauer's comments, his charm, and the impeccability of his French; the high calibre of the pianists' performances; and the enthusiastic reactions of the audience. It always credited and expressed gratitude to Long, whose idea was at the root of this exciting week. On all counts, it was another important feather in Long's pedagogical cap. When Sauer died in the spring of 1942, Long wrote a lengthy article about him for the *Comoedia* of May 23, 1942.

Long did not limit her teaching to advanced students or to those who were clearly destined for a performing career. Throughout her life she enjoyed teaching amateurs and young children. She founded her own school so that amateurs and professionals could benefit from the same sound training:

> [The school] is open to young men and women who want to dedicate themselves to a pianistic career; then there are classes designed for "amateur-professionals," those who pursue other primary studies and careers, but who are committed to the discipline of learning how to play the instrument and the richness of its repertoire to the best of their ability; and finally, there are classes for children who make their first acquaintance with the keyboard.[11]

Long emphasized that her school was one of *piano-playing:* "What I mean is that, after basic rudiments, we do not study solfège for six years here!" This was a none-too-subtle dart at the regional conservatories in France, which would not let children (or adults) touch an instrument without first enrolling in years of the almighty solfège. After suffering through these esoteric acrobatics, they would have lost all desire and love for music.

For Long the piano was the ideal vehicle for gaining a knowledge of music, particularly for amateurs, and that is why she valued the teaching of nonprofessionals:

> What instrument can compete with the piano as a tool for developing one's broad musical culture? The piano, being so widespread, has a far-reaching influence on people, and this is why teaching piano to amateurs is a great responsibility. [*Phono-Radio-Musique,* January 1931.][12]

With the advent of the phonograph and the radio, Long was often asked if the new technology would put pianists out of business. She believed quite the opposite:

> To appreciate a concert, a recording or a radio broadcast best, one ought to have a good musical knowledge. And the best way to acquire it is to study the piano . . . so in fact, there will always be a need for people to teach piano well, which is to teach music.[13]

With her characteristic optimism, Long turned a pessimistic viewpoint into a positive outlook: "The phonograph is in every way a stimulant, an ally of music and a wonderful means of propaganda."[14]

Long concluded her interviews on the state of pianists and piano teachers by saying that in recent years (the 1920s and 30s) their role had become subtler and perhaps even more important. Amateurs who came for piano lessons did not wish to learn just one or two effective pieces. They were asking to be initiated into the beauty of music, in order to develop their taste and enable them to appreciate the great concerts that their records had made them want to hear.

The sincerity of Long's commitment to amateur music making in general was further exemplified by her collaboration, in 1948, with the orchestra of the Société Nationale des Chemins de Fer Français, France's nationalized railroad company. Long appeared as guest soloist with an orchestra formed of its employees. The Chief Executive of S.N.C.F. wrote to her on April 22, 1948, expressing the players' gratitude for her participation in their concert at the Palais de Chaillot: "Your admirable performance moved the audience very much, and our players felt all the more pride from the trust you had invested in them."[15]

Long's dedication not only as a teacher but as a champion of new music through her pupils grew with the years. While she was premiering the Concertos by Ravel and Milhaud, touring Europe with the composers, and traveling to Brazil, Long maintained her Classe Supérieure at the Conservatoire and her school, and continued to stage recitals and master classes.

By the beginning of World War II, the careers of some of her most prominent Premier Prix laureates were well launched. Jacques Février, Jean Doyen, and Lucette Descaves would soon hold their own posts at the Conservatoire.[†] Among the younger generation, Nicole Henriot and Samson François were to make superb debuts in New York, while others were faring well at the 1938 Queen Elisabeth Competition (then known as Concours Ysaÿe) in Brussels. Of the 88 pianists competing in the Concours Ysaÿe, nineteen, from ten different countries, were chosen for the semifinals. Among the nineteen were five French pianists, two of whom advanced to the finals.[16] Four of the five French semifinalists were members of Long's Conservatoire

[†]Jacques Février became Professor at the Paris Conservatoire in 1952. Jean Doyen was to inherit the Classe Supérieure at the Conservatoire when Long resigned in 1940. Lucette Descaves was Yves Nat's assistant from 1941 until she was promoted to her own class in the early 1950s.

class;[‡] this was a considerable feat, for in the semifinals, with the exception of Russia and France, each country was at best represented by one candidate. Proud of this remarkable achievement, the Association des Anciens Elèves du Conservatoire (the Conservatoire's alumni association) organized a concert at the Salle Erard to enable Paris to hear these young talents. This concert was very important to the French, for a few days earlier the two Russian pianists who had won first and third place at the competition made spectacular debuts in Paris. Composer Henri Sauguet wrote:

> The extraordinary qualities of the young Soviet virtuosos were for so many of us such a dazzle that soon rumor had it that there could be no possible contest between our French school and such artists. . . . This concert at the Salle Erard was therefore a great service to our young artists, who had just exhibited a considerable effort and could realize, judging by the ovations each received that night, that they knew how to touch both the hearts and the ears of their audience. This concert also proved to those who might have doubted that our French school of piano playing is the most solid . . . the most "human," resting on a tradition . . . that will continue to flourish because it is in good hands. [*Jour,* June 26, 1938.]

In *Le Temps* of June 25, 1938, Paul Landormy gave a glowing review of each artist's share of a rich program: Chopin's B-flat minor Sonata, Schumann's *Carnaval* and *Symphonic Etudes,* Brahms's *Paganini Variations,* Chopin's F minor Ballade, Saint-Saëns' Toccata, and Szymanowski's *Thème Varié.*

Long never lost track of her pupils. Her pedagogical commitment did not end when the lesson was over or the degree was granted. Everyone who studied with her and who showed promise was for her a responsibility, someone who would benefit from her support and the tangible opportunities she was able to offer. Whether it was the Salle Erard master classes, the lectures followed by student performances, the 1938 concert featuring the five Queen Elisabeth semifinalists, the assistantships in her school, or the encounters with composers, all were ways Long had devised to follow up on her students beyond their Conservatoire years, to help their careers as best she could. In the next two decades, starting during World War II, her energy increasingly focused on

[‡]Charlie Lilamand, Nicole Rolet, Jacqueline Potier (now Landowski), and Colette Gaveau. The fifth semifinalist was Monique de la Bruchollerie, a brilliant pupil of Isidor Philipp.

assisting blossoming careers and on devising creative ways for her students to be heard, thanks to the large and influential following she had gathered. Reciprocally, she would reap the benefits of her disciples' success: her reputation as one of the greatest piano pedagogues at home and abroad was firmly established.

8

The War Years: 1939–1945

In October 1940, four months after the Germans occupied Paris, Marguerite Long submitted her resignation to the Paris Conservatoire. Did she not wish to work for the French state during the occupation, and would rather keep her distance and independence? Or was she motivated by feminine vanity, as some of her detractors have intimated? Approaching mandatory retirement, was she bowing out gracefully, so as not to reveal her age to the public? Perhaps she simply wished to concentrate on her own school.

Long had faithfully served the Conservatoire for 34 years, since 1906. She moved out of her apartment at 18 Rue Fourcroy, where she had lived since she was a young bride and where her school had occupied the ground floor for most of that time. After several temporary arrangements during the war, Long finally settled in 16 Avenue de la Grande Armée, only a few steps from the Arc de Triomphe de l'Etoile: this apartment became the stage for the events of the next 25 years and remained indelibly engraved in the memories of many contemporary pianists.

Jacques Thibaud

Just before the war a new person entered into close collaboration with Long, the violinist Jacques Thibaud (1880–1953). He was a native of Bordeaux (like Marliave, Roger-Ducasse, and Déodat de Séverac) and was six years younger than Long. He did not teach (except for occasional master classes, such as the Ecole Normale's 1921 *Ecole de maîtres*), and his career was truly international. In the United States he is mostly remembered for the historic trio of Jacques Thibaud, Pablo Casals, and Alfred Cortot. Thibaud was very handsome, kind, and affable, a man of irresistible charm. Everyone loved him, and several have laughingly suggested that he was the opposite of Long, for she had many enemies and was not physically attractive.

It is not clear exactly when or how Thibaud and Long became acquainted. They were both leading musical personalities in France, and Long's students recall that in the late 1930s Thibaud was part of their mentor's entourage. He occasionally played sonatas with Long's pupils, and for them (the women in particular), it was an unforgettable experience. A very colorful correspondence between Long and Thibaud also began in the 1930s. Thibaud's letters are wonderfully spicy. A letter dated October 8, 1937 opens with "Very dear friend, . . . I haven't had the pleasure of seeing you since the Hundred Years' War!"[1] and ends with "My old and sincere friendship." A much later letter, written from Paris on July 29, 1947, could only have seduced its addressee:

> Marguerite Darling,
>
> Your Baby just returned from a short trip. . . . What in the world are you doing in Aix [-les-Bains, a health spa]? Please do not heal your rheumatism which enabled you to play the piano the way you did the night of that unforgettable Fauré quartet . . . but rather, cherish it!

He would often sign "le Jacquot" after a playful ending such as: "It has been too many years since I've stuck my fat lips on your fraternal cheeks, and I have the firm intention to make up for it soon. . . . A big kiss in tenor clef" (October 16, 1947). Thibaud's eccentric effusions were never intended to have romantic overtones, but rather expressed fraternal affection.

The January 8, 1939 issue of *Jour* carried an article by Pierre Berlioz with the headline "Jacques Thibaud and Marguerite Long open a school: it will focus on the teaching of [violin-piano] sonata playing." The article is in the form of an interview with Jacques Thibaud, who was asked how the idea came to him:

> A violin school makes no sense unless it is in conjunction with the coaching of [violin-piano] sonatas, that is, the study of piano.
>
> All my life I have performed sonatas with Cortot, Planté, Busoni, Rubinstein, Diémer, Rosenthal, Moysevitch. I have a lot of experience and I

> wish to teach, for they [violin-piano sonatas] are the most beautiful literature of our musical heritage.
>
> To have pianists I immediately proposed a collaboration with our great artist Marguerite Long.

This "school" would meet in the studios above the Salle Gaveau. Thibaud explained that they would hire some of their former students as assistants so as to ensure consistency of musical thought: Jean Doyen, Jacques Février, and Tasso Janopoulo for the piano; and Gabriel Bouillon, Roland Charmy, and Joseph Calvet for the violin. It is not clear whether this school actually got off the ground. Long's students have no recollection of a school focused on the study of violin-piano sonatas. What did in fact happen was the opening of another Ecole Marguerite Long–Jacques Thibaud, two years later, in October 1941. It found its home at 46 Rue Molitor and remained Long's teaching headquarters until 1960.

When Long moved out of her living quarters on Rue Fourcroy, she also lost the spacious first-floor rooms which housed her school. About the same time, a long-time friend, Marcelle Lyon, was widowed and wished to help Long as a way of filling the recent vacuum in her own life.

Lyon was a music lover and a good amateur pianist herself. Two of her daughters had attended Long's school in the 1920s, and one of them, Gilberte, had gone on to the Conservatoire and earned her Premier Prix in the 1930s. Through the years, Long had been a frequent houseguest of the Lyon family, particularly in the summers. During the war, Lyon was living in the second floor of a large *hôtel particulier,* on Rue Molitor, in the heart of the then fashionable Auteuil neighborhood. When the first floor of the building became available, Lyon offered the space for Long and Thibaud's school. In the same breath, the devoted "Madame Lyon" (as she was always referred to) offered her services as Director of the school, entirely out of the goodness of her heart and without any remuneration. She scheduled classes and lessons, and kept the accounts of the school, the master classes, and the many other activities that took place at the Ecole Rue Molitor over the next two decades. When the Concours Marguerite Long–Jacques Thibaud was established a few years later, Madame Lyon automatically became its Executive Director. She assumed all the administrative responsibilities of Long's endeavors, whatever they were.

As a way of previewing and attracting attention to their upcoming

Ecole, Long and Thibaud joined forces in organizing six public master classes in the Salle des quatuors of the Gaveau building, from May 22 to June 25, 1941. At these highly successful classes solo piano pieces were interspersed with the great violin-piano repertoire, such as sonatas by Beethoven (the "Kreutzer"), Brahms (the D minor), Franck, and Debussy. The same pianist could be heard one day in the Franck Violin Sonata and the next day, solo, in Schumann's *Kreisleriana.* The classes provided much-needed opportunities for young artists to perform in public at a time when musical life was greatly reduced. Long and Thibaud found in each other a soulmate and an accomplice in doing what they could to encourage the younger generation. A passer-by wrote to a Paris newspaper after one of these classes:

> I admit to having stepped in just by curiosity, to spend ten minutes in the hall . . . and to having stayed, quite thrilled, until the end of the whole class. Marguerite Long and Jacques Thibaud have such a vibrant passion for music. . . . To listen to them is enrapturing: their comments are so clear, so human, so well articulated, they can only make converts out of us.[2]

As planned, the new school opened its doors in October. At the inaugural concert on October 28, the "Tout-Paris" of music was present, including the Secrétaire Perpétuel of the Académie des Beaux-Arts, Louis Hautecoeur. Speeches preceded the program. Former Premier Prix laureates played Debussy's Violin and Piano Sonata, followed by Ravel's *Ma Mère l'Oye* (for piano four-hands).[3] The evening ended with Fauré *mélodies* sung by Pierre Bernac and accompanied by Jacques Février. Debussy, Ravel, and Fauré—the masters at the heart of Long's career—formed the core of this inauguration.

A four-page glossy flier outlined the instrumental classes to be offered at several levels: *cours d'enseignement et de virtuosité, cours supérieur, cours secondaire, cours préparatoire, cours élémentaire.* It indicated that there would be monthly inspections by Marguerite Long and Jacques Thibaud, and quarterly juries, which would be open to the public. Year-end juries would award diplomas to those who qualified. A more modest flier, probably designed for wider circulation, indicated that branches of the school were planned throughout France, from which students could come to Paris for the school's end-of-year examinations. Having branches of the school meant that a former student of Long would have her private studio in a provincial city in France, at which Long would make occasional appearances.

The published fees for these classes were substantial. The Ecole Marguerite Long had acquired a considerable reputation over the years, and it was very fashionable and prestigious to send one's child there. Long was very good at taking money from people who were eager to spend it, yet she often gave a whole day to someone she deemed worthy of her time and did not expect any payment. This partly explains how she could devote so much of her life to young rising stars, who could not possibly afford what a person of her reputation would charge. It was, in a sense, an indirect form of patronage. Long was unofficially raising money through the school to subsidize pianists who needed support. That was true at all levels: she would teach especially gifted children for nothing if they showed promise. She had a "sixth sense"—instantly identifying striking talents and following them thereafter. Since the French government did not allocate funds for programs to aid artists (except for providing two or three tuition-free years at the Conservatoire), Long took matters into her own hands, particularly during the war years.

The Long-Thibaud master classes of May–June 1941 were so successful that a series of seven classes was scheduled for the spring of 1942. The last two were accompanied by the Orchestre du Mouvement Musical des Jeunes, conducted by Thibaud's close friend and disciple Joseph Calvet. The session on June 12 was devoted to J. S. Bach: the D major Piano Concerto, the Double Violin Concerto, and the Concerto for Three Pianos. The one on June 19 was devoted to French music, with Fauré's Ballade and Franck's *Variations Symphoniques* for the piano, and Chausson's *Poème* and Saint-Saëns' *Rondo Capriccioso* for the violin. These classes provided the rare opportunity to work with orchestra; but they also served to propel Long's and Thibaud's protégés onto the stage. The large audiences probably would not have traveled to hear unknown youngsters, but they came because Long and Thibaud were the *têtes d'affiche* (headlines).

These events were limited to those whose careers were burgeoning and who had had previous professional experience. A 1944 program, for example, contains the names of students who were enrolled in Emil Sauer's classes, of semifinalists from the 1938 Queen Elisabeth competition, and of participants in the 1930s public master classes. During the war, Long was helping pianists who had received their Premier Prix during the 1930s, her last Conservatoire "vintage." The added dimension to the recent *Cours de Haute Virtuosité et d'Interprétation* was the presence of Thibaud and the violin repertoire. On the 1944 program, for instance, Poulenc played the piano part of his own Violin Sonata with violinist Françoise Soulé (who had played at the inaugural concert).

The war notwithstanding, the combined personalities of Long and Thibaud created an active musical environment for those at a critical point in their careers. In a letter of September 16, 1938, for example, Thibaud asked Long's assistance for a young pianist:

> Do you know Tasso Janopoulo, who for the past sixteen years has accompanied my concerts all over the world? I would love for you to see him and help him in his life with your wisdom, your advice: Tasso is like a young brother for me . . . . In any case, he is a sweet man and a beautiful artist . . . but he needs a Marguerite Long.

Long and Thibaud were a source of team spirit and encouraged a fruitful camaraderie and competitiveness among their disciples. And the young musicians were grateful to Long for her genuine support of their careers. As the violinist and conductor Jean Martinon wrote to her on August 10, 1945:

> Very dear Madam
>
> It is very difficult for me to express the immense gratitude I owe you; I am infinitely moved by the active kindness that you have shown me and I am filled with happiness and pride to have found in you a genuine guide. All the more so since I know from experience how rare it is to stir the interest and to find the support of great artists whose fames create all too often a wall of indifference.
>
> Jean Martinon[4]

The war years revived in Long the emotional suffering she had endured during World War I. They also reminded her how much music and hard work had helped her to emerge from her grief. Composers and friends such as Debussy, Chevillard, and Roger-Ducasse had gently and trustingly given her back what she had lost, encouraging her to return to the stage in 1917. In the 1940s Long wanted to nourish the young pianists around her and not let international events squelch their potential fire and optimism. This mission was her guiding force throughout those years: she had found a wonderful collaborator in Thibaud, who, with inner resources as rich as Long's, was as generous and optimistic as she was dedicated. As she reminded her students: "If my career has been what it is, it is because I never gave up, I always worked. My joy in life is work, because *it* will never betray you."[5]

Concert Activity during the War

When Long communicated to her pupils that art should remain the ultimate refuge and consolation, she not only believed it but was herself an example of this axiom. More than ever, music was necessary to her spiritual strength. She continued to appear in public with orchestras, even though some of them had to be reduced in size. She premiered a new work by Ernesto Halffter, a young Spanish composer, who had written a rhapsody for piano and orchestra in honor of his teacher Ravel. Feeling increasingly patriotic, she never missed an anniversary of Fauré, Debussy, or Ravel to restore pride in the French spirit: it was her form of resistance to the enemy. Finally, she was often asked to perform at concerts for the benefit of prisoners of war and always graciously offered her participation.

The year 1940 opened with a trip to Belgium, where Long appeared with the Association des Concerts du Conservatoire of Brussels, under Désiré Defauw. She played Beethoven's "Emperor" Concerto in the first half of the concert and Fauré's Ballade in the second half. The program also included Mozart's Overture to *Idomeneo* and works by Paul Dukas and the Belgian composer Guillaume Lekeu. Both Belgian and French newspapers reviewed the performance with enthusiasm and praise.

On May 3, 1940, Long and some of her colleagues gave a concert of Fauré's chamber music for the benefit of the Conservatoire. She played both Piano Quartets with Jacques Thibaud, Maurice Vieux, and Maurice Maréchal. The song cycle *L'Horizon chimérique* and the *Elégie* for cello constituted the rest of the program. Twenty years later, Long vividly recalled that evening: "Menacing shadows darkened the horizon . . . and a few days later, everyone was dispersed . . . it was the end of an era."[6] "A few days later" was May 10, when the Germans invaded neutral Netherlands and Belgium, and with this invasion began the whole movement toward France.

May 10 was also the date for Long, Thibaud, Vieux, and Pierre Fournier (who had replaced Maréchal) to record Fauré's Second Piano Quartet for Pathé Marconi. The news came over the radio that morning. Long was filled with anxiety as she and Jacques Thibaud traveled to the recording studio together: his son, Roger, was stationed on the front line in that region.

> Controlling our dreadful anguish . . . we began our recording session in an extraordinary atmosphere. Never had Thibaud's sound been more gorgeous. We were all devastated. Elevated by the music, beyond the reach of present times, we succeeded in the *tour de force*, of recording the whole quartet in one day.[7]

In 1903, Fauré himself had written in a letter to his wife: "For me, music elevates us as far as possible above what exists here."[8] His Second Piano

Quartet did just that at one of the most tragic moments in all four players' lives: Roger Thibaud was killed two days later, on May 12. Many years later, when Long listened to this recording in the company of Emil Gilels, the Russian pianist said with emotion: "Here, Madame, is one of life's grand moments."[9]

After the Germans took Paris in June 1940, a large part of the city's population fled. The country was in disarray, and artistic life came to a complete halt. In the fall of 1940 Long did not return to the Conservatoire and instead devoted herself to her own school, so as not to work for a state under enemy occupation.

By the fall, some orchestras had resumed their activity, and the Pasdeloup Orchestra, under Philippe Gaubert, invited Long to play her two "warhorses" on October 27: the Fauré Ballade and Ravel's G major Concerto. The hall was packed. The other works on the program were Debussy's *Nocturnes* and Chabrier's *Bourrée Fantasque*, and in the midst of all this French music, Beethoven's Fifth Symphony.

Finally, either to close the old year or to welcome the new one, the Société des Concerts du Conservatoire, now under the direction of Charles Münch, gave an all-Beethoven program on December 31, which was repeated the next day, at the Salle de l'Ancien Conservatoire. Long played Beethoven's C minor Piano Concerto, preceded by the *Egmont* Overture and followed by the "Eroica" Symphony.

In 1941 Long collaborated on several other occasions with Münch, the future conductor of the Boston Symphony, who was then at the height of his career in Europe. In March they gave the first performance of Ernesto Halffter's *Rapsodia Portuguesa* with the Société des Concerts. Halffter was a Spanish composer who lived mostly in Portugal, had studied with Manuel de Falla, and had sought advice from Ravel, for whom he composed this new work for piano and orchestra. In an appreciative letter, Halffter expressed his delight that Long had accepted his request to premiere the *Rapsodia.* She was always excited at the prospect of a new work. (In the album compiled for Long by foreign composers during the 1937 World Exhibition, Halffter's contribution had been a piece called *Espagnolata.* Long remembered the work fondly: "It is a truly delightful piece, full of life and charm."[10]

Long learned the *Rapsodia* in manuscript. Using popular Portuguese melodies in a very colorful and brilliant orchestration, it exudes a fire and temperament characteristic of the Iberian peninsula. The piano part is very rich and virtuosic. It also contains passages of wonderfully tender nostalgia. It is surprising that this work has not become more popular, taking the place of the concerto that Granados never wrote, as it is indeed a very successful and appealing piece.

The concert was held in the grandiose hall of the Palais de Chaillot. Although the Salle de l'Ancien Conservatoire was the home of the Société des Concerts, Münch chose to give concerts honoring a special occasion in the Palais de Chaillot. A full house came to hear a rather long and flamboyant concert: the Bach-Respighi *Passacaille*, the *Rapsodie Espagnole* and the G major Concerto by Ravel, *Danse des Morts* by Honegger, and the new piece by Halffter. The critic Suzanne Demarquez called the *Rapsodia Portuguesa* a "success of rare quality" (*Le Monde musical*, March 23, 1941) and praised the artistry and showmanship of both Long and Münch, who received well-deserved ovations. The same two artists and orchestra performed the work again in 1943. The recording they made for Columbia soon after the première has an exceptional acoustical quality for a 78 rpm record.

Long and Münch shared the stage frequently. Their collaboration during these sad times marked the beginning of their lasting friendship and mutual esteem. Münch conducted one of Long's last public appearances, her June 1956 Jubilee Concert, when she was over 80 years old.

On February 14, 1941, Thibaud joined his artistry to that of Long and Münch in a Beethoven Festival held by the Société des Concerts in the Salle de l'Ancien Conservatoire. Because of the curfew, this concert for the benefit of prisoners of war and the French Red Cross, was scheduled for 6:15 P.M. The emotion-packed program included three of Beethoven's greatest works: the Seventh Symphony in A major, the C minor Piano Concerto, and the sublime D major Violin Concerto. Thibaud was the soloist in the last work, only a few months after the war had taken his son.

Six weeks later, Long participated in another benefit concert for prisoners of war in Clermont-Ferrand, a town in the heart of France's Massif Central mountains. On April 3 she played the Beethoven C minor Concerto again and the Fauré Ballade. The Clermont-Ferrand newspaper *Le Moniteur* lauded this "Concert de Gala" and noted "the very good work of the orchestra, in spite of the numerous empty spaces caused by the absence of first chairs and professors, presently prisoners of war" (April 4, 1941). The orchestra was made up of professors and students at the local conservatory.

On March 9, between the two benefit concerts, Long performed the "Emperor" Concerto at the Salle Pleyel, with the Lamoureux Orchestra conducted by Eugène Bigot. There was no French music on this program, but rather Bach (Orchestral Suite in B minor), Beethoven, and Brahms (Fourth Symphony).

The spring of 1941 was indeed an active season for Long, after the quiet and ominous year of 1940. Münch chose to end his season as director of the Orchestre de la Société des Concerts with three Grand Festivals in the hall of the Palais de Chaillot: a concert on June 13 devoted to Debussy, one of Ravel's music on June 20, and an all-Beethoven concert on June 27. (The first such Festival had taken place on March 12, 1939, honoring Fauré on the 25th anniversary of his death. On this occasion Long had played his Ballade.)

For the 1941 Festivals, an extensive and artistic publicity was sponsored by La Voix de son Maître. The program for the Debussy festival included *La Mer* and the *Martyre de Saint-Sébastien*; the Ravel concert featured *Rapsodie Espagnole*, *Boléro*, *Daphnis et Chloé*, and the Concerto for the Left Hand with Jacques Février at the piano. The third and last concert, in honor of Beethoven, consisted of the "Emperor" Concerto, with Long at the piano, and the Ninth Symphony. As *Paris-Midi* wrote, in announcing the three Festivals, "This beautiful way of ending the season explains why these concerts had to leave their Salle du Conservatoire in favor of the huge auditorium of Chaillot" (June 12, 1941).

Long was invited to play the "Emperor" Concerto again by the Orchestre Pasdeloup in the fall of 1941. During this year, she appeared with almost every orchestra in Paris: Société des Concerts, Lamoureux, and Pasdeloup. It is curious to note the conductors' frequent choice of Beethoven in time of war. Would Beethoven's music restore pride to the listeners? Would it inspire strength and power, hope and faith?

On May 19, 1942 three of France's most-celebrated artists joined forces in a program of music by Gabriel Fauré at the Salle Gaveau: Pierre Bernac, Francis Poulenc, and Marguerite Long. Long played four piano pieces; and Bernac sang, accompanied by Poulenc. The program opened with four *mélodies*: *Lydia*, *Tristesse*, *Aurore*, and *Après un rêve*. Long then played the Second Nocturne and the Second Barcarolle. Bernac and Poulenc came back to perform the entire cycle of *La Bonne Chanson*, one of Fauré's most beautiful works. The great Sixth Nocturne and Third Valse-Caprice for piano followed, and Bernac and Poulenc closed the concert with another set of four *mélodies*: *Le Don silencieux*, *Prison*, *Le plus doux chemin*, and the enchanting *Mandoline*. The review in *Paris-Midi* describes an admirable evening:

> Marguerite Long surpassed herself. . . . Pierre Bernac . . . showed his overflowing musicality, his delicate nuances and his keen intelligence in all of his interpretations. Francis Poulenc is not an accompanist but an enchanter: his touch, his musical sensitivity intensify the beauty of this music.

Even though Poulenc (1899–1963) was of a younger generation, Long knew him because of her unfailing interest in young composers and because he was a pianist. Poulenc was a man of irresistible charm; wherever he was, his presence dominated the room. Before World War I, he had studied piano with Ricardo Viñes, but he turned primarily to composing when he returned from the army. Poulenc and Long exchanged letters and had a warm and friendly relationship. Poulenc addressed the following to Long, evidently after she had congratulated him on a recent radio performance:

> Dear Madam and friend,
>
> You are just too kind to have written to me in this way. I can see that the radio is a rather lenient medium, because, unless you are even more lenient than it, I played in a rather pitiful way, with clumsy fingers on a heavy Steinway. Do you know that more and more I am coming to appreciate old Erards again, for one gets drowned in their beautiful sound quality. . . .
>
> . . . I have started working again. I will complete my violin sonata and then write a concerto for two pianos and ten instruments commissioned by the Princesse de Polignac. I think you will like the first movement, in D minor, for the piano is treated in sound effects.
>
> I am really proud that you are playing the *Caprice Italien* and am looking forward to hearing it played by you, particularly since I was not able to play it myself.
>
> Poulenc[11]

Many years later Poulenc congratulated Long on her performance at the Edinburgh festival of 1950 (see below, p. 170). Even through his pen one can sense his sunny personality:

> Dear friend,
>
> How well you played in Edinburgh the other night. You almost made me a Fauré fan, and the Ravel was, once again, unparalleled. Why did you never record the *Tombeau de Couperin*, which people distort recital after recital? . . . I am sending you my "naughty boy" concerto. . . . To be forgiven and not just because such is my nature, I am writing a Stabat [mater] for choir and orchestra. I feel very much at home with it, and I hope I can touch those who like prayers. . . . Have a good summer and receive my affectionate admiration.
>
> Francis[12]

This letter is signed "Francis," whereas the first one, written by a young 32-year-old, was still signed "Poulenc."

Inspired by the success of the 1941 Festivals, Charles Münch decided to give his last concert of the 1941–42 season with the Société des Concerts in the same hall, at the Palais de Chaillot. The event on June 4 was a Festival Fauré-Debussy, with Long playing a late work by Fauré, his *Fantaisie pour piano et orchestre*, Op. 111. It had been premiered in Monte Carlo on April 12, 1919 by Marguerite Hasselmans; and Alfred Cortot, its dedicatee, played it at the Société Nationale in Paris a month later. Before her performance, Long gave a little talk introducing this obscure work:

> Perhaps it is the success of the frequently performed divine Ballade . . . which has somewhat dampened the memory of the *Fantaisie*. . . . If the *Fantaisie* does not offer the same appeal upon first hearing as does the Ballade . . . it possesses on the other hand the refined gifts of wisdom and is a product of the discipline the composer imposed upon himself at the end of his life. . . . Let me point out . . . the precision and fluidity of the themes, the ease with which they are developed and the classical sobriety reflected in the writing. . . . Let us hope that today's performance will honor this *Fantaisie* and will allow it to be reinstated on the programs of our great orchestras.[13]

A warm letter from Münch to Long, dated August 2, 1943, announced a Festival Ravel for the opening of the next season:

> Chère Grande Amie [Dear Great Friend]
>
> I wanted to ask you if you would play the season opener at Chaillot with me. I would like to start with a "Festival Ravel," where the Concerto which you play in such a distinctive way must absolutely be featured. . . . I kiss you very tenderly.
>
> Charles Münch[14]

In the summer of 1942, Long and Thibaud were again the center of attraction in a benefit concert for prisoners of war. Entitled Gala de la Valse, the whole program was built around waltzes.

> The most sensational "number" was without a doubt the "Duo" Jacques Thibaud–Marguerite Long. Our international Jacques, at the podium, conducted (and with what a subtle baton!) the orchestral accompaniment of a lovely

> Strauss Waltz, in which Long was the soloist. Never did the great interpreter of Fauré's art touch the keyboard with more wit, more grace, more charm and spirit. [*L'Information musicale*, September 25, 1942.]

The large hall of the Palais de Chaillot was sold out, and a considerable sum of money was raised. The *L'Information musicale* article opened with the words "Finally an event worthy of our prisoners of war! Unforgettable hall of the Palais de Chaillot packed with a huge crowd." The Secrétariat des Stalag X sent a very appreciative letter of thanks to Long, assuring her that her generosity would never be forgotten, that it would remain associated with the benefits that this gala was able to provide for those in need.[15]

By 1943 the international conflict had escalated, and during the last two years of the war Long's public performances were more sporadic and reserved for special occasions. One of those was a series of three concerts of piano and violin sonatas with her dear friend and collaborator Jacques Thibaud. On May 3, 7, and 11, 1943 the two artists presented works by Bach, Mozart, Fauré, and Debussy at the Salle Gaveau. They made their own fun during rehearsals. When Long would end a brilliant run, Thibaud would put a coin on the piano with a teasing nod and say "Well done! " She would break out in laughter each time.[16] A short while later, the two artists performed at the Société des Concerts, with Thibaud as conductor and Long as soloist in Mozart's A major Piano Concerto (K. 488). During the spring of 1943 Long and Thibaud were also planning their first piano and violin competition, which was to take place in the fall (see below, p. 136).

Except for another performance of the "Emperor" Concerto with the Société des Concerts in December 1943, Long's public performances were now limited to celebrations of Fauré's music, of which she was still considered the prime interpreter. In November 1944, Long, Thibaud, and their quartet partners, Vieux and Maréchal, gave a concert at the Salle Gaveau on the twentieth anniversary of Fauré's death. They spontaneously agreed to donate the proceeds of this concert to families in the Eighth Arrondissement whose members had been part of the Underground. Why the Eighth Arrondissement? Possibly because the Salle Gaveau was located there or because of personal connections with the musicians. The mayor of the Eighth Arrondissement expressed his gratitude to Long for the musicians' initiative:

> République Française, Comité Local de Libération du VIIIe arrondissement, Paris, 22 Novembre 1944:

> Dear Madam,
>
> Thank you for the magnificent concert . . . benefiting families of F.F.I.s† of the Eighth Arrondissement. My colleagues and I were very moved by your spontaneous offer and the meaning you gave to this event by associating our great patriotic musician, Gabriel Fauré, to the F.F.I. and the symbol of November 11th. . . . Please let me add my congratulations for the way you averted, during the last four years, the most tempting and Machiavellian offers on the part of the Germans.[17]

The last sentence is but a hint of the tension within France between hard-core Underground members and ordinary citizens, who tried to carry on a normal life as best they could during the German occupation. Particularly at the end of 1944, after France was liberated, Underground members were quite forthcoming and tended perhaps to overstate their role in the liberation of France.

A few days before the benefit concert Long and Thibaud were interviewed by the music critic of *Parisien libéré.* Thibaud advised him to devote more of his time to writing about the young virtuosos for whom each public appearance is a major undertaking. "You are very kind to give us so much attention," said Thibaud, "but frankly, Madame Long and myself are a bit embarrassed to see so many papers writing about our concerts, whereas they do so little, or nothing, for musicians who are just beginning."[18] Having made the support of young careers their main activity during the war years, Long and Thibaud were hoping for more help and encouragement on the part of the press. They deplored the lack of coverage of debut recitals. When asked about his immediate projects, Thibaud answered warmly:

> I believe the one I cherish the most is about to be realized. I was asked to give a series of concerts—over sixty of them!—for the soldiers at the front. . . . I will be able to play for those who are fighting: and do not think they requested light music. They all demanded serious music. [*Le Parisien libéré*, November 9, 1944.]

In November 1944, Long celebrated her 70th birthday. Paris was at last liberated, and the end of the war was in sight.

The year 1944 had been the twentieth anniversary of Fauré's death, and 1945 was the centennial of his birth. A whole week of programs marked the event, from May 11 to May 17. The celebration included a performance of

†Force Française de l'Intérieur, which combined all underground organizations, except the Communists, during the German occupation of France.

Fauré's opera *Pénélope* at the Théâtre National de l'Opéra, a concert version of *Prométhée* (a lyric tragedy in three acts) by the Orchestre National, a concert by the Société des Concerts under Charles Münch's direction, and performances of chamber music. The week was more than a grand celebration of music: on May 7, just four days before the first concert, Germany had surrendered unconditionally to the Allies, and on May 8, a sea of men and women had gathered around the Arc de Triomphe in exultation over the victory.

The Société des Concerts, Münch, and Long opened the festival on May 11 at the Théatre des Champs-Elysées. On the program was the *Suite de Pelléas et Mélisande,* a delightful and sunny orchestral work written at the end of the nineteenth century. It came as no surprise that Long would play "her" Ballade—for by now the piece was associated as much with Long as it was with Fauré. The program concluded with one of Fauré's greatest masterpieces, his Requiem, which is not as somber as most compositions of the same name. As Long wrote, it would "glow from the rays of hope of its In Paradisium."[19] Long and her quartet colleagues—Thibaud, Vieux, and Maréchal—met on May 16 at the Salle Gaveau for a performance of Fauré's First Piano Quartet. The same evening, Long and Thibaud played the First Sonata for Violin and Piano in a larger program of chamber music, which also included *mélodies.*

The Fauré centennial, with the participation of some of the most prominent personalities and musical institutions in Paris, signified that French musical and artistic life would soon return to its past glories.

Throughout World War II, during most of which France was occupied by the enemy, Long tried, as did many, to show that life could still go on and that things could be accomplished. She concentrated her efforts on the younger generation, to ensure that the political climate would not shatter their dreams or discourge their ambitions forever. She found an equally energetic, generous, and inspiring accomplice in the person of Jacques Thibaud, whose foremost interest at that time was also to assist and launch young musicians. While there was fighting on the front and people at home were trying to feed their families, Long and Thibaud joined forces in leading their school on Rue Molitor and in founding the competition which still bears their names today.

Although gradually slowing down the pace of her public performances, Long continued to play on special occasions, particularly when she could provide help to prisoners of war. In this initiative, she found in Charles Münch a musician and conductor whom she esteemed highly and whom she befriended for the rest of her life.

9

The Concours Marguerite Long–Jacques Thibaud

The Genesis of the Concours

Although the Concours Marguerite Long–Jacques Thibaud was inaugurated in 1943, the idea of creating a competition had been in the back of Long's mind since before the war. She had attended the 1938 Ysaÿe Competition in Brussels, which four of her students had entered: "To see all those dedicated young people with so much talent . . . had simply exhilarated me. . . . Ever since that time, I have wanted to create a competition and have waited for the proper timing to do it."[1]

The Ysaÿe Competition had been founded by Queen Elisabeth of Belgium, a genuine music lover and violinist, in honor of her teacher Eugène Ysaÿe (1858–1931), whom she revered dearly. Her interest in music was so well known that Fauré dedicated to her his Second Violin Sonata, Op. 108. The first Concours Ysaÿe took place in 1937 for the violin, and in 1938 for the piano; the first two winners were David Oistrakh and Emil Gilels.

In the middle of the German occupation and a seemingly never-ending war, Long felt sorry for the young generation of musicians whose careers were stalled and who could not travel or perform abroad. Now was the time to create a competition to revive their hopes and stimulate their artistic and spiritual energies. In collaboration with Jacques Thibaud, who wholeheartedly

Long and Jacques Thibaud, 1946.
Photo Roger-Viollet, Paris.

shared Long's concerns, the two set out to organize the first Concours Marguerite Long–Jacques Thibaud in November 1943. There would be a first and a second prize in each violin and piano category. The cash prizes were modest but the professional rewards would be considerable: concert engagements with some of the Paris orchestras, a recording contract with Pathé Marconi for the pressing of one commercial record, and concerts with the Jeunesses Musicales (see below, pp. 141–42). Thanks to the renown and dedication of the founders, several institutions offered their support of the Concours, including the record company Pathé Marconi and the Salle Gaveau, which made the hall available for the event.

The first Concours was of relatively small proportions, due to political circumstances, and no foreigners were able to attend. There were ten entrants each in the violin and piano categories, and only two rounds for each, one a day, from Monday, November 15, through Thursday, November 18, 1943. The repertoire requirements were much simpler than they were to become later. The first round of the violin competition consisted of one concerto chosen among those of Beethoven, Brahms, Tchaikovsky, the Mozart D major, and the Saint-Saëns B minor; the second round was a J. S. Bach Fugue and a Paganini Caprice. Compared to current standards, these rounds seem to be in reverse order. In the piano contest, the first round required one of three sonatas: Beethoven's "Appassionata," Chopin's B minor, or Weber's A-flat major. The second and final round included Chopin's First Ballade; an etude by Chopin, Liszt, or Debussy; and one major work by Fauré, Debussy, or Ravel. The two first prize winners were Michèle Auclair, violin, and Samson François, piano.

Long was very pleased with the way the whole event unfolded.

> It was a very interesting Concours, with a well-chosen jury composed essentially of conductors and composers, chaired by Henri Rabaud [Director of the Paris Conservatoire]. It was altogether very solemn and captivating, and a very much needed distraction during the tragic period through which we were living.[2]

Despite the success of the first Concours, Long and Thibaud decided to wait until the end of the war for further trials, and then turn their Concours into an international competition which would take place every three years. "This is how it all started," said Long.[3]

As soon as the war was over they began to plan the first Concours International, scheduled for December 1946. "We were rather courageous, because since the competition had not been established before the war, and the borders of countries had just recently opened up, we had no notion of how it would turn out."[4] Actually, 23 countries were represented. Long explained that young people obviously wanted to travel, and this was an excellent opportunity to come to France. But they were not tourists, for they had to work very hard: 52 candidates entered the violin division and 93 the piano.

Both winners were foreigners: the American Arnold Eidus in violin and the Hungarian Hedi Schneider in piano. The prestigious jury of twenty was presided over by the composer Jacques Ibert, then director of the French Academy in Rome. Among the jury members were the violinist Zino Francescatti (of Italy); Walter Legge (of England), then Director of the Columbia Gramophone Company; the conductor Felix Weingartner (of Austria), Heinrich von Kralik, Director of Vienna Radio; the composer Joseph Jongen (of Belgium), then Director of the Brussels Conservatory; Eduard van Beinum (of Holland), then conductor of the Amsterdam Concertgebouw; Geza de Krecz, Director of the Budapest Conservatory; the Polish pianist Witold Malcuzynski; and the composer Alexander Tcherepnin. This list exemplified Long and Thibaud's ability to attract distinguished musicians, and it reflected their good sense in inviting conductors, directors of radio or record companies, and composers to hear the promising young talents, for these people were in a position to help performance careers. Long had finally realized her dream: to give France its first international competition.

The 1949 Concours

It took only one round to establish the reputation of the Concours International Marguerite Long–Jacques Thibaud. For the 1949 competition, which took place from June 20 to 27, the awards were considerably more important, including larger cash prizes and numerous concert engagements in France and abroad, as well as the recording opportunity with Pathé Marconi. The increase in cash prizes reflected the international interest in the competition, for many prizes were offered by private individuals, by music publishers (including Durand and Heugel), and by festival directors. There were also some "Anonymous U.S.A. prizes." The concert engagements grew out of the connections Long and Thibaud had among conductors and festival directors.

Both juries were quite large: 20 members judged the violin competition and 23 the piano, representing twelve countries in all. Some served on both juries, for example, Sergiu Celibidache of the Berlin Philharmonic; Edward Lockspeiser, then Director of Music at the B.B.C; the composers Francesco Malipiero (Director of Venice's conservatory), Georges Enesco (of Rumania), and Ernesto Halffter (of Spain); and Pierre Agostini, Director of Pathé Marconi. The juries also included directors of foreign conservatories, some prominent conductors in Paris, and (on the piano jury) Nadia Boulanger, Magda Tagliaferro, and Lazare-Lévy.

This gathering of prominent European musicians only hints at the magnitude of Long and Thibaud's initiative. It must be remembered that there were very few international competitions at the time. One of the oldest, the Queen Elisabeth in Brussels, had been created a mere decade earlier; and the only other international contests were the Chopin Competition in Warsaw and the Geneva Competition. Therefore, an international event of this stature held in Paris would quickly gain prominence.

Long was once asked about Thibaud's role in planning the competition, for the violinist traveled quite often and was known for his artistic temperament more than for his administrative gifts. She answered that indeed he was away very often but that when he came back they would talk about their project and she would assign him various responsibilities. On his next visit Thibaud would inevitably stick his head through the door of her boudoir and say, with his irresistible charm: "Marguerite, I have done nothing of what you told me to do, but do not scold me, give me a kiss and a hug!" "And of course, we would gladly kiss him!"[5] Long explained that the competition was his pride and joy and that Thibaud publicized it on his concert tours. But even more important, during the rounds themselves, his presence brought great charisma to the event.

Needless to say, this endeavor represented an enormous administrative task. Credit must be given to the faithful Madame Lyon, who had not only opened up her house on Rue Molitor for the Ecole Long-Thibaud (inaugurated during the war), but had also devoted her time to the organization of Long's various enterprises. It was the same Madame Lyon who kept track of applications, stayed in touch with embassies, and arranged housing for foreign candidates. The Concours received modest state subsidies; Long remarked that although "the French state may not be wealthy enough to fund such a project, we must admit that even if it was, music is not a priority in France."[6]

Among the 1949 piano laureates who have achieved international careers and have become familiar names are Aldo Ciccolini (of Italy) and Ventsislav Yankoff (of Bulgaria), who tied for First Prize (both subsequently taught at the Paris Conservatoire until 1988 and 1991 respectively), Daniel Wayenberg (of Holland), Paul Badura-Skoda (of Austria), Yuri Boukoff (of Bulgaria), Pierre Barbizet (of France), and Maria Chairo-Georges (of Greece). In violin, the winner was Christian Ferras.

Long proudly reminisced about 1949 and its outcome:

> When Ciccolini arrived in Paris, he was a short, charming little Italian man, and he did not speak a word of French. He was completely unknown, and he won the competition. A week later he gave his recital at Salle Gaveau: all of Paris was there. This is when I felt that my efforts were rewarded, for the goal had been met.[7]

Growth of the Concours: 1951, 1953, and 1955

After the banner year of 1949, the Concours was solidly established as one of Europe's main piano and violin competitions, and its founders decided that it should occur every two years starting with 1951. Mounting interest in the event by patrons of the arts as well as by the French government resulted in substantially increased cash prizes. The Prix de la Ville de Paris (second place), for example, doubled twice, from 50,000 francs in 1949, to 100,000 francs in 1951, and 200,000 francs in 1953. The Prix de la Société des Compositeurs de Musique increased from 25,000 to 50,000 francs. The First Prize, or Grand Prix Marguerite Long, went from 100,000 francs in 1949 to 200,000 in 1951, 300,000 in 1953, and 350,000 in 1955. By 1955 all eight finalists received generous financial rewards in addition to offers of concert engagements.

The juries, which averaged twenty members, also reflected the growth of the Concours: in 1951 Francis Poulenc, Arthur Honegger, and the Czech pianist Rudolf Firkusny joined the ranks. Artur Schnabel had to decline the invitation to judge the rounds; as he wrote to Long in February 1951, from New York:

> I would have loved to accept your kind invitation if I had been certain I would be in Paris at the time you mentioned. Unfortunately, as of now I do not see it as a possibility.
>
> If by any chance my plans changed, I would be thrilled to let you know as soon as possible in the event that my collaboration were still desired.
>
> My best wishes for the success of your interesting competition,
>
> Artur Schnabel[8]

A milestone in the history of the Concours Long–Thibaud was the first participation of Soviet candidates, in the spring of 1953. Long admitted that the Russians' entrance gave the contest another scope; 1953 was also the year that the Soviet Union was represented in the jury, by David Oistrakh and Lev

Oborin. A Soviet violinist, Nelli Shkolnikova, won the Grand Prix Jacques Thibaud. In the piano contest, the results were controversial, for instead of one first prize, the Soviet Evgeny Malinin and the French Philippe Entremont tied for second place. In the violin juries of 1953 and 1955, the names of David Oistrakh and Henryk Szeryng added considerable luster to the list. For the piano, participation by Artur Rubinstein and Guido Agosti in 1953 and by Claudio Arrau, Emil Gilels, Alexander Brailowsky, Annie Fisher, and Witold Malcuzynski in 1955 indicates the importance this contest had gained. Leading conductors, composers, and conservatory directors from France and abroad continued to serve on both juries, year after year.

As committed as Long and Thibaud were to the cultivation of performing careers, good intentions were fruitless without actual concert engagements. In addition to the various concerts in France and abroad promised to winners in previous years, a new prize was offered starting in 1951: extensive concert tours with the Jeunesses Musicales de France (Musical Youths). The idea of the J.M.F. originated with René Nicoly, who wanted to help young musicians' careers and at the same time promote live music among children. The J.M.F. concerts featured a solo artist and a distinguished lecturer, who would introduce the music to the young audience by making interdisciplinary connections between the arts, history, and politics. Nicoly's plan provided a way for recent competition winners to be heard and known throughout the country. The J.M.F. concert tours consisted of 30 to 50 concerts, at a rate of close to one concert a day. All of Long's laureates benefited from the J.M.F., and all of them were grateful for it. They unanimously deplored the fact that nothing of the sort exists now. Whereas today's young competition laureates wait for rare engagements with major symphonies under world-famous conductors, the J.M.F. enabled them to season a program by playing it many times in the small towns of France and to earn fees in the process. This organization was in perfect agreement with Long's philosophy. From its very beginning, during the war, Long encouraged Nicoly in this venture, which took a few years to become well established. In the early 1950s, the J.M.F. also had exchange programs, so that a French pianist could tour the United States or Brazil while an American or Brazilian pianist toured in France. According to Philippe Entremont:

> If there is in the world a precious artistic organization among all others, it is undoubtedly the Jeunesses Musicales de France. Admirable initiative which

> educates the audiences of tomorrow, unmatched proving ground for young artists—we can never say enough how much music and musicians are indebted to this prodigious organization. For my part, the J.M.F. was at the base of my career, giving me the opportunity to play both in France and abroad.[9]

Daniel Wayenberg expressed similar feelings:

> Should we underline to what extent [the J.M.F.] has helped us, and continues to help young artists at the beginning of such a difficult career? . . . I want to point out especially to what extent a J.M.F. tour gives us the experience of the stage and the audience, and enables us to mature the pieces that we perform.[10]

The Jeunesses Musicales de France was one of the strongest assets of the Long-Thibaud competition, along with the Pathé Marconi recording contract. Above and beyond the official rewards came others, such as concert management. One of Long's dearest and oldest friends was Marcel de Valmalète, who owned one of the two most important concert management offices in France (still famous today), the other being run by Gabriel Dussurget. Dussurget, also a friend of Long, was the founder of the Aix-en-Provence Music Festival. He had great influence on the music business and an even greater reputation as a powerful impresario; he later became the Director of the Opéra. As the Concours continued to develop, Long relied on both Valmalète and Dussurget to help her laureates.

In ten years the Concours had come a long way in every respect. Long and Thibaud could contemplate with satisfaction the fruits of their labor, while continuing to dream up new ways of improving and magnifying their endeavor. But a tragedy struck this dream on September 1, 1953, when the plane carrying Thibaud on tour to Japan crashed into a mountain, leaving no survivors. The news plunged France's musical world into mourning; and it devastated Long. Since the first days of World War II Thibaud had been her close friend, her partner, her soulmate. They complemented each other: Long was the guardian of discipline and perfection, and Thibaud was charm personified. Everyone who knew Long and Thibaud could appreciate the deep sorrow that this news inflicted on the pianist. Long received letters from all over the world, expressing sympathy and affection while encouraging her to

Long with Artur Rubinstein and André Cluytens, during the 1953 Concours. Photo Roger-Viollet, Paris.

continue the work with the strength of two people. Magda Tagliaferro, one of the first to write to Long, sent a letter from São Paulo on September 4, 1953:

> My dear friend,
>
> What a horrible accident! I am distressed beyond what I can express and think dearly of you in such a devastating moment. One remains disconcerted when faced by the terrible doom of Providence and overwhelmed by such a tragic end. Please let me hear from you.[11]

Only a few weeks later classes resumed at the Rue Molitor, in the school Long and Thibaud had started during the war. His absence left an immense vacuum, but she continued on her own to pursue their common goal.

Long's biggest challenge was to prepare for the 1955 competition without her partner. But after the Soviet participation in 1953 and all the other signs of the steadily growing prestige of the Concours, the French government decided to take an active part in the upcoming contest. On November 24, 1954, Jacques Jaujard, Directeur des Arts et des Lettres at the Ministère de l'Education Nationale, and M. de Bourbon-Busset, Directeur des Relations Culturelles at the Ministère des Affaires Etrangères, held a press conference. In the presence of foreign ambassadors, French and foreign cultural attachés, and press attachés, they declared the competition one of France's most important artistic and international endeavors.[12] Jaujard opened with a brief history of its inception, paying due homage to its two founders and deploring the untimely death of Thibaud. He then described the French government's increased commitment to the organization of this international event and to its financial support. On behalf of the Ministère des Affaires Etrangères, Bourbon-Busset spoke in the same tone, urging foreign ambassadors and cultural attachés to promote the Concours abroad. Long closed the press conference by thanking Jaujard and Bourbon-Busset for their continued support and for having included the competition in the national budget. She also acknowledged the invaluable assistance of Pathé Marconi and the Maison Gaveau, without whose generous support this biennial event would not have attained its considerable prestige.

As a result of this recognition by the French state, the cover of the application and rules booklet for the 1955 contest reads:

> Concours International Marguerite Long–Jacques Thibaud under the auspices of the President of France, the Ministre des Affaires Etrangères, the Ministre de l'Education Nationale, the Président du Conseil Municipal de Paris. . . .[13]

The Concours and the Marguerite Long Foundation

The Ministère de la Culture started sponsoring the Concours in 1957, and members of the French government took an active role on its board of directors. For the first time the event was shown in its entirety in several countries over French television. The Hungarian Peter Frankl was the First Prize winner. On September 6, 1957, Rudolf Firkusny wrote to Long from Aspen, Colorado:

> Dear Madam,
>
> I would like to tell you once again how touched and proud I was to be one of the judges in your competition; also, to thank you for the kindness you have expressed toward me during my last stay in Paris. It is a rare privilege to know you and every contact with you signifies a new source of inspiration and admiration. Thank you for all that you give us so generously.
>
> Rudolf Firkusny[14]

Long wanted to ensure the permanence of her competition. Until then, it had been a private organization to which the government lent political support and modest subsidies. Her idea was to bequeath her estate and the Concours to the French state in order to create a national foundation which would continue her mission of encouraging and nurturing young careers by means of the Concours.

Long expressed her intentions to her many friends and supporters among France's ministers. In a letter dated March 24, 1960, Louis Joxe, then Ministre de l'Education Nationale, acknowledged her wish that he head the new foundation:

> Dear friend,
>
> I am deeply touched by your thoughtfulness in asking me to assume the presidency of the Foundation which you are about to create to perpetuate the Concours.
>
> I have enjoyed your friendship for a long time. Its testimony today is too valuable to be expressed in words. It is therefore with a great deal of joy that I tell you how delighted I am to accept the proposition you made me.
>
> I also want to tell you that I will intervene with M. [André] Malraux with all possible urgency to make sure that under no circumstance should the Concours ever suffer from lack of support by the powers that be.
>
> Louis Joxe[15]

Joxe had stood by Long when the Concours was first started and had supported her many endeavors ever since. As the French ambassador to Moscow, he had been her host during her trip to the Soviet Union. Joxe was president of the Long Foundation's Board of Directors until his death in April 1991.

In the spring of 1961, a press conference held at the offices of the Direction Générale des Arts et des Lettres was an important landmark in the history of the Concours. Long made public her assignment of the foundation to the French state:

> At the press conference . . . M. Jacques Jaujard, Secrétaire Général du Ministère des Affaires Culturelles, made public the conferral by Marguerite Long, of a Foundation that she has endowed with considerable capital. The revenues of this foundation will serve to assure the First Grand Prize for Piano . . . (in addition to engagements with the great French and foreign symphony orchestras, an engagement with the R[adiodiffusion] T[élévision] F[rançaise], a series of concerts with the Jeunesses Musicales de France and a recording with Pathé Marconi). . . .
>
> M. Jacques Jaujard added that the State would make its own contribution to this magnificent institution. Thus, for the first time and thanks to the generosity of its founder, a private competition will become a State competition, and the Concours Marguerite Long–Jacques Thibaud is henceforth guaranteed to pursue its wonderful mission.[16]

Moved by this turning point in the history of her own competition, Long spoke with great emotion:

> I am overwhelmed to hear such praise on my behalf; I could in turn praise you even more when I think of your so effective and thoughtful collaboration.
>
> Thank you . . . for the faithfulness of your presence and for the interest you have shown toward this project. This Concours, which brings us closer internationally every two years, encourages my desire to support young talent. . . . It is with that in mind that I took the steps M. Jaujard spoke of earlier in order to secure the continuity of the effort I have made for the last eighteen years.
>
> The institution which grew from it could only be entrusted to people of great value, who generously helped me at the origin of my initiative, which enables me today to express publicly all my gratitude to M. Louis Joxe, Ministre d'Etat, and M. Jaujard, Secrétaire Général des Affaires Culturelles, who accepted with enthusiasm to be the guardians of my mission.[17]

As with all governmental and legal activities, the steps involved to finalize the Marguerite Long Foundation took several months, and it was not until April 28, 1962 that the decree-law was enacted by Georges Pompidou, then Prime Minister, and Roger Frey, Ministre de l'Intérieur.[18] In the May 5, 1962 issue of the *Journal Officiel de la République Française,* it appeared under the section "Ministère de l'Intérieur": "Par décret en date du 28 Avril 1962, la fondation dite Fondation Marguerite Long, dont le siège est à Paris, est reconnue comme établissement d'utilité publique" (p. 4548.)

By this time Long was already planning the 1963 Concours: "I take care of all the planning, more then ever. I am reconsidering the dates of the next rounds . . . modifying repertoire requirements. . . . I would like it so much if the Chinese could one day participate, but it is difficult."[19] (Long's wish was realized posthumously: Chinese candidates participated in the Concours Long–Thibaud for the first time in 1981.)

In 1963, the tenth Concours Long–Thibaud marked the twentieth anniversary of its creation. Long asked Darius Milhaud to be president and Henri Sauguet vice-president. At a press conference and reception on February 18, 1963 Long said that her recent action regarding the Concours was that of "a mother, whose child had grown . . . and who must, without melancholy and as is necessary, let him live his own life."[20]

There were to be no changes in the way it would be run except that it would take place from November 12 to 30 instead of in the spring. And the finals, traditionally staged at the Salle Gaveau, as were the other rounds, would be held at the larger Théâtre des Champs-Elysées. The preliminaries and semifinals would take place at the traditional Salle de l'Ancien Conservatoire.

The 1965 Concours was the last one that Long attended; she was 91 years old. An affectionate card from Aldo Ciccolini endearingly recalled earlier days of this international event:

> Dear Madam,
>
> On the eve of the tenth Concours International which holds your illustrious name, my thoughts are with you, filled with gratitude, admiration and tenderness. It is with the greatest emotion that I will be part of your jury in this same hall where, sixteen years ago, your marvelous prize was awarded to me. I embrace you with all my heart,
>
> Aldo[21]

The Concours still thrives. Each year 8,000 brochures are sent all over the world; an average of 60 contestants are selected from about 250 applicants, by means of dossiers and tapes. Since 1983, the Concours has been on a three-year cycle: the first for piano, the second for violin; and on the third year, a gala concert with orchestra is held in the Théâtre des Champs-Élysées or the Salle Pleyel. The winners of the two previous years make their Paris debuts with orchestra, and a number of laureates from the past collaborate in ensemble performances, such as double or triple concertos. The present administration of the Concours strives to perpetuate Long and Thibaud's mission: more than merely managing the contest itself, it aims to assist the careers of its laureates and help their reputations grow. In addition to subsidies from the French government, the Concours now has among its private sponsors the Banque Nationale de Paris and the Fujisankei Communications Group of Tokyo.

The Concours continues to draw on the world's leading musicians for its juries. In December 1989, Leon Fleisher chaired the piano jury, which selected two American First Prize Winners, Brian Ganz and Jeffrey Biegel; in the fall of 1992 Lorin Maazel conducted the finals of the piano competition; and the 1993 Concours will celebrate its 50th anniversary with the participation of Yehudi Menuhin and Isaac Stern.

10

The Postwar Decade: 1946–1955

Though Long was in her 70s when the war ended, she was entering what may be called the "golden age" of her pedagogical, political, and artistic influences. Her allegiance to the Conservatoire had ended. Her school and her persona henceforth radiated their own enormous prestige throughout France, Europe, and overseas. Through the international competition she and Jacques Thibaud had founded, she attracted to Paris pianists and violinists from all over the world. In the late 1940s and the 1950s, an impressive roster of musicians gravitated around her, particularly in connection with the weekly master classes she instituted in 1947.

The Golden Years of a Pedagogue

In December 1946, after the prizes had been awarded at the Concours Marguerite Long–Jacques Thibaud, Long spoke to the Bulgarian pianist Ventsislav Yankoff, whose talent she had recognized during the competition rounds[1] (he went on to win First Prize in 1949). "Why don't you come by, 46 Rue Molitor, the first Friday of January [1947] to play for my class? I am trying something new; it will be very informal. I have no idea who will turn up. We will just see."[2] He came and played Beethoven's "Waldstein" Sonata and Debussy's *L'Isle joyeuse.*

Long at her writing desk, with a photo of Marliave in the background, 1953. Photo Roger-Viollet, Paris.

Thus began Long's illustrious international public master classes. They were held weekly in the first floor salon of 46 Rue Molitor, the home of the always caring and affectionate Madame Lyon. The salon was a typical double living room of a Paris home, with glass double-doors in the center, which were kept open. Even though it was a large room, it soon became crowded, as this event gained popularity in Paris. Through the next decade and a half, these classes attracted pianists from all over the world, as well as an assiduous following of fans who not only delighted in Long's pedagogical "one-woman show" but also came to witness burgeoning careers. The classes were occasionally attended by foreign critics, including those from the *New York Times,* who would report on the young "colts" of the moment; and the Paris press regularly reported on the afternoon happenings at Rue Molitor, which were a *rendez-vous* not only of music but of high society.

Long played her grand role to the hilt. Her royal entrance would be 15, 30, or 45 minutes late. Wearing extraordinary hats, furs, and jewelry, always impeccably elegant, and more often than not carrying a large bouquet of flowers, she would greet her aristocratic friends, on her right and on her left, with fluffy chatter. The pianists would be sitting in the front row, anxious and ready to perform, all hoping strongly that "Madame Long" would be in a good mood.

Whether the pianists were of Yankoff's generation or a few years younger, they all spoke of Long, the classes, and the atmosphere generated as the strongest influence in their lives. Well in her 70s, Long was at the peak of her form and took an all-embracing personal interest in each one of her "children," as she called them.

An outpouring of stories has come from the group of pianists who began working with Long in 1947, who prepared for the 1949 Concours together, and who thereafter remained in her entourage. The core of this group were Yuri Boukoff and Ventsislav Yankoff (of Bulgaria), Daniel Wayenberg (of Holland), Maria Chairo-Georges (of Greece), and Pierre Barbizet, Nicole Henriot, Marie-Thérèse Fourneau, and Janine Dacosta (of France).[3] Among the younger pianists, who appeared on the scene in the early 1950s, were Philippe Entremont, Bernard Ringeissen, and Gabriel Tacchino. Aldo Ciccolini began participating in the master classes only after he won his First Prize in the 1949 Concours.

The Vendredis d'Auteuil (Fridays at Auteuil, as they were known) lasted a good four to five hours, without interruption. (The day was later changed to Tuesday.) The classes had their worldly and ceremonial aspect: countesses, marquesses, and ministers' wives were there to be seen. Long enjoyed her role of "Grande Dame" and acted it out wholeheartedly. Officially, one had to pay an entrance fee in order to perform at these sessions, but Long never asked or expected a penny from a pianist who aroused her interest.

Among the auditors attending these classes was a pianist who had won a Premier Prix at the Conservatoire. After a few sessions, Long asked him if he would like to play. He replied that he could not afford it, but she had him play anyway. At the next class she had her devoted Madame Lyon tell him that he could play as often as he wished and at no charge. This young man became one of her protégés and went on to win the Concours a few years later. The same arrangement was true for many of his peers, all of whom reported that Long was generous with her time and that none of them ever paid for a single lesson. The pianist Gabriel Tacchino also told a beautiful story, which also dismisses some unreliable gossip. While preparing for the 1957 competition, he had a number of private lessons at Long's home, in addition to the public classes. Long knew that his family was of modest means. A few days before the first round, as his lesson ended, she slipped a large bill into his hands (the equivalent of $100 to $150 today), saying:

> My child, I want you to take a cab to the first round. The Russians are put up by the embassy. They will be driven to the hall, and I do not want you to become tired unnecessarily. You may not take the subway, and furthermore, I want you to eat steak every day this week.[4]

Long's students testify to her generosity, but many jealous souls have perpetuated stories about her greed and miserliness. There were certainly some less-magnanimous aspects of her personality, but when it came to supporting promising young careers, Long gave of herself wholeheartedly.

One matter on which all her students were in agreement was that Long terrorized them. Jacques Février confessed:

> I was terrified. My mother always took me to my lessons to see in what state I would be when I came out. Actually, it was never so bad because though Madame Long was severe, she was always the first one to recognize good work and encourage us if an effort had been made.[5]

Even the mature pianists of the Rue Molitor group made similar admissions. Long was extremely demanding and exacting and would not tolerate the least weakness on anyone's part. The pianists who were working with her at that time were all quite accomplished, with First Prizes from the Paris Conservatoire or the equivalent in their own countries. They were all "in training" for international competitions, and Long was their "trainer": the analogy was made by one of them to describe the unrelenting intensity with which she pushed them. One either knew one's piece or one did not: there was no middle ground. Long did not hesitate to criticize someone harshly in front of a large crowd. Her students had to be very strong. Forty years later they agreed that they had acquired excellent habits and had learned about life, not merely about piano playing. At the same time Long was very sensitive to individual personalities and never tried to impose her own pianistic technique on them. The result is evident in the wide range of musical temperaments displayed in her disciples: Ciccolini, for example, who came to her from Naples with an extremely digital technique, as opposed to Yankoff who played more like the Russians, utilizing the power of the whole body. Psychologically she could also adapt and occasionally soften her approach: Samson François, "my last Premier Prix" (1940), as she called him, was an extremely eccentric individual and got away with things no one else could. One day, quite exasperated with him, she threw him out of the class. He left, but he came back to the door a minute later and said: "Please, Madam, do not condemn me, I am only seventeen." "You are right," she said, "come back to the piano and let us get back to work."[6]

Long expected all her students to be able to play any piece, any time. Occasionally they would be contacted in the morning and told to play a specific piece at that afternoon's class. One pupil recalled occasions when she asked him to play *Gaspard de la nuit* late the same day because the Ambassador of such and such a country and his wife would be there, and Long wanted them to hear that performance. The student would complain that he had planned to bring a Brahms Sonata that day and had not looked at the Ravel work in several weeks. She would simply remind him that he had two hours to bring it back into his fingers, and there was no more discussion.

Along with her strict discipline and high standards, Long had a great capacity for warmth and affection. She loved her students as if they were her own children. "You were like a mother for me in Warsaw, and never will I forget that afternoon when you played for me the whole F minor Concerto [by Chopin] to help me, to give me an idea of how to practice it and play it," wrote Paul Badura-Skoda from Vienna on December 17, 1949.[7] Long encouraged camaraderie among her students, and they were all good friends and supportive of each other. She saved postcards collectively signed by her pupils or colleagues when they were traveling. A card from Vicenza, dated April 19, 1951, opened with a note from Thibaud: "Mon cher Petit [My dear little one], All gathered here, we think of you. For my part I kiss you damn hard. See you soon, Jacques Thibaud." Several pupils, conductors, and the composer Malipiero scribbled short notes and signed the same card.[8]

Among the fans who faithfully attended the master classes were a number of women, themselves pianists and good musicians, who would often host Long and her pupils. It was not uncommon for the class to end and move to one or another of their salons, where the group would continue to make music on into the night. Or they would go to a concert together and discuss it afterwards. If Long could not go along, she would ask for a report the next day.

One of her pupils explained that Long had been a part of her life for 30 years, from the day she entered the Conservatoire to the day Long died. And it seems that this feeling was reciprocal: many said how much she cared and how much time she devoted to them, in addition to the weekly five-hour public sessions. When her students asked her to hear a particular piece, she never refused, but looked for a time to meet privately. She always tried to attend her pupils' orchestral rehearsals and, of course, their concerts; and the next day she would go over the performance in meticulous detail. Conversely, the students spoke of their frequent opportunities to hear their mentor perform in public. Long insisted that her pupils come to hear her. They remarked with admiration that she always played very well: her mature age did not interfere with her solid technique. She demanded of herself the same perfection she asked of her disciples.

As harsh and demanding as Long was, she was equally capable of praise when it was deserved, particularly in front of the whole class. Many of her pupils said with beaming expressions that when that happened, it was pure bliss. Some of them reminisced about her keen sense of humor, musing that with "Madame Long" a smile was never very far away. This was usually the case with her male students. Women had a harder time, and she often provoked their tears. Only the very strong and gifted women endured Long's tyranny. But men, particularly if they were charming, had an advantage. Daniel Wayenberg—whom she nicknamed "Il bambino," for he was the youngest of the group—was the recipient of some effusive hugs: he would inevitably knock off the elaborate hat she was wearing, but despite her caring about elegance, she did not mind at all. She was capable of being moved to tears when Wayenberg or his peers performed well. The tears would ruin her makeup, but she did not mind that either.

For many of Long's disciples, the most memorable feature of her teaching was her ability to bring alive stories and reminiscences about Fauré, Debussy, and Ravel. It established an atmosphere, the setting and the image of another epoch:

> What was important was not so much her comment about a particular piece. When she would tell us about the day she first read through Ravel's Concerto while he was standing next to her, she made a much bigger impression on us than if she had said "do this here, do that there."[9]

Those extramusical memories about composers opened their eyes and sparked their imaginations. Long also spoke frequently about her husband, which was rather surprising, for she had been a widow for over 30 years. She would refer to him as the Marquis de Marliave with a certain deference: that, too, contributed to her exuding an atmosphere of times past. "It was at the end of her life that she seemed to unleash all that she knew," said one of her pupils. Long traveled during an epoch when people did not travel, particularly women who were alone.

Long was not beautiful but she had an irresistible charm. One student admitted, "We were all a little bit in love with her." She held a great fascination for them, and she was always extremely elegant. "She loved it when we spoke to her about her outfits, for her interest in the whole subject of dress and fashion was legendary! She knew how to charm more than anybody."[10] Lessons at her home were a colorful matter. Long would appear from her boudoir in one of her many floor-length robes. Her boudoir had a balcony covered with flowers, and she was always picking a leaf, watering, smelling a fresh blossom. "Her apartment was a greenhouse," wrote Barbizet.[11] Her two Gaveau pianos were horribly out of tune: when Jacques Thibaud would come to rehearse at her home, as he was about to tune, he would ask: "Just give me the *A* you want!" But she insisted that there were no bad pianos, only bad pianists, as she also repeated there were no bad tools, only poor artisans. Long is remembered as more than a teacher or mentor. Jacques Février declared:

> I am indebted to her for having learned the Concerto for the Left Hand and worked on it with Ravel. I was one of the last pianists to work with Ravel and the first French pianist to play the piece, which had been played only once by its Austrian dedicatee, to the great dissatisfaction of the composer.[12]

To help her students' careers, Long would arrange musical salons at the homes of her aristocratic friends, such as Germaine de Jouvenel or the Marquis de Gontaut-Biron, where conductors, composers, festival directors, and other influential people would be present. In July 1948, she organized a concert at the Salle Gaveau featuring eight of her foreign pianists and two French ones.

The concert was presided over by Louis Joxe, Directeur Général des Relations Culturelles, whose presence officially endorsed the initiative. Even more to the point, Long was guaranteed two or three dates a year with each of the main orchestras in Paris (Société des Concerts, Pasdeloup, Colonne, Lamoureux) and was therefore in a position to secure engagements for those of her disciples she deemed ready for that opportunity. As the Hungarian pianist Geza Anda wrote on July 3, 1949:

> Dear Madam
>
> . . . Nothing reveals your generosity to me more than your kind offer to help me in my career. I am extremely grateful for this and I asked Mr. Dussurget—as you suggested—to contact you. I know that a word from you will suffice in order to obtain an engagement with the Société [des Concerts] du Conservatoire and I am certain that I will be worthy of your recommendation.[13]

Gabriel Dussurget was one of France's two most important impresarios. Anda was not alone in benefiting from Long's friendship with him. In a letter of May 20, 1951, an enraged Jacques Thibaud called on Long to rectify a gross injustice committed by Dussurget: the winner of the First Prize in violin from their Concours was not asked to perform at the Festival d'Aix, whereas the First Prize in piano was. Thibaud demanded in no uncertain terms (and sparing the impresario no epithets!) that Long intervene and summon Dussurget, the founder and director of the festival, to remedy this problem promptly. He ended his letter with his usual panache: "Je vous embrasse à tire-larigot"[14] (kiss you to death).

By the time they entered the 1949 competition, most of the pianists who had attended Long's weekly international classes and studied with her had already made their Paris debuts with orchestra. Long knew from her own experience how difficult it was for budding pianists to get such engagements, in a country where only seasoned artists would be asked to perform with the principal orchestras of Paris. Now she made it her responsibility to make such opportunities possible for deserving young pianists.

In 1948 two of Long's youngest pupils, Nicole Henriot and Samson François, made their American debuts with the New York Philharmonic under Charles Münch. They had both earned their Premier Prix at the Conservatoire shortly before the war. Münch was so fond of Henriot that he performed with her many times after her debut. Rudolf Firkusny reported to Long on Henriot's playing in a letter dated April 1, 1950, sent from Washington, D.C.:

Dear Madam,

I finally had the pleasure of hearing Nicole Henriot when she played the Ravel Concerto in New York with Münch. I was so impressed that I must write to you to congratulate you and to share with you the enormous success Nicole enjoyed and which was so well deserved. She played admirably and it was for me a real joy to be able to applaud her.

I always think of you, your great kindness toward me, and your good advice. I regret very much that I cannot come to Paris this year, but I will be there next year and I am looking forward to seeing you again.

Rudolf Firkusny[15]

Being one of Long's chosen pupils also meant being exposed to a rich artistic milieu. A number of composers gravitated around her: Francis Poulenc, Henri Sauguet, Darius Milhaud, Heitor Villa-Lobos, Marcel Landowsky* (who married one of Long's pupils, Jacqueline Potier). The pianist Jacques Février was very much a part of this entourage, and Long sent many of her disciples to study with him. One of her students, Yuri Boukoff, remarked that these artists were part of a generation of musicians which is disappearing nowadays, not for lack of talent but for lack of time. They were extremely witty and well read, and they talked about many subjects other than music. "It was thrilling to spend an evening around them," said Boukoff. Long herself had wide-ranging interests; she had learned much about philosophy, literature, and history through her husband, who had left her a handsome library.

Boukoff described this milieu as the "opposite" of the Conservatoire. When he arrived from his native Bulgaria, he had attended the Conservatoire in the class of Yves Nat, who did not have particularly tender feelings toward Long. Long had left the institution in 1940, and by now her successors (except for Jean Doyen, who was her own protégé), including Ciampi, Lazare-Lévy, and Nat, behaved like rivals. As one of Long's friends astutely observed, they were more jealous of her worldly successes than of her purely pianistic ones.[16] Truthfully, Long was a political as well as a musical personality. She had friends in the French government, among French and foreign ambassadors, among members of the Académie des Beaux-Arts (one of the five Académies which constitute L'Institut de France), all of whom gave their support and official recognition to her undertakings, mainly her competition. "She had the whole Ministère wrapped around her little finger," remarked Boukoff.

For her pupils she was "Madame Long," and she became their friend. After their careers were launched they enjoyed coming back periodically to the Rue Molitor classes; it was an occasion to see old friends and to steep themselves in that unique atmosphere. At that time no one else in Paris was giving regular master classes for international virtuosos. Wayenberg was especially proud of a photograph Long inscribed to him: "A mon cher Bambino, de la part de son maître et de son *amie*" (To my dear Bambino, in memory of his mentor and *friend*). When her pupils traveled they would write detailed letters to her, reporting on the audiences, the performances, the cities they were visiting, and how they felt—all this in a moving and affectionate style. She kept all those letters and amassed an enormous stack of correspondence. Two particularly charming letters were sent to her by Pierre Barbizet. On November 11, 1953 he wrote:

> Madame and Dear *Maître*,
>
> Finally a little moment of calm and the joy of telling you that I think of you every day, that I dedicate to you every practice session, not only because I love you and admire you with all my heart, but also because I *need* that. . . . The Germans are happy. They asked me to come back. You see, dear Maître, I try to realize your formula: "what matters is not to play but to *play again.*"

The second, dated July 18, 1954, was written on an airplane as Barbizet was on his way to Lisbon:

> My Beloved *Maître!*
>
> I will not have enough of a lifetime of work, of meditation, of enthusiasm always renewed to express to you with dignity my gratitude, my affection, my faith in you, in all that you represent of greatness, of enlightened kindness, of unmatchable refinement, in one word—of Adorable—. . . . You are Adorable because you are divine. This is why I always say "the Divine" when I speak of you. . . . Well! I have tears in my eyes because I just finished reading all the mail that you had the exquisite kindness to entrust to my friend [Christian] Ferras. Forgive the sloppiness of this note . . . it is as though it were coming out of my guts! You must receive my letter very soon. We will be in Lisbon in one hour. Tomorrow São Paulo around 5 P.M. . . . You will be with me everywhere and . . . never have I felt—understood rather—the value of the title of "Disciple" with which you are willing to honor me. . . . I kiss you with all my heart and all my tenderness,
>
> Pierre[17]

The letter also goes into great detail about previous concerts as well as upcoming plans in São Paulo. The idolizing tone, if telling of her student, is even more telling of the epoch. Few students today would ever speak to their

Long in Burano (near Venice). Bibliothèque Musicale Gustav Mahler, Paris; Marguerite Long Archives.

mentors in those terms, and Barbizet was not alone in writing assiduously to his teacher in such an adoring manner.

In the summer of 1948, Long took four of her pupils to Venice, where she had been invited to give master classes. As one of them reminisced:

> We spent an admirable month together. We would go to concerts, we would visit the islands. We got to know [the composer] Francesco Malipiero, who was a good friend of hers. When I think that she was 73 years old! She went to all the museums with us. She never tired, but more important, she was completely at ease with us, 20- to 25-year-olds that we were.

Long's playing was characterized by extreme clarity, stunning ease, and attractive elegance. Her students were mesmerized by the ravishing quality of her passagework; several mentioned that her performance of the Rondo of Beethoven's Third Piano Concerto was electrifying. They praised her understanding of Beethoven's music. Boukoff particularly remembered lessons on Op. 111, Op. 57, and the "Emperor" Concerto. In addition to French music, Chopin occupied an important place in her teaching. Long had chosen the Polish composer's B-flat minor Sonata (Op. 35, "Funeral March") as the only piece for the preliminary round of her competition. She believed that nothing was more difficult to play well than Chopin, and that this particular Sonata embodied all the technical and musical challenges of piano playing. "One day," she said, "we wondered, Busoni, Sauer, and myself, which was the key work for the piano: it is that piece."[18] For many, her interpretation of Chopin's F minor Concerto was unforgettable.

Long's technique was French, a technique inherited from the eighteenth-century *clavecinistes* and transmitted through the nineteenth century by pianists such as Saint-Saëns, Marmontel, and Diémer. Specifically, it was an extremely digital way of playing, in which the fingers did all the work with very little involvement of the arm and upper body. Long's Conservatoire pupils described this training as a very solid and reliable base, which prepared them for anything else and which, alone, gave them a very clear and sparkling sound, if not a "big" technique. This French technique was quite popular abroad, notably in Germany. It was a crystal-clear way of playing, and its proponents repeated: "Do not forget that you play the piano with your fingers." Gabriel Tacchino said:

> But what Long managed to do with her fingers was rather extraordinary. She had an extremely wide sound palette, and each note was a pearl. I was always struck by her stage presence. She was really the kind of artist who was incomparably more effective on stage than through recordings, particularly those old recordings.[19]

Barbizet used the same analogy: "All her notes were singing pearls." He compared her delivery to that of the great actresses of her time, such as Sarah Bernhardt: "Each note was interesting and intelligent. Marguerite Long's notes were coquettish personages. . . . In passagework, in a cadenza, each note spoke. Her trills were out of this world." A third pupil, Marie-Thérèse Fourneau, remarked on the astonishing flexibility of her thumbs. Long always used them with remarkable ease. And when she was not playing, her thumbs were in constant motion, looking as if they were made out of rubber. This style of playing was already considered *passé* in the 1950s, when Russian and American pianists were winning competitions with forceful Brahms, Tchaikovsky, and Rachmaninoff Concertos.

Long's playing was intimately linked to the aesthetic of the pianos she used: nineteenth- and twentieth-century French instruments. Was not Debussy's ideal "a piano without hammers"? The Pleyels and Erards of her day had slightly shallower and lighter keyboard actions than do modern Steinways. Their sound could be delicate or loud but never thundering, and they demanded a very clear and articulated kind of playing. Long's technique was ideally suited to those instruments. Before World War I France was skeptical of the Steinway instruments. Debussy, Ravel, and Poulenc liked their French Erards and Pleyels, and as long as France was building good pianos, why import foreign ones? France considered the Erard a modern piano, for it was this firm which had invented the double-escapement early in the nineteenth century. But French pianos did not evolve: Erard was still building concert grands with parallel strings in the 1930s, whereas Steinway, in both Germany and America, had been making concert grands with crossed strings since the 1880s. Long was quite aware of the modern Steinway, and she had an immeasurable admiration for Russian pianists. Ever since she had heard Gilels at the 1938 Queen Elisabeth Competition, she held him in the highest esteem. She often remarked to her students about Gilels and Richter: "That is piano playing, that is just fantastic." But it was obviously too late for her to change her technique and style: she had inherited the old French tradition, a tradition that was not without merit.

Barbizet, a celebrated solo artist as well as a world-class chamber musician, gave his mentor credit for his own chamber music talent: "I listened to her practice the Piano Quartets of Fauré. It was marvelous: never fast, each note sang and all of the voices were as clear as a mountain spring. I learned by simply watching and listening to her." Her legato was exemplary and an inspiration: "She insisted on perfect legato playing without pedal." Another testimonial, not by one of her students but by a pianist who attended one of her very last public performances, adds a perspective to Long's playing. Eric Heidsieck said:

> Although Cortot's students were perhaps prejudiced against Long, I must say that I remember being very impressed when I heard her play Fauré's Quartet in C minor at the Salle Gaveau in 1957 [concert of May 10 with the Pasquier Trio, see below, p. 188]. I had a stage seat with a clear view of her left hand, and I remember the exceptional quality of her tone, together with the evenness of her fingers. Although people have criticized her and her students for having a "surface-y" approach, I was convinced on that occasion that she was really getting into the keys. . . . This made a strong impression on me because I didn't think it was characteristic of her style.[20]

Alfred Cortot's playing was very different from Long's. Cortot strongly encouraged the use of arms and shoulders. He played abroad much more than Long did, and he performed on Steinway pianos from an early date. Although he had been trained under Diémer and therefore was the product of the same school as Long, Cortot revised his technique to adapt to the heavier pianos. The result was an altogether different style of playing and sound, not to mention temperament. And regardless of personal preferences or allegiances, most would agree that Cortot was not a typical French pianist. The rivalry between Long and Cortot is put in perspective in letters to Long from Cortot's wife, Renée. One in particular, dated June 23, 1957, addresses this issue very openly. After expressing sincere regrets that she and her husband had not been able to attend a reception in Long's home, she writes:

> The two of you, both Elders of an Art which animated your lives with the same love and commitment—that of serving it by making others discover it and love it!—many points in common, many links bring you ever so close and connect you beyond all the divergences of a past where people took pleasure in confusing and misrepresenting many things between you. Human Sordidness. But the truth remains, privilege of all that is Beautiful and Real! May I hope, Madame, that you will come and see us in Lausanne? We would both be so happy.
>
> We know how particularly interesting and revealing your Concours was this year, and how the young Russian, Boris Goutnikov, proved to be *extraordinary*. Once more, a discovery of that ilk and a successful stepping stone for this young artist was guaranteed because of you![21]

An extremely friendly and warm letter from Cortot himself, dated June 4, 1961, shows how the wisdom of a lifetime could close rifts and dissolve rivalries. He was then a few days from his 84th birthday; Long was 86.

Even though Long did not play the big Romantic repertoire herself, such as Brahms and the Russian composers, she taught it very well; her keen musical intelligence and intuition enabled her to absorb a wide range of music, much wider than her performing repertoire would lead one to believe. Wayenberg said it was very rare to hear her say she did not like certain composers. She loved the Rachmaninoff concertos, for example, at a time when in France many professional musicians considered this music second-rate. She often said: "I regret very much never having learned Rachmaninoff's Second Piano Concerto, for there is in this music, particularly in the second movement, a Slavic nostalgia that moves me deeply."[22] Her pupils fondly remembered: "Between all of us we covered all of the Brahms, Rachmaninoff, Tchaikovsky, and Prokofiev concertos." Entremont and Wayenberg took turns accompanying their classmates; both knew the orchestral scores so well that they would play the second piano entirely from memory. Long delighted in such a *tour de force.*

If in the past her pedagogy had suffered from a certain technical rigidity, her intelligence and open-mindedness enabled her to broaden her horizons when she was exposed to modern pianists and their new style of playing. Not content with being a mere spectator, Long actively participated in learning and absorbing ideas not familiar to her. It is this philosophy of life which provoked her to say at age 91, when coaching one of her disciples' students: "I have the feeling I am still improving."[23]

This portrayal of Long would be incomplete without an account of some of the colorful and less-flattering aspects of her personality.[24] As a *quid pro quo,* her support gave her unlimited rights to the services of those she took under her wing. Long had the distinctive reputation of never having taken a cab in her life. She could always count on one of her devoted friends or pupils to drive her to the dentist, to the railroad station, or to her dressmaker. "When she came home from a trip, we would all meet her at the train; it was a real event," remarked many of them. In a letter dated October 10, 1954, to the Brazilian pianist Magda Tagliaferro, Madame Lyon vividly describes Long's arrival in Paris after her second trip to Brazil (see below, pp. 175–79):

> My dear Magda,
>
> The arrival at the train station under a dazzling sunshine was charming (although the night before, our friend [Long] had someone phone from the boat

> that she had the flu and that her doctor should come and diagnose her immediately upon her arrival). She looked extremely well, happy to see around her those who interview her on the Radio [list of names], Descaves, Doyen, Février, the Daniel-Lesurs, her friends F . . ., Mlles S. from the Affaires Étrangères, Entremont, Wayenberg, Barbizet, Claude Kahn, Tasso, Szeryng, professors, and your servant![25]

Long was notorious for asking her pupils to mail letters that had not yet been stamped. "She took very good care of us but she had us at her beck and call. She had a very good memory: she never asked the same favor from the same person twice." She was capable of putting on a whole dinner party without lifting a finger or paying a single bill. All she had to do was to pick up the telephone. With so many people devoted to her and an uncanny ability to make others perform services for her, she could have a whole dinner party prepared, delivered, and served entirely by her entourage. One pupil remembered, not so fondly, having been involved in one of these elaborate maneuvers. On this occasion Long did not even have to dial the telephone numbers. He would dial for her, and when the call went through, she would begin: "The ambassador of such and such a country is coming tonight. I am having fifteen people for dinner. I remember the sherbets at your house the other night were absolutely exquisite," and pretty soon the person at the other end would promise to bring the sherbets herself. The whole meal was orchestrated on the telephone, from caviar from the Soviet Embassy to the after-dinner liqueurs, served by white-aproned help, all graciously offered by one or the other of Long's friends and admirers. It was her indubitable charm and personality that enabled Long to depend on others to perform services for her for which she never felt indebted. One of the most extraordinary examples of such a relationship was the fidelity of Madame Lyon.

When Long was invited to Brazil in 1954, she asked one of her pupils to drive her from Paris to Le Havre, a trip of four to five hours. When he saw how much luggage she and her maid were taking, he asked a friend, also a pianist, to help, for they needed two cars to accommodate everybody and everything. They loaded up at the Avenue de la Grande Armée early in the morning, leaving Paris at 7 A.M. in order to arrive in Le Havre by midday. The two young men carried the baggage to her cabin and put roses into a vase ("for one always brought roses to Madame Long"). All was ready for the "Grande Dame's" crossing of the Atlantic. They found Long on the ship's bridge conversing with the captain. She greeted them and said, "Thank you very much, my children. Now drive safely and I will see you later." Surprised, the captain stepped in and invited the two to join them for lunch, for it was unthinkable to let these young men drive back without a good meal. A few minutes later, as the party walked to the main dining room, Long took one of her pupils aside and said: "Did you see how I succeeded in getting you an invitation to dine at the captain's table?"

At the 1954 Naples Competition, where Long was chairing the jury, she was staying with an extremely wealthy family in a superb estate overlooking the bay. As a gesture to her hosts, she gave a few piano lessons to their daughter. At the end of the competition there was a luxurious meal in the home, to which several laureates were also invited. Long admired the highly valuable Capodimonte china with which the table was set; and with no hesitation she told her hosts that if they wanted to give her a gift for having taught their daughter, a set of this china would make her very happy. Six months later, a complete set was delivered to her apartment at the Avenue de la Grande Armée.

Long could get anyone to do anything for her. Because of the boundless admiration and the aura that surrounded her, she was able to arrange concerts for her pupils, get cash prizes for her competition, and remain at the center of musical, social, and political life in Paris for years. Even after her death in 1966, the Concours continued to be managed for more than a decade by her dear friends Marcel Fournet and his wife without remuneration, out of deference to the memory of the woman they admired and revered so much. It was not until 1981 that a full-time professional staff was appointed by the French government to administer the competition.

It is relevant to note that Long was born into a modest family and that her father worked for the railroad. When she married, she became the Marquise de Marliave and gravitated to another echelon of French society. But even before her marriage she assiduously frequented the salons of the aristocracy, exhibiting her talent and slowly gaining access to a world she enjoyed being a part of. "She had a genius' instinct for success," said Jacques Février: success not only in her craft, but in politics, in society, and as a celebrity. Long was not merely the Marquise de Marliave or the renowned French pianist; she was the Personage of an epoch, toward whom the aristocracy, the pianists, the composers, and the politicians were attracted, a woman simultaneously esteemed and feared.

The Centennial of Frédéric Chopin

In 1949, the centennial of Frédéric Chopin's death was the occasion for a national celebration in France. As president of the National Organization Committee, formed under the honorary chairmanship of Vincent Auriol, then president of France, Long had the task of planning musical and cultural events honoring the Polish composer throughout the year.

In March, Long and the eminent critic and musicologist Bernard Gavoty gave lectures at the Salle Gaveau preceding performances by other pianists.[26] Long's lecture, on March 24, covered Chopin's life from 1810 to 1838: Warsaw, Stuttgart, Vienna, and Paris. Her former pupil Jean Doyen, then her successor at the Conservatoire, performed some early works of Chopin, composed up to 1837, including the Fantaisie-Impromptu; Nocturnes, Op. 27; the First Ballade; Three Etudes, Op. 25; a Polonaise; and a Mazurka. The evening closed with the Larghetto of the F minor Piano Concerto played by Long and Doyen. At his lecture, on March 31, Gavoty discussed the last twelve years of Chopin's life: Majorca, Nohant, Edinburgh, and Paris.

On April 26, 1949 Long officially opened the festivities with a lecture at the Conservatoire:

> At the hour during which Warsaw celebrates the memory of the musician whose voice never ceased to cry the mournings and to exalt the hopes of its oppressed country, France, which was his shelter and which now watches dearly over his ashes, owes him its fervent homage. . . . In the millenary friendship which unites France to Poland, Chopin was a living symbol. . . . To Poland belongs the glory of Chopin's genius, and to France that of having welcomed him with passion at the flower of his youth.[27]

In October, the month of Chopin's death, there was an official pilgrimage to the composer's resting place in the Père Lachaise cemetery in Paris. Many celebrities were present, including the general secretary of the Franco-Polish alliance, members of the Polish Embassy, and Aurore Sand, granddaughter of the novelist George Sand. At the end, the delegations and the faithful admirers of Chopin filed past his monument, which was covered with an astounding abundance of flowers. Long closed her brief oration by offering "the fervent homage of all those whom Chopin's genius has guided, inspired, exalted, this genius that Debussy considered the greatest of all, for, with the piano alone, he said, he had discovered everything."[28]

During the last week of October there were five concerts at the Salle Gaveau at which almost all of Chopin's piano works were performed. The programs were shared by six laureates from the June 1949 Concours Long–Thibaud—Ciccolini, Yankoff, Barbizet, Wayenberg, Boukoff, and Fourneau (all familiar names from Long's international master classes)—and four laureates from the Warsaw Chopin Competition of September 1949.

Long had spent two weeks in the Polish capital as a member of the Chopin Competition jury. Responding to the Polish people's insistence on hearing French music, she played the Ravel Concerto at a concert in Warsaw, the proceeds of which would benefit a Polish contestant. She expressed radiant enthusiasm about her visit and the warmth of the Polish people, in spite of the conditions of their cities, which still lay in ruins. Finally, she announced with pride that the Centennial Committee would raise the necessary funds for her Concours to award a large cash prize (equal to the First Prize) to the candidate who gave the best performance of Chopin's music, regardless of his or her overall ranking in the competition.

On November 5, Long organized a concert of forgotten or unpublished pieces by Chopin. They were performed by pupils under the age of fourteen (the young Philippe Entremont was one of them). "Small pieces by Chopin, almost all of them unpublished or forgotten, discovered and reproduced in several Polish musical journals."[29]

> The young children of the Ecole Marguerite Long recently honored the memory of Chopin at the Salle Gaveau. It was truly charming to listen to these young talents, playing almost standing up in order to be able to reach the pedals and interpreting with extreme sensitivity the unfamiliar pages of the composer. [*Parisien libéré,* November 8, 1949.]

11

Ambassador of French Music

French music of the twentieth century was central to Long's life as a pianist. That, combined with her wisdom and her talent for befriending high-ranking ministers and politicians gave Long's career ambassadorial overtones. After World War II her presence abroad was more frequently requested, and she delighted in fulfilling this role. She gave speeches that could win over an electorate, and she would wholeheartedly share with her audiences the passions of her life. Georges Soria wrote in *Lettres Françaises* of February 17, 1966, shortly after her death:

> For me, what will remain of . . . Marguerite Long is this energy, this unquenching curiosity, this love for her art . . . which made her . . . live, in a word, intensely live her passion: music. Marguerite Long lived for music the way others have lived and now live for science, or any other great human passion.

She represented a passion not just for French music but for a specific epoch of French music: the first half of the twentieth century, which was the richest and most prolific period in the musical history of France. The international reputation of her Concours also enhanced her postwar career.

During this period she was often asked to serve on the juries of major international competitions: 1949 in Warsaw, the 1952 and 1954 Casella Competition in Naples—where she was chairman of the jury—and the 1952 Queen Elisabeth Competition in Brussels, the year that American pianist

Long surrounded by Jacques Ibert, Georges Auric, Georges Tzipine, Arthur Honegger, and Marcel Mihalovici. Bibliothèque Musicale Gustav Mahler, Paris; Marguerite Long Archives.

Leon Fleisher won. On April 27, 1952, on the occasion of her first stint on the Naples jury, Aldo Cĩccolini, who won First Prize at her 1949 Concours, wrote in his most effusive Neapolitan style:

> Dear Madam,
>
> Naples at last has the honor and joy of welcoming you! . . . Never has a visit been as eagerly awaited and desired by Neapolitan musicians as yours, and I wish with them that it be the first of many. . . . I will finally be able to say

> everywhere that Marguerite of France has been to Naples. Yes, Marguerite of France, for, even in a republic, you are a queen whose power overwhelms but also comforts the little artists that we are!
>
> I practice my piano with the same concerns as always and hope to see you one of these days, soon.
>
> Aldo[1]

This letter is one of hundreds written by Long's disciples, pianists whose careers were growing and whom she loved as her "children." They always came back to her for advice. Ciccolini had already toured extensively in Europe and America for three years, but he still continued to seek "Marguerite de France" as mentor and friend.

Other foreign pianists, who did not necessarily study with Long but came to Paris for other reasons, would inevitably come in contact with her, and she would always welcome and support them. As Van Cliburn wrote on July 1, 1958:

> My very dear Madame Long,
>
> I want to express my deep appreciation for your kindness to me and my family in the expression of the reception at which I not only had the distinct pleasure of meeting you but also become acquainted with all the distinguished members of the musical life of France.
>
> I shall never forget your thoughtfulness and shall value your continued interest.
>
> Most sincerely,
>
> Van Cliburn.[2]

On August 1950 she played the opening concert of the Edinburgh Festival with the Orchestre National de la Radiodiffusion Française. Both the Ravel Concerto and the Fauré Ballade were on the program. The concert was broadcast to a very wide audience, and her admirers—pupils, friends, composers, politicians—sent her innumerable letters after the occasion. The same year she performed in Madrid for the first time, with the Orquesta Nacional, to great acclaim.

On January 20, 1952, the twentieth anniversary of the première of Ravel's G major Concerto was marked by a commemorative concert in the same hall, Salle Pleyel, and with the same orchestra, Orchestre Lamoureux. Every year since 1932 Long had played the work at least once, but this anniversary concert was a special celebration. Jean Martinon, who had been the concertmaster at the première, took Ravel's place at the podium. René

Dumesnil wrote in *Le Monde:* "Twenty years already! No one could have guessed it upon hearing the Concerto executed with the same agility, the same bright spirit and the same emotion in the Andante. . . . The audience requested an encore of the last movement."

The Brazilian Connection

For over 30 years, Long had very strong ties with Brazil. Several Brazilian pupils came to study with her in Paris as early as the 1920s. Two of the most famous were Souza Lima (a classmate of Jacques Février, Jean Doyen, and Lucette Descaves) and Eleazar de Carvalho, who later became an important Brazilian conductor. When Long visited Brazil in 1932, the welcome extended to her was overwhelmingly affectionate. She had been given so many flowers, that she admitted to feeling very nostalgic when she left Rio de Janeiro: "This bay . . . is an enchantment I hope to return to soon" (*Candide,* November 24, 1932). She was equally enchanted by the people of Brazil. Her sojourn not only sealed friendships but also initiated a lifelong love affair between Long and Brazil.

During August and September 1932 Long gave eight lecture/master classes entitled "Curso de Interpretaçao e virtuosidade," in which her lectures were followed by student performances of a very high caliber.[3] Long delivered an eloquent and exuberant opening speech:

> The Brazilian school of piano playing is now famous, due as much to its renowned teachers as to its virtuosos. . . . Many of them came to our country, earned immediate successes and, in so doing, united and made triumphal both our pedagogies. From this remarkable school came Magda Tagliaferro, whose brilliant career is justly recognized; Mme. Guiomar Novaes, whose precocious debut in Paris was such a resounding success that my praise joins that of all her compatriots. To cite more names would take too long, but among those who were my dear disciples, I owe a special thought to Souza Lima, great virtuoso and exceptional musician. . . . I came, strengthened by the hours of work and intimacy [with Fauré and Debussy] to share with you not my thoughts but *theirs.*[4]

Although French music held a central position in this project, Long's overall theme was the evolution of piano music. Her handwritten notes indicate the scope of each lecture. The first one, entitled "The Piano, Its

Technique and Evolution," was illustrated by the performance of works by Mozart, Beethoven, Schumann, and Liszt. Long stressed that thorough knowledge of the individual techniques of these composer-pianists and of the way each of them approached the instrument was indispensable to a faithful interpretation.

The second and third lectures were devoted to Chopin's music. Long believed that "We must simply listen to Debussy's music to have an idea of what Chopin must have been for his contemporaries. In the astonishing Barcarolle all of the Debussyism already floats in suspense."[5] The Chopin programs covered a great deal of the composer's repertoire: the B-flat minor Sonata, eight Etudes, two Ballades, two Scherzi, Barcarolle, Berceuse, several Preludes, and the A-flat Polonaise.

The last five sessions were devoted to French music: two on Debussy, one on Ravel, one on Fauré, and one on composers "from Franck to the present." The last one included works by Franck, Chabrier, Gabriel Pierné, Florent Schmitt, Roger-Ducasse, Ibert, Delanoy, and Poulenc. The programs were generous and covered a broad cross-section of each composer's music. Long concluded: "The French composer who received the most enthusiastic response was Maurice Ravel. . . . As to the younger ones, Poulenc and Ibert were the most warmly appreciated" (*Candide*, November 24, 1932). In addition to the lecture/master classes, Long performed the new Ravel Concerto, premiered merely months earlier in Paris, as well as the three other works most often associated with her: Beethoven's "Emperor" Concerto, Chopin's F minor Concerto, and the Fauré Ballade.

"Let us hope that her artistic mission, which has given marvelous results, will be renewed next year," wrote a Brazilian newspaper. In spite of promises made on both sides, Long was not to return to Brazil until 1954, even though she kept up a regular correspondence with her South American friends and former pupils.

One of them was the pianist Magda Tagliaferro, with whom Long had a relationship that was more cordial and professional than intimate. Opinions and accounts disagree on the sincerity of their friendship, which had its ups and downs. In Tagliaferro's own words: "It was between 1949 and 1958 especially that I had the closest ties with her [Long], whereas we grew apart from each other during her last years."[6] Nevertheless, the two women maintained an extensive correspondence, and Tagliaferro was an essential contact in planning Brazilian tours for Long's students. Indicative of Tagliaferro's efforts is a letter to Long written on September 28, 1948 from Rio de Janeiro:

Dear friend,

. . . Unfortunately, I was unable to do much for him [Samson François] because here, like everywhere, one needs to plan well ahead of time . . . but he certainly has a great deal of talent and seemed to me quite endearing. . . . I was able to do more for Charlie Lillamand, who had warned me of his visit and seems to be happy, on the whole, with his South American tour.[7]

Tagliaferro was a member of the jury of the Long–Thibaud competition every year between 1949 and 1955, and again in 1975 and 1977, after Long's death. But she had to decline the first invitation in 1946. As she wrote to Long from Rio on November 20:

My dear friend,

I am very disappointed not to be able to . . . be a jury member for your International Competition this year, but important commitments oblige me to stay here until the end of December. . . . All my warmest wishes for a complete success of your magnificent initiative and please tell Jacques [Thibaud] that I am deeply sorry not to be able to be there.

Magda Tagliaferro

Among the numerous letters from Long's Brazilian students, one in particular, from Souza Lima, illustrates the student-mentor relationship and exemplifies Long's pupils' reliance on the "Grande Dame" at important junctures in their careers. Souza Lima was notorious for very lengthy missives, telling his esteemed teacher about family news, career developments, and Brazilian music politics. On May 18, 1950 he wrote to her from São Paulo:

Very dear Madame,

Last month I played Villa Lobos' Second Piano Concerto for its world première, under the direction of the composer. It was an artistic event that people still talk about. . . . This provoked an enormous curiosity, for it was an unpublished work and one of the composer's latest works. . . . The piece is quite interesting not only from the point of view of the conception but also pianistically. . . . Concerning the performance of this piece, I take the liberty of asking you if you would approach Charles Münch, who is now in Paris, about my playing the concerto in Boston. I am convinced that a recommendation on your part to the conductor would be all that is needed to see my dream of playing in the United States come true. It would be an American première of a work which is well worth it. Thanks to your help (and God knows how great and sincere my gratitude is for all that you have done and continue to do for me) I will be able to pursue my career which has started so well in France.

There is no record of the outcome of Lima's request, but it is known that Long's professional and personal friendship with Münch, dating back to the early days of World War II, eased the way for two of her pupils to make their New York Philharmonic debuts in 1948.

Long was very fond of Brazil's leading composer, Villa-Lobos, and had regular contacts with him. During her sojourn in Brazil in 1932, he dedicated a concert he was conducting to Long. In appreciation for her interest in contemporary music, Villa-Lobos dedicated a collection of children's pieces to the students of the Ecole Marguerite Long. Entitled *Francette et Pià,* this charming set of ten "easy pieces for piano based on popular French and Brazilian tunes" told the story of a Brazilian Indian boy, Pià, who had come to France and who had met a little French girl, Francette.[8]

In the spring of 1952, when Villa-Lobos was in Paris, Long held a formal reception in his honor at her home. On this occasion, Louis Joxe, Directeur Général des Relations Culturelles, bestowed upon the Brazilian composer a bronze medal displaying his portrait, in recognition of his 50 years of musical activity. Although the reception was private, many government dignitaries were present, lending an official atmosphere to the event. Among those in attendance were the Brazilian Ambassador and his wife, the President of UNESCO, the Consul Général of Brazil, the Director of the Paris Conservatoire, the Inspecteur of the Beaux Arts, and the composers Jacques Ibert and Florent Schmitt. Also present were some of Long's prized pupils: Doyen, Ciccolini, Wayenberg, Descaves, and Sequeira-Costa; as well as three prominent Paris music critics: Bernard Gavoty, René Dumesnil, and Marcel Schneider. The focus of the evening was the performance of several Villa-Lobos works by the young Brazilian pianist Anna Stella, who was then studying with Long.[9]

Long was scheduled to return to Brazil in the summer of 1952. Letters she exchanged with Tagliaferro provide ample details of her plans, which would begin with a concert in Rio de Janeiro on August 30. A series of lectures, receptions, and various social functions would follow. But on July 22, Long wrote to her colleague that she could not undertake the long and demanding journey. She was almost 78 years old.

> The truth is that I have been so tired lately, that I, and my friends and colleagues fear it would not be safe for me to take this trip—a pleasure trip,

Heitor Villa-Lobos, in a photograph inscribed on September 19, 1954, "To Marguerite Long, the most divine artist and dear friend, with my eternal admiration." Bibliothèque Musicale Gustav Mahler, Paris; Marguerite Long Archives.

granted, but also one involving hard work, considering all the activities your letter described. . . . It is wiser for me to give up the idea and go for a rest at a health spa (a "cure"), rather than rediscovering your country, which I was so anxious to visit again. I hope perhaps . . . next year after the Concours [of 1953] I will be able to realize this trip.[10]

In July 1954, shortly before she was to embark on her second trip to Brazil, Long organized a concert of Villa-Lobos's piano music at the Salle Marguerite Gaveau (a small hall in the same building as the Salle Gaveau). Four of her pupils were on the program: Wayenberg performed *Rudepoema;* and Ringeissen, Entremont, and Ivete Magdaleno shared a complete performance of *Cirandas,* a suite of sixteen pieces based on Brazilian popular tunes. *Le Monde* of July 2, 1954 saluted the idea and the success with which it was executed, thanking its originator not only for her noble initiative but for the high level of artistry of her disciples. Before the music began, Long opened the concert with a short but eloquent speech honoring the Brazilian composer, who was present. Her tone reveals the ease and joy with which she assumed this kind of political role:

> My dear Villa-Lobos,
>
> I would like to give you a great speech, enumerate your glorious merits, retrace your prestigious career. But everyone here knows you, loves you, admires you. You even have citizen's rights here, since you are a member of L'Institut de France. However, what we will never know enough about is what you do for our country, your tireless efforts to promote French music, and the invaluable help you provide to all our French artists in Brazil.
>
> My dear friend, I will simply tell you it is a great joy for us to have you here tonight—the joy of our young pianists, who, in spite of feeling nervous, I am sure, are so happy to play your music for you, this music born of the Brazilian soul, so rich in harmonies and instrumental colors, speaking to us of the magnificent nature of Brazil. During your sojourn in Paris, you have recently heard concerts with large choral and instrumental groups. Tonight, with one piano, these young artists will try to express the poetry, the varied and powerful rhythms of this art which reflects your intense personality.[11]

Invited by the Brazilian government, Long finally returned to Brazil in August and September of 1954 for a series of lectures on French music and four concerto performances in Rio de Janeiro and São Paulo. As much as she was looking forward to these two months in South America, it was not without a little trepidation that she wrote to Tagliaferro on July 27, 1954, shortly before her departure:

> My very dear friend,
>
> I was very touched by your affectionate letter and I assure you that if it were not for your presence and the comfortable security of having you near me, I would not have the courage to take this far-away journey. Certainly I am looking forward to it and I wish to go very much. But just now I find myself a

little foolhardy and I will tell you again "at my age!!!" My eyes are better but now I have hideous problems with my teeth. . . . But when I think of our Isidor Philipp, who at the age of ninety-two travels the skies, alone . . . I realize I am making a lot of fuss about nothing.

So "à bientôt" my dear Magda,

Marguerite[12]

In this long-overdue visit Long was treated as a high-ranking dignitary. She was greeted on the dock by Brazil's Minister of Education, and from that point on, was never neglected by journalists' pens or photographers' lenses. Nearly 800 items appeared in the newspapers in one month; and the photographic coverage was even more telling than the verbal one.

Her hotel suite virtually exploded with flower arrangements, and the accompanying greeting cards were meticulously saved. Among them were messages from Guiomar Novaes: "To the great Marguerite Long, with all my best wishes and high admiration"; from Brazilian students: "With admiring and respectful tribute from the répétitrices and pupils of the Magdalena Tagliaferro School in São Paulo"; from Villa-Lobos and his wife, Mindinha: "Welcome! To our dearest friend, the joy of having you home."[13]

At the opening reception at the Fine Arts Academy in Rio de Janeiro, Long addressed the crowd in a grandiose manner:

> It is for me a great honor that the Brazilian government has invited me to this beautiful country, and it is with legitimate pride that I salute the people of Latin America, with whom we are united through strong and subtle ties of art and thought. . . . Political treaties, military pacts and economic agreements are all too often of small influence and short term, simply because they do not rest on what is essential in human beings. Cultural exchanges are of another nature. . . . Music, where the soul of a people can express itself so freely, holds a special place; and it is in this sense that I am particularly thrilled to have contributed modestly in the ever-growing search for a Franco-Brazilian cultural community. . . . You know all the admiration and affection I hold for [Villa-Lobos] . . . his art has the force and truthfulness of . . . Brazil's colossal nature. He knew how to elevate it to universality while remaining profoundly attached to popular sources, such rich sources as Brazilian music; and if Debussy called himself "musicien français," Villa-Lobos can sign "Villa Lobos, musicien brésilien." They each personify the glory of their country. . . .
>
> I will end this long message by saying that all this is not about influences, propaganda or planned strategies, but rather about attractions, sentiments and affinities which are historical between our two countries. . . .
>
> It is important that artists and writers of the same spiritual family fight against what divides people and fight instead for what unites them.[14]

On August 13, Magda Tagliaferro hosted a large cocktail party for Long in her Copacabaña residence in Rio de Janeiro. The guests included ambassadors, ministers, radio directors, conductors, cultural attachés, music critics, composers, painters and poets, impresarios, and members of Rio high society. Nearly 90 people were present and even more had been invited.[15]

The many letters exchanged by Tagliaferro and Marcelle Lyon, back home, document Long's triumphal visit to Brazil. These letters also reveal the frustration of the devoted Madame Lyon at Long's neglect of her. Madame Lyon ran Long's school and had undoubtedly poured a great deal of energy in helping Long prepare for her trip, but the pianist did not seem to give her friend any thought while abroad. On August 22 Madame Lyon wrote to Tagliaferro:

> I received your letter yesterday; without it, when and how would I have gotten any news of the arrival of our dear Marguerite, who does not trouble to send me any, knowing nevertheless with what anticipation I was awaiting them![16]

Two weeks later, on September 4, another letter to Tagliaferro from Madame Lyon expresses more unhappiness:

> I just got home and found your letter as always, keeping me abreast of what is going on. I too love her, find her endearing, *géniale*—the fact remains that since she has been in Rio, I have not received the least bit of news from her whatsoever, not even a small mark of affection on a postcard, but what can you say, one cannot expect from her more than she can handle! But I feel quite hurt and, I must admit a bit of resentment brewing inside.[17]

Long was notorious for not being considerate of her friends. These little incidents explain why Madame Lyon's friendship eventually eroded and their collaboration ended irremediably in 1959. In Tagliaferro's letters to Lyon there are also occasional hints of friction between the two pianists and subtle allusions to Long's temper. For example, in a letter of August 21, 1954 Tagliaferro stated: "I am not sending any photographs because alas they are not very good and that has been the cause for a veritable drama—this is just between you and me——."[18] Earlier in the same letter she wrote: "My joy would have been complete if you know who had not found a way to behave toward me in a very shocking way. . . . I realize that an unfortunate set of circumstances gave her reason to get a little irritated but. . . ." In the same letter, however, Tagliaferro praised Long's energy, enthusiasm, and good health, masking whatever tensions there may have been. Here too the friendship was not to be everlasting. Tagliaferro admitted that she and Long drifted apart in the late 1950s; she did not take part in Long's Concours after 1955, after having been asked to be on the jury every year since 1946.

Artists' frictions notwithstanding, by the time Long left Brazil in September 1954, she had received several honors and decorations, the most important being the Cross of the South, in recognition of her services to Brazilian music. In addition to giving concerts, lectures, and master classes, Long presided over the inauguration of a national piano competition that would bear her name. Letters and flowers had welcomed her arrival in August, and they marked her farewell a month later. Villa-Lobos and his wife wrote from Rio on September 22:

> To our dear friend,
> Sad to see you leave Rio, our sincere wishes for a good journey and hoping for the great pleasure of seeing you on our land very soon.
> Your friends who embrace you very affectionately,
> Mindinha and Villa-Lobos[19]

On her return to Paris on October 7, Long had only enthusiastic reports from her trip, according to Madame Lyon's letters to Tagliaferro. One written on October 10, 1954, three days after Long's return explained:

> The first thing she told me was "Magda was wonderful." . . . Shortly after, she showed me your gorgeous bracelet, the brooch purchased at "Magda's jeweler," another bracelet, etc. . . . Today [Sunday] I had lunch with her and I just now got home (it is eight o'clock!). . . . Your kindness toward her was, from all accounts, astounding . . . often in the course of the afternoon I heard . . . that without Magda I would not have gotten through it! . . . About your students, she only made excellent comments on the way you teach them. Altogether enchanted by all that had to do with you, she was particularly moved by your farewell on the boat, where, to her great joy, you joined her for dinner.[20]

Long expressed her warm feelings toward Tagliaferro in a letter dated November 10, 1954. The first page is devoted to her frustration at the inefficiency of the post office, which had been so slow in delivering her earlier letters. Then, she wrote:

> In my mind, in my heart you dominate my memory of this trip, you can be sure, and I derive great pleasure from admitting that.

> Believe it or not, I took a silly fall, which has just forced me to rest for three weeks. I cross the seas, travel through continents, and then I run aground on the carpet of my own boudoir . . . it is just ridiculous. And I had returned in such good form, a crowd at the train station, flowers. Everyone was flabbergasted by my healthy looks—Can you believe it?[21]

Long made a third and final trip to Brazil in September 1957, when she was two months shy of her 83rd birthday. She gave lectures and master classes, played concertos with orchestra, and presided over the jury of the piano competition inaugurated during her previous visit.

Further testimony to the friendship between Long and Villa-Lobos are the letters she received from his wife, Mindinha, after his death. Mindinha was unconsolable and shared her grief with Long: a letter written on June 2, 1962, three years after the composer died, can be compared to the letters Emma Bardac wrote to Long following Debussy's death.

> Very, very dear friend,
>
> I never forget you. You are always in my thoughts. My soul is empty without the presence of our unforgettable Villa-Lobos, but *in spite* of everything, my health is fine. . . . The government created the Villa-Lobos museum . . . and I am in charge of a radio program for the Ministry of Education called "Villa-Lobos, his life, his work." . . . I insist on writing to you about this because I cannot have a program about Villa-Lobos without having your contribution. . . . It would make me very happy and the program would be all the better for it. It is because of the deep friendship *he had* with you . . . for his sincere admiration for your art, well, everything, that I hope to hear from you soon. . . . You can understand how I feel, without the one who represented everything to me: my immense love, my mentor, my friend, and how difficult it is to live. . . . I do not understand how it is possible that I am still here, but, alas, life goes on. I miss you very much and now that the competition is going on here, I am sad that you are not with us. I hope your health is the best possible and that you are happy, as you deserve. I hug you strongly.
>
> Your sad and unhappy friend,
>
> Mindinha[22]

The Soviet Union

In the spring of 1955, Long had the chance to travel to the Soviet Union for the first time. Her friend Louis Joxe, who was Directeur des Relations Culturelles au Ministère des Affaires Etrangères in the late 1940s, during the early days of her competition, was now the French Ambassador in Moscow. Long had planned to stop in Warsaw on the way, where she was to be a member of the jury for the Chopin Competition. But a bad cold convinced her doctor that at her age she should give up her visit to Poland. She took a train directly to Moscow, where a warm welcome awaited her. She was greeted by her 1953 laureates, Evgeny Malinine and Nelli Shkolnikova, and she later visited her friends Emil Gilels and Leonid Kogan. Gilels was to be a member of the jury for Long's Concours in June; and Kogan was to be on the jury for the violin rounds in 1957.

The program of the opening concert, with orchestra, was to include "her" Ravel Concerto and the Fauré Ballade. Because of Long's flu, the concert was postponed a few days, and the Ballade was dropped. At the concert the response to the Ravel Concerto was so enthusiastic that the last movement had to be repeated. The audience and the orchestra were insatiable; the applause would not stop. Kyril Kondrashin, the conductor, and Long exchanged a few words, and then the orchestra and the soloist broke into a triumphal performance of the Fauré Ballade after all, which they had read through only once, days earlier. "Of all my memories, this one about the Ballade remains one of my most precious," wrote Long.[23]

At the Tchaikovsky Conservatory Long gave lectures on Fauré, Debussy, and Ravel in the form of dialogues with the audience. Her visit made a lasting impression on the Moscow musicians, as indicated by a letter dated April 22, 1956 from a young pianist, winner of the First Prize in the 1955 Chopin Competition:

> Madame,
>
> Just a year ago I had the great honor to play Debussy's *L'Isle joyeuse* for you in the small hall of the Moscow Conservatory. I keep faithfully in my memory your advice on interpretation of this beautiful work. . . . In August 1955, I participated in the International Piano Competition in Warsaw . . . and won first prize. . . . *L'Isle joyeuse* was on the program. . . . I am sorry you were not able to come. We were told you would be in the jury, but, unfortunately, you were not. . . . The music world in Moscow remembers your visit here and, above all, your very inspired interpretation of the Ravel Concerto at the Great Hall of the Moscow Conservatory. Our students ask constantly if you will come back to see us.
>
> [Signature illegible][24]

To cap her successful ambassadorial trip to the Soviet Union, the Moscow Conservatory bestowed on Long its highest honor, one rarely awarded to a

Long with Georges Auric and David Oistrakh, 1958. Photo Roger-Viollet, Paris.

woman. On April 19, 1955, in a formal ceremony, Long received the title of Honorary Professor of the State Conservatory in Moscow.[25]

On October 25, 1956, Dmitri Shostakovich, then editor of *Soviet Music,* wrote to Long asking if she would participate in an interview to be published in that journal. He sought Long's opinion on the evolution of contemporary music, on how to arrive at a better understanding between avant-garde musicians throughout the world, and on which recent works had made the most significant contribution to contemporary art. The tone of this questionnaire suggests that Shostakovich, then the leading Soviet composer, regarded Long as a world authority on contemporary music. Many leading Soviet musicians continued to show their respect toward the "Grande Dame," sending numerous telegrams on momentous occasions in upcoming years.

The United States of America

Long never traveled to the United States. Although her close friend Charles Münch was Director of the Boston Symphony Orchestra for many years, and several of her students toured the United States regularly at her encouragement and often because of her help and connections, Long herself never visited the country.

However, letters document the fact that at least one opportunity was offered to her in the early 1950s. It is not clear why Long declined, if she did, or what interfered with this apparently firm proposal. Pierre Bourgeois, the president of the French recording company Pathé Marconi, wrote to her on November 27, 1953:

> My Dear Friend,
>
> You know all the efforts we are presently putting forth to disseminate our French music abroad, and, particularly, the magnificent accomplishment of our Associated Company in New York, directed by Monsieur Dario Soria, who just released its first catalogue under the brand name "Angel," on which I think you would be pleased to see appear your recording of the Ballade by Fauré and the Concerto by Ravel. . . .
>
> He informs me that he would be extremely happy and honored if you would be willing to consider a visit to the United States, in the course of 1955, a visit he hopes for very strongly considering your quite exceptional position in the French music world. This trip could be organized by Monsieur William Judd, Vice-President of "Columbia Artists Management," for a duration of approximately six weeks, between January and April 1955, including concerts with the greatest American orchestras.
>
> I would personally be thrilled to hear your opinion regarding this matter, and I take this opportunity to enclose a pamphlet which will enable you to judge for yourself the merits of "Columbia Artists Management," a company entirely independent of the recording company of the same name.
>
> Pierre Bourgeois[26]

Six weeks later, Long had apparently not responded. Bourgeois, acting again as intermediary between Long and the New York office, reiterated the proposal on January 12, 1954:

My Dear Friend,

I take the liberty of reminding you of the terms of my letter of November 27. . . . I received from Monsieur Soria a second letter in which he renews his proposal, in the hope that you will be kind enough to give him an answer as soon as possible. For my part, I would be very happy to learn that you are willing to accept the idea of this project.

Pierre Bourgeois[27]

No further correspondence pertaining to this matter has been found. Perhaps Long's age was a factor in declining such an extensive trip. On the other hand, Long did travel to Brazil in 1957, at the age of 82. Another friend who wished to see Long play in the United States was Eugene Ormandy. He wrote to her on July 2, 1952 expressing this wish:

Dear Madame,

Just a line to tell you what a great joy it was for me to play with you last night, a pleasure I had been waiting for ever since I had heard you in Edinburgh two years earlier. I hope I will have this great honor many more times and not only in France, but . . . I wish ever so strongly, in the United States.[28]

Why Long never visited the United States remains an unanswered question.

Long turned 80 on November 13, 1954. About that time she began a series of twenty radio talks, or interviews, as if to celebrate the beginning of her ninth decade by reflecting on her life over the microphone. These half-hour programs, entitled "Mes maîtres, mes amis, mes élèves" (My mentors, my friends, my pupils) were broadcast weekly between October 12, 1954 and February 22, 1955.[29] On the last broadast she invited three of her oldest students, Lucette Descaves, Jean Doyen, and Jacques Février, all of whom were now tenured at the Paris Conservatoire. Her closing remarks expressed her happiness at seeing her pupils travel to foreign countries; it gave her the feeling that parts of her ten fingers were playing on all the keyboards of the world. But what moved her most was to realize that her unrelenting work as a pedagogue was being continued by her disciples, in whom she had complete trust, no matter how disparate their personalities. Her last words to the three in the studio were: "I hope that when it is your turn to speak on the radio some day you will evoke the memory of me with the same tender affection I have always felt toward you."[30]

12

The Last Ten Years of Long's Life: 1956–1966

Even though her repertoire was restricted to a handful of concertos and a few chamber works, Long had been performing regularly, in France and abroad. Now, past 80, she gradually retired from the concert stage, her appearances reserved for a few rare and momentous occasions. The only composer whose music she played in public until the end of her life was Fauré. According to her doctor, Long was in exceptionally good health for a woman of her age; but she was beginning to experience certain weaknesses—failing eyesight and a stooped back that slowed her pace. Her travels ceased after her last journey to Brazil in September 1957, but her mental vitality did not diminish in any way. During her last years she ensured her legacy by writing and publishing several books. All the while, her Concours continued to flourish; it was officially recognized and endowed as a National Foundation by the Ministère de l'Intérieur on April 28, 1962.

Long's Last Public Performances

As if to welcome her into the last decade of her life, a grandiose National Jubilee concert was organized by the French government at the Grand Amphitheater of the Sorbonne on June 4, 1956. The first page of the concert program contained a tribute by Darius Milhaud:

> Marguerite Long is not only the admirable performer we are celebrating today, but also the artist who has devoted herself to the cause of French music and played the works of Debussy, Ravel and Fauré with ardor, and finally a teacher with prodigious energy who, for half a century, has communicated a passion for music to her innumerable students. In this passion, she always included contemporary composers, and this is why today, with a deep feeling of gratitude, using the letters of her name, we have braided—Auric, Dutilleux, Françaix, Lesure, Poulenc, Rivier, Sauguet and myself—this garland of homage with all our hearts.[1]

The concert celebrated the 50th anniversary of Long's first appointment at the Conservatoire in 1906. But more to the point, it recognized a great artist's multifarious career, one that had touched and influenced many generations of musicians. Conceived and implemented by the French government, this event brought together an audience of more than 2,500, including

> ministers, ambassadors, old and young pupils, high- and low-ranking government officials, friends, enemies, those who loved and admired her, those who were consumed by jealousy toward her and came anyway, those for whom she was everything. . . . In short there was a whole world . . . all that world that Marguerite Long created around her throughout a life which has spanned 82 youthful years.[2]

Performing on the program were the Orchestre National under the direction of Charles Münch, who had come back from Boston for the occasion, and Long herself, who chose to share the stage on this festive evening by playing once again "her" Fauré Ballade. Before she made her entrance, the orchestra exploded into a frenzied *Marseillaise* followed by Berlioz's *Le Carnaval Romain.* After the Ballade came the piece written expressly for the occasion by the eight composers listed in Milhaud's homage: *Variations sur le nom de Marguerite Long.*[3] Ravel's *Daphnis et Chloé* brought the celebration to a close.

Variations sur le nom de Marguerite Long, despite its name, actually consists of eight independent short movements, each one written by one of the eight composers. The result is a lovely work, whose charm is due to the quality and variety of the whole as much as to the individual contributions. The order of movements was as follows: Jean Françaix's three-minute-long *Hymne Solennel*; Henri Sauguet's *Variations en forme de Berceuse pour Marguerite Long,* based on the four-note theme E A G G derived from her name; Darius Milhaud's *La Couronne de Marguerites* (The crown of daisies), a waltz in rondo form (French *marguerites* = English *daisies*); Jean Rivier's *Nocturne;* Henri

Dutilleux's *Sérénade sur le nom de Marguerite Long,* which uses all fourteen letters of her name to construct the theme: Daniel-Lesur's *Intermezzo;* Francis Poulenc's *Bucolique;* and Georges Auric's *Allegro Final.* (The piece was performed only once more, eighteen month later, at the Chatelet Theater, by the Orchestre Colonne conducted by Georges Tzipine.)

The reviewers marveled at Long's youth and vitality. With a glass in hand, Long was still present, past midnight, at the festivities following the concert. Surrounded by flowers, she greeted her numerous admirers. Those who could not attend, notably her Soviet friends, sent telegrams, with messages full of deference and gratitude:

> I deplore not being able to attend the celebration of gratitude on the part of France and the music world at large, organized on the occasion of the fiftieth anniversary of your magnificent pedagogical and artistic work. I present you my best and most sincere congratulations on this day. I am with you with all my soul.
>
> Emil Gilels[4]

> The Director, Professors and students of the Moscow Conservatory warmly congratulate the Honorary Professor of our Conservatory, the remarkable musician Marguerite Long for her fifty years of outstanding pedagogical activity. They wish her good health and many many years ahead.
>
> Professor Svechnikov, Director of the Conservatory[5]

> Please let me cordially and sincerely congratulate you, revered Madame Long, distinguished pianist and beautiful pedagogue with a sensitive and tender soul. . . . The rise to prominence of so many talented artists is linked to your name. I wish you health and the brilliant continuation of your noble and precious enrichment of the musical culture of the world.
>
> With my profound respect.
>
> Professor Georgui Orvid, Vice Minister of Culture in USSR[6]

After she played the Fauré Ballade, Long announced that this would be her last public performance. She had to rescind her words, for a mere two months later she appeared at the annual Music Festival of Menton, on the French Riviera. A year earlier, in August 1955, Long had come to hear her pupil Samson François play at this festival. The concerts took place on the square in front of the Church of Saint-Michel of Menton, on balmy Mediterranean evenings. Long had exclaimed that this setting would be an ideal one in which to play Fauré's music. Promptly, a Fauré concert was organized for the following year, and Long was asked to participate. On August 10, 1956, surrounded by the Trio Pasquier, she played Fauré's sublime First Piano Quartet in C minor, no small feat. *Nice-Matin* wrote: "On hearing and watching her, one is astounded by her unabating vitality. For, in the Quartet she was not content with merely holding her part energetically: she led the group in the performance" (August 14, 1956). The rest of the program consisted of Fauré's String Quartet and a set of his *mélodies.* Among the letters hailing the event, a hasty note from Jean Cocteau, written on August 6, 1956, a few days before the concert, expressed his hope to attend:

> Very Dear Marguerite Long,
>
> I must go to Lebanon, where a French Festival is being organized. . . . I will do my best to come on the 10th to the admirable Square in Menton. If I do not make it . . . do not hold it against me.
>
> Your faithful,
> Jean Cocteau[7]

Within the year 1956, Long recorded the First Piano Quartet for Columbia with the three Pasquier brothers, immortalizing her chamber music appearance in Menton. This was her last recording.

On May 10, 1957, an evening of French music celebrated the 50th anniversary of one of Paris's most prestigious concert halls, the Salle Gaveau. Presided over by Jacques Bordeneuve, Secrétaire d'Etat aux Arts et Lettres, the occasion promised to be a meeting of France's best musicians, past and present: Fauré, Debussy, and Ravel interpreted by Pierre Bernac, Francis Poulenc, Marguerite Long, the Pasquier Trio, Jean-Pierre Rampal, Lily Laskine (harp), Luben Yordanoff (violin), and Jacques Lancelot (clarinet).

The printed program contained a history of the hall by Claude Rostand, who reminded the audience that Etienne Gaveau's father, Joseph Gaveau, had started building the first Gaveau pianos in 1847. In 1957, Joseph's grandsons, Marcel and André, were still keeping the family enterprise strong and healthy:

> Such continuity, from both an artistic and family perspective, is rare in the history of music. . . .
>
> In 1907, Etienne Gaveau gave our capital this concert hall, which, throughout the last half century, has been one of the vital centers of Paris's artistic and intellectual activity. Of today's illustrious virtuosos, most recall with emotion and nostalgia that . . . on this stage, they met, along with their first stage fright, their first triumphs. . . .

> From Saint-Saëns—who gave his farewell concert here—to Pierre Boulez, who, a few weeks ago, at the dawn of his young career, produced the most audacious harmonies of our time, including Fauré, Debussy, Ravel, and the musicians of the epoch of the *Groupe des Six,* the great names and dates of the history of contemporary music sparkle . . . on the walls and balcony of this hall . . . where instrumental and vocal music find their ideal setting. . . .[8]

Indeed, a beautiful choice of instrumental and vocal chamber music honored the 50-year-old Salle Gaveau. Jean-Pierre Rampal opened with Fauré's *Fantaisie,* Op. 79, for flute and piano; then followed Ravel's *Introduction and Allegro* for harp, string quartet, flute, and clarinet; and before the intermission Bernac and Poulenc performed Debussy *mélodies,* including *Beau Soir, L'Echelonnement des haies, Le Promenoir des deux amants,* and *Trois Ballades de François Villon.* The evening was brought to a close with Fauré's First Piano Quartet, in C minor, interpreted by Marguerite Long and the Pasquier Trio again. It was Long's very last performance of the piece.

On her return from her third trip to Brazil, in September 1957, Long became the first recipient of the national honor of Commandeur de l'Ordre des Arts et des Lettres, which had only recently been instituted by the Secrétariat d'Etat aux Arts et Lettres.

A few months later the city of Paris chose to reward Long for her extensive contribution to the musical life of France's capital. On February 7, 1958, she received the prestigious Grande Médaille de Vermeil de la Ville de Paris at a ceremony held at the Hôtel de Ville. After a long speech by René Fayssat,[9] vice-president of Paris's municipal assembly, Long accepted the award with her usual eloquence and sense of humor:

> The honor which Paris bestows on me moves me deeply. . . . For, like many Parisians, I committed a youthful sin, that of being born in the province. . . . I have done my best to repair it, for at the age of twelve . . . I left Nîmes, my beloved and beautiful city, not knowing that I was never to return. . . . I entered the world of music as one enters a religious order, I tried to perform, I tried to teach—the only way to continue learning—. . . . This medal . . . I receive it not as a consecration, but as an encouragement to always keep the youth that age cannot touch.[10]

In the spring of 1958, the Philadelphia Orchestra under Eugene Ormandy gave a concert in Paris, at the large hall of the Palais de Chaillot, celebrating the tenth anniversary of the State of Israel. During the intermis-

Long and Eugene Ormandy. Bibliothèque Musicale Gustav Mahler, Paris; Marguerite Long Archives.

sion, in an intimate ceremony, Long awarded Ormandy the Cravate de Commandeur de la Légion d'Honneur and reminisced about a performance of the Ravel G major Concerto they had given together, years earlier.

During the same spring, Louis Joxe, Ambassador of France and Secrétaire Général des Affaires Etrangères, presided over a concert given by ten foreign virtuosos at the Salle Gaveau. Long had been granted the use of the hall for the evening, free of charge. The pianists, all participants in Long's international master classes, were thus given the opportunity to perform on one of Paris's most coveted stages. Nine countries were represented: Lebanon, Brazil, Turkey, the Philippines, Cuba, Jamaica, Japan, the United States, and Argentina. Several premières were performed in a program of twentieth-century composers from Fauré to Jolivet and Messiaen, including Villa-Lobos, Albeniz, Sauguet, Auric, Milhaud, Daniel-Lesur, and Rivier.

The last concert appearance by Marguerite Long occurred on the occasion of the twenty-fifth anniversary of the Orchestre National, on February 3, 1959, when she was 84 years old. The Orchestre National de la Radiodiffusion Télévision Française was created in 1934, thanks to the sole initiative and perseverance of its conductor Désiré-Emile Inghelbrecht.* Originally conceived exclusively for radio broadcasts, it soon encouraged public attendance of its performances and became one of the pillars of Parisian musical life. It earned an international reputation with its many successful tours, including one in the United States in 1948. An illustrious roster of guest conductors contributed to its renown: Manuel Rosenthal, Jean Martinon, Pierre Dervaux, Paul Paray, Bruno Walter, Wilhelm Furtwängler, Charles Münch, and André Cluytens. Its equal dedication to contemporary and classical repertoire gave it a place of distinction among French orchestras.

A special three-month series of concerts in honor of the orchestra's twenty-fifth anniversary was presented at the Théâtre des Champs-Elysées, sponsored by French Radio, the Director of the Theatre, and Pathé Marconi. On February 3, 1959, the series opened with Désiré-Emile Inghelbrecht on the podium and Long as soloist. The program consisted of Inghelbrecht's *Vézelay*, Debussy's *La Mer,* Fauré's Ballade, and Ravel's *Daphnis et Chloé.*

Long's physician, Jean Thin, confided in a personal interview that although her health had been remarkably strong for years, it was starting to weaken. Long was now 85; her eyesight was failing, and her increasingly stooped back was beginning to hinder her breathing and would eventually put stress on her heart. When she was asked to play for this momentous occasion, she consulted Dr. Thin. He was well aware of her physical condition and admitted to being worried, but he also knew that discouraging her from this last appearance "would simply kill her." He claimed to be as nervous before the performance as she was: "All of Paris was present; half the audience had come to honor Fauré and Long, who had retired from the stage for years; the other half had maliciously come to witness a catastrophe, to watch Long fall from the keyboard."[11] As she was adjusting her bench, Thin noticed that she was trying to avoid the spotlights, which were blinding her. He was very concerned, but as soon as her hands touched the keyboard, everything went very well, and her last Fauré Ballade was a triumph. Lengthy ovations called her back to the stage a dozen times to bow and wave her last farewell. "The stage was transformed into a garden from the avalanche of flowers she received."[12] In *Le Guide du Concert,* musicologist Pierrette Mari described the concert and its purpose in glowing terms:

> Giving in to pressing solicitations for this exceptional occasion, Marguerite Long agreed to come out of her retirement from the stage. It was to offer us with her velvety touch Fauré's Ballade, which she had performed for the first time over half a century ago.
>
> The success became triumph, and there was, in the endless ovations which honored Marguerite Long and D.-E. Inghelbrecht, a great deal of admiration and gratitude. . . . One could not hope for a more brilliant opening of the celebration of this twenty-fifth anniversary, which marks a milestone in the history of music in France. [February 13, 1959.]

A letter from Ida Rubinstein (1885–1961) added luster to Long's memory of this special celebration. Rubinstein, an important personage in France's twentieth-century artistic life, had come to Paris as an unknown dancer with the Russian ballet and had created a sensation at her debut performance of June 4, 1909. More than a dancer, she was also a mime. Her exotic beauty and extraordinary stage presence exerted such fascination on fellow artists that countless authors and composers were inspired to create stage pieces for her. The first such work was Debussy and d'Annunzio's *Le Martyre de Saint-Sébastien.*

Long was acquainted with Ida Rubinstein through Ravel, for the dancer was part of his intimate circle during the last decade of his life. Their relationship dated back to at least 1927, when Rubinstein asked Ravel to write a ballet for her. From this commission came *Boléro,* which she premiered on November 20, 1928 at the Paris Opéra, along with a performance of *La Valse.*

Ida Rubinstein was one of very few women Long genuinely admired and respected. She was grateful for all that the dancer had done in the difficult last years of Ravel's life, when few people could truly help him. On the day after Long's last public appearance at the Théâtre des Champs-Elysées, Ida Rubinstein, 74 years old, wrote:

> My dear and great friend,
>
> You were *divine* last night! How can I thank you for all that you gave us. The musicians who were with me were as dazzled and wonderstruck, as was I. Please receive my faithful and deepest affection.
>
> Ida Rubinstein[13]

Other letters from Rubinstein to Long express the esteem the two women had for each other. When Rubinstein died in 1960, Long devoted a lengthy article to her in *Le Figaro littéraire* of January 21, 1961, tracing the life of this remarkable woman and recounting in detail her love for and devotion to Ravel.

In January 1960 it was Spain's turn to honor Long with its National Award: the Cross of Isabelle the Catholic. The Count de Casa Rojas, the Spanish Ambassador to Paris, bestowed the decoration on Long in the sumptuous salons of the Embassy:

> Your merits, Madame, are known worldwide, but let me share with you the gratitude Spain feels toward you for the efficient help you have always so graciously given to all the Spanish musical events in France, and particularly for having made mandatory for all entrants of the Concours Long–Thibaud a performance of works by our great composer Isaac Albeniz.[14]

Long responded with her characteristic eloquence and charm:

> Yes, I love Spain, and this love did not begin the day I discovered its music. I am from Nîmes . . . and as a child, I was an ardent *aficionada* of bullfights, so much that, when I deserved a punishment, it was from this exalting spectacle that I was deprived. . . .
>
> I was prepared for Spanish music, if I may say so, by the genial "Air du Toréador" from *Carmen.* As a very young child I used to sing it at the top of my lungs. . . . I heard *Iberia* by Albeniz for the first time by a Spanish pianist of great talent. It was superb. Later I got to know the dear, very dear Isaac Albeniz. . . . So, Your Excellency, this decoration with which Spain honors me today makes me relive a whole period of my past.[15]

But what delighted Long most was to learn that her new distinction entitled her to enter Spanish churches on horseback!

In the summer of 1959, Long was approached by Jean Fournier, a businessman who had grand plans to transform her school into a "Piano Academy." The arrangements at the Rue Molitor had become marred; differences had arisen between the pianist and the devoted Marcelle Lyon, director of the school. The situation was difficult, since the Rue Molitor quarters were Lyon's residence. Part of Fournier's idea was to take charge of the operations as a business and manage its finances himself. Essentially, Fournier was buying Long's name to create a prestigious and lucrative enterprise, in a glamorous *hôtel particulier,* Rue Freycinet, an elite Paris neighborhood. Long would appear at her whim for well-publicized master classes, and the teachers at the school would include younger artists chosen from among Long's disciples: Aldo Ciccolini, Lucette Descaves, Jean Doyen, and Ventsislav Yankoff. The Académie de Piano would also offer chamber music, theory and analysis, sight-reading, and solfège with professors from the Paris Conservatoire: Gabriel Bouillon, Tony Aubin, and Yvonne Desportes. An elaborate glossy flier reflected the grand scale of Fournier's vision. It advertised concerto classes with the participation of one of the Paris orchestras (Colonne, Lamoureux, Société des Concerts, Pasdeloup). Piano instruction was to be available at all levels, for young beginners up to those preparing for international competitions. A hierarchy of diplomas were to be granted, and so on.

By the spring of 1960, the plan was well in place, and the Académie was to open its doors in the fall. Long's friend Louis Joxe, the former French Ambassador to Moscow, now Ministre de l'Education Nationale, had agreed to preside at the inaugural ceremony. In the fall of 1960, Long's international master classes resumed in this new location, and they were to continue for the next several years. One of Long's last protégés was the Argentinian pianist Bruno Leonardo Gelber, a favorite laureate of the 1961 Concours.

What became of the Académie de Piano Marguerite Long after her death in 1966 is unclear. Apparently Fournier's vision did not withstand the test of time. Some of the principal players interviewed, including Descaves and Yankoff, were very evasive in their responses. Was it financial difficulty or conflict of personalities? It might have been a bit of both. By the end of the decade, the Académie no longer existed.

Chopin's 150th Anniversary

Just as the centennial of Chopin's death was celebrated in 1949, in 1960 France was gearing up for the 150th anniversary of his birth. A National Committee was placed under the honorary sponsorship of three ministers: André Malraux (Affaires Culturelles), Maurice Couve de Murville (Affaires Etrangères), and Louis Joxe (Education Nationale). Marguerite Long again presided over the National Organizational Committee, just as she had in 1949.

The National Committee sponsored musical events and concerts throughout the year, opening with a pilgrimage to Chopin's grave at the Père Lachaise Cemetery on February 22. Many Chopin recitals were scheduled, featuring Artur Rubinstein, Witold Malcuzynski, and other Polish artists, as well as Jean Doyen and Samson François. Exhibits of documents from the composer's life were presented in some of his residences, including a ceremony in Nohant. There was even a pilgrimage to the birthplace of Nicolas Chopin (the composer's father) in the village of Marainville (Vosges). Programs were broadcast live over the B.B.C. and Polish, French, and Austrian radio. From February 22 through the month of August, there was an imaginative and abundant schedule of Chopin events in France.

Long's contribution to this six-month festival was to conceive and organize concerts on April 1, April 26, and May 23, each of which had a special attraction. Stanislas Gajewski, the Polish Ambassador, attended all three events.

For the concert on April 1, Long replicated the program of Chopin's Paris debut, on February 26, 1832 at the Salle Pleyel. Chopin had performed his F minor Piano Concerto, which had been an instant success. A copious potpourri of chamber and orchestral music had surrounded the concerto. Long chose the largest stage in Paris, the Opéra, to reenact that momentous concert. The orchestra was that of the Théâtre National de l'Opéra, conducted by Pierre Dervaux.

The evening opened with Beethoven's String Quintet, Op. 104, performed by the first chairs of the Opéra orchestra. Two arias from Bellini's *Norma* followed. The first half closed with Chopin's F minor Piano Concerto, with Bernard Ringeissen as soloist. A pupil of Long, Ringeissen had won First Prize at both the Chopin Competition in Warsaw and the Concours Long–Thibaud in 1955.

The *pièce de résistance* came after the intermission. On that same concert on February 26, 1832, a Grande Polonaise for six pianos by Kalkbrenner had been performed by Chopin, Kalkbrenner, and four other artists. As Chopin wrote to his friend Titus Woyciechowski, back home: "I will give a concert on December 25 [1831]. . . . I will play my F minor and my Variations in B-flat major. . . . I will give, in addition, with Kalkbrenner, a March followed by a Polonaise, for two pianos and four other pianos accompanying. It is somewhat crazy!"[16] (The concert was actually postponed to February because Kalkbrenner was ill.) Long was very eager to revive this piece for the occasion, but she could not locate the score. Finally, the themes Kalkbrenner used were discovered in the Conservatoire library, and Tony Aubin agreed to "reconstitute" the Polonaise in Kalkbrenner's 1830s style.

No one will ever know how close to the original Aubin's version was, but Long's wish was not to be denied, and the program featured "Grande

Polonaise for Six Pianos on a Theme by Kalkbrenner, by Tony Aubin, in Homage to Frédéric Chopin." The six pianists were laureates of the Long–Thibaud Competitions: Yankoff (1949), Wayenberg (1949), Ringeissen (1955), Toyoaki Matsuura (1959), John Blot (1959), and Alain Motard (1957); and, French piano manufacturers were also well represented: Gaveau, Erard, and Pleyel pianos were all on that stage.

There was more music on this program: a Rossini aria, *Solo de concert* for oboe and orchestra by Henry Brod (principal oboe in the Opéra orchestra), and Chopin's variations for piano and orchestra on "La Ci Darem la Mano," Op. 2, performed by the most recent winner of the Concours Long–Thibaud, the Japanese pianist Matsuura.

The evening created a stir in Paris. The Opéra was flooded with flowers, compliments of the city of Menton:

> staircases wrapped in giant bouquets, the stage's banister disappeared under lilacs, tulips, roses and hawthorn, while trees of hydrangea surrounded the orchestra, on stage. Cypresses on an infinite background of sky formed the set. Never had the musicians played in such Eden![17]

Hélène Jourdan-Morhange was very much impressed by the execution of the Polonaise:

> Tony Aubin, with his usual skill and musicality, certainly knew how to reconstruct, in the style of the author (Kalkbrenner), a Polonaise for Six Pianos, quite provocative, romantic and extremely brilliant. . . . Yankoff replaced Kalkbrenner, Wayenberg took the place of Chopin. . . . It was a memorable match, with runs, trills and winning rhythms. And what ensemble! The last scale in unison (going from the lowest to the highest registers of the piano) was truly a miracle of precision. The audience, enthralled, encored the Polonaise.
>
> . . . Evoking Chopin at the piano (he is thin, charming, and his poetic playing makes the comparison appropriate), Bernard Ringeissen performed the Concerto in F minor. I like his Chopin, not distorted by excessive rubati . . . Ringeissen is a true musician; his success was great.[18]

The second concert arranged by Long, on April 26, was a recital shared by Samson François and a Polish singer, Stefania Woytowicz. It took place in one of the largest halls of the Louvre Palace, Salle Daru, with paintings by Delacroix hanging on the walls, including the famous portrait of Chopin. It was a splendid setting in which to hear a set of Chopin's songs, followed by the

Fourth Ballade, the First Impromptu, four waltzes, and the "Funeral March" Sonata, in B-flat minor. Long made her intentions explicit in the program:

> Today, it is in the prestigious Louvre Palace that I wished, in the name of the National Committee, to honor officially the two great figures of Chopin and Delacroix, who shared such brotherly ties through art and its expression. This is how, thanks to Edmont Sidet . . . Executive Director of the Museums of France, where so many treasures have accumulated, I conceived this event, both as a concert and an exhibit, the face of Chopin being inseparable from the portrait Eugène Delacroix made of it.[19]

On May 23, "by popular request," Long presented a recital by pupils under the age of fourteen, at the Salle Gaveau, as she had done at the celebration in 1949. Here again, the young pianists performed early pieces by Chopin, several of them unpublished or forgotten. A few titles were recognizable from the earlier centennial program, while others were drawn from Chopin's more standard repertoire: a Ballade, a Scherzo, an Impromptu. Among the thirteen young performers was Katia Labèque, who has since achieved international renown. This recital was introduced by Pierre Barbizet. All three concerts were televised by Radiodiffusion Télévision Française.

In November 1960, Long was 86 years old and still a pillar of French musical life. A birthday card from the American composer Virgil Thomson addressed her with playful deference: "To Her Majesty, Happy Birthday, from her faithful servant Virgil Thomson."[20] His correspondence usually opened with "Chère Reine" (Dear Queen) or "Chère Majesté," and he sent her sunny greetings from Spain, Venice, or wherever he was traveling.

About this time, Long encountered difficulties with her landlord, who complained that the piano playing was disturbing the neighbors. He attempted to evict her, after the "Grande Dame" had occupied the apartment for twenty years. Long promptly sent her lawyer and friend, Maître Hauer, to take care of the dispute. When he came back and proudly announced that the matter was taken care of, and that the lease was guaranteed for the next ten years, she exclaimed: "Well, and what after that? "[21]

In July 1963, Long officiated at the International Jazz Festival of Juan-Les-Pins, on the French Riviera. *Nice-Matin* wrote under the headline "Historical soirée, Marguerite Long presides at the gala":

Long on the Riviera, on a motor scooter, waving a bottle of Coke. Bibliothèque Musicale Gustav Mahler, Paris; Marguerite Long Archives.

The person music history will remember as the great interpreter of Fauré, Debussy and Ravel is staying at the Grand Hotel. Her hotel-room neighbors are Miles Davis and Sarah Vaughan. She is having breakfast two tables away from Sammy Price, who is sipping his orange juice. . . . And she takes the elevator

> several times a day with "the drummer" Tony Williams . . . or Virginia, the angel of the Harlem Beggars. . . . That is not all. Marguerite Long will preside in person at tonight's gala. [July 30, 1963.]

The gala was a showcase of French jazz musicians: The Claude Bolling Sextet and the violinist Stéphane Grappelli, accompanied by a trio; and to close the evening, the great American singer Sarah Vaughan. Long was delighted with the idea of participating in the Festival. She was quoted as saying with vivacity:

> Jazz has been a form of musical art for a long time. . . . I, myself, derived great pleasure, years ago, from playing jazz for fun. And some of my students, among them Samson François, give jazz an important place in their activities. [*Nice-Matin*, July 30, 1963.]

Le Piano and Other Writings by Long

After teaching thousands of young pianists for over 60 years, Long wished to leave a written record of her experience. Her intellectual curiosity had also led her to explore writings on piano playing by virtuosos of the previous century and a half. In addition, she had given many lectures on the development of piano technique and on the styles of certain composer-pianists. Armed with the wealth of her library, her lecture notes, and the wisdom of a lifetime, Long envisioned her book on piano playing as a far-reaching pedagogical manual.

Le Piano was published in 1959 by Salabert. The frontispiece is a reproduction of Long's autograph thanking Jacques Février and Jean Bérard for their good humor and advice in helping her complete the volume. Her closing remark is a quotation from Debussy: "It is unnecessary to make technique austere in order to appear more serious . . . a bit of charm never ruined anything."[22]

The book offers an exhaustive array of exercises and drills for developing a sound piano technique: Chapter I, five-finger exercises, repeated notes, and trills; Chapter II, double notes; Chapter III, scales and arpeggios; Chapter IV, wrist, octaves, chords, tremolo, and glissando. Long worded her directions very carefully, encouraging sensible practice of her exercises and good judgment in choosing drills adapted to one's hand, in order not to cause physical stress. She did not hesitate to draw on the experience of her predecessors where appropriate, borrowing or referring to exercises by Tausig, Thalberg, Czerny, Clementi, Mendelssohn, Liszt, Brahms, Busoni, and Moszkowski.

Long warned the student against doing all this technical work first thing in the morning; instead, she suggested spreading it throughout the day, interspersing repertoire work with attention to a specific technical difficulty. "When healing at a spa, one does not consume all at once the volume of mineral water prescribed for the whole day."[23] She insisted that practice be musical at all times, with constant attention to producing a beautiful sound. Long hoped that by careful reading of her comments, directions, and historical explanations, the student would learn the art of practicing critically and efficiently.

Beyond the 95 pages of densely laid-out pianistic exercises, the most interesting part of *Le Piano* is found in Long's 21-page Foreword. It is a testament of faith of the great pedagogue, a place where she condensed her thoughts about her life and career as pianist and teacher. Philosophical and perspicacious, these well-written lines bring her personality and genuine culture to life. First, in describing some of her guiding forces in teaching music, she approached the subject of nationalism:

> I obeyed another secret impulse of my conscience. I wanted to pay homage to the art and science of the "French" piano. . . . I do not have the silly pretension of placing our professors and artists above their foreign colleagues.
>
> But, while claiming universality, which should be a quality of all works of art, I believe that each country, each nation, each race, each culture honors them in its own way. . . .
>
> In spite of the diversity in temperaments of our great virtuosos, one can detect among them certain common features. Pianists as different from one another as Planté, Diémer, Pugno, Saint-Saëns, were united by a secret technical and stylistic kinship, made of clarity, ease, measure, elegance and tact. . . .
>
> If France is the country of Descartes and, in painting, of Jean Fouquet, it is also that of Racine, Baudelaire, Verlaine, that of Chardin, Delacroix and the impressionists. If all of these great artists had the same concern for elegant logic, can we not see that this logic never took away their fire of inspiration, or the nuances of their sensitivities?
>
> As to our pianists, they owe the character of their talent to our composers. From Couperin to Ravel, they developed in the art of the piano the sense of color and timbre. Composers such as Fauré and Debussy revealed to us subtle and precious secrets in the search for voluptuous harmonic resonances . . . their compatriots had to benefit from it when they studied their works. French

> playing, at once vigorous and mellow, brilliant and delicate, has thus an easily recognizable personality . . . (Debussy requested softness in strength and strength in softness).[24]

Approaching the subject of technique more directly, Long was convinced that:

> The study of piano requires a great deal of effort. But it does not mean fighting against nature. A normal hand is made to play the piano and any pianist who does not share this conviction is unworthy of his art. . . . Our fingers are not only a miraculous muscular mechanism, they are also prodigious organs of perception endowed with their own sensitivity, almost their own creative gift.

Later she quoted the great surgeon Thierry de Martel: "There are countless things our hands understand before our brain does, and those who manipulate while thinking will discover more than those who think without manipulating."

Long's observations are often corroborated by the comments of older masters, such as Chopin, whom she quoted on the subject of finger dexterity and evenness. For Long, clarity in performance was of the utmost importance: "Fingers must pronounce notes the way lips pronounce syllables. . . . A way of playing which is well articulated and without dryness is for the pianist an asset as precious as good diction is for an actor." After discussing technical considerations from a more mechanical viewpoint, Long then defined good piano technique: "Technique is the whole of all our pianistic knowledge: it is the mastery of sound control and color, it is ease in execution . . . it is touch, the art of fingering, of pedaling, of phrasing, the possession of a vast expressive palette." In a word, technique was music making. She quoted Albeniz's ironic but perceptive remark: "The pianist who likes exercises too much is simply lazy." Long insisted on the value of slow practice, slow but always expressive and musical, listening attentively and objectively. Even when one knew a fast passage well, one should never refrain from playing it slowly again. She reminded the reader that Liszt would say: "I do not know this work well enough to play it slowly."[25]

A lengthy section is devoted to the pianist's most precious quality: tone quality. It goes without saying that in order to have a good sound the pianist should develop a good ear:

> How I love Montaigne, who wanted children to be awakened by the sound of a virginal. . . . The best thing you can do for a young child . . . is to teach him to discover a beautiful tone, to enjoy it, not to hit the piano, but to search with his finger a way to make the string vibrate gently. That says something about how, in our epoch of deafening noises and loudspeakers, parents must protect their children's ears as much as possible.

Finally, Long addressed the life-style of artists who must protect their health—their mental and physical balance—in order to sustain years of self-imposed discipline and hours of practice. She warned young pianists against the impatience of the times, in which recent graduates were expected to be instantly propelled into the limelight. She believed that the learning process continued indefinitely, and that it was most important to take the time to learn to know oneself: "They must know that, like genius, talent is a long stretch of patience, and patience alone magnificently rewards the artist." After covering a wide range of subjects, Long ended with words borrowed from two great artists whose views she espoused wholeheartedly:

> And if sometimes . . . you are overcome by discouragement, remember this advice from Liszt, who was nonetheless a man blessed with all the world's gifts and facility: "Have patience with yourself."
>
> Also meditate over these words from the great French painter André Dunoyer de Segonzac: "It takes a whole lifetime to build one's house."

She reiterated these thoughts as a sort of epilogue to *Le Piano*, after the four chapters of drills and exercises: "To learn one's craft, a great deal of work and patience are required. One also needs a lot of modesty and the respect for tradition. These are the simple truths I will give as a conclusion to my book."[26]

Le Piano was received with great enthusiasm by pianists and musicians, some of whom had encouraged Long to write such a book for years. The scholar and critic René Dumesnil wrote a lengthy column in *Le Monde* of July 2, 1959, shortly after the final rounds of the 1959 Concours Long–Thibaud. "The aftermath of this concert, given by two finalists of the Concours, seems to be the perfect occasion to talk about *Le Piano* by Marguerite Long: it is much more than a method, it is the very soul of an instrument and the spirit of its artist." On May 6, 1959, Mica Salabert, owner and manager of the publishing firm, wrote a personal note to Long, who had dedicated *Le Piano* to the memory of Mica's late husband, Francis Salabert:

My very dear Marguerite,

It is with great emotion that I will submit your *Piano* to you today. It represents . . . the completion of a unique and monumental work which will remain current through the times.

Your Mica[27]

Of greater interest is a letter from Rosina Lhevinne, congratulating her French colleague on her achievement. The letter, dated New York, June 10, 1960, is in French, with a number of charming mistakes:

Dear Madame Long,

Please excuse me for not having written to you earlier. . . . Now, I have had the opportunity to examine your book with great interest. It is with great pleasure, Madame, that I tell you that I found this book quite unique in the combinations [of exercises] . . . so well organized and with superb remarks which should help every pianist who will apply himself to understanding all the magnificent advice you give.

Please receive all my admiration for your work and my best wishes.

Rosina Lhevinne[28]

Le Piano circulated widely and was adopted in Russian translation by the Moscow Conservatory as its official piano-technique manual. Surprisingly, *Le Piano* has not been translated into English.

Long organized her recollections of her collaborations with Fauré, Debussy, and Ravel in the form of three little books, *Au piano avec Fauré, Au piano avec Debussy*, and *Au piano avec Ravel.* Having transmitted through her teaching the tradition of these three composers, she felt it was now time to record her experience on paper for future generations. René Julliard was ready to publish her accounts as soon as they were written. Unfortunately, the books misrepresent their author in both content and form. Although each one offers some valuable information, the facts tend to be overstated and her rapport with each composer exaggerated. In doing so, Long discredits herself rather than reflecting the real stature of her career. Furthermore, the writing does not exhibit the elegance of language that her notes, lectures, and letters do, suggesting that she relied heavily on the pens of others. It is unfortunate that these three books are all that has been translated into English by or about Marguerite Long, for they present a distorted view of the pianist.

Au piano avec Debussy, published in 1960, was dedicated to Long's friend Paul Léon, a member of L'Institut de France. As in many of her endeavors, Long enlisted the help of a devoted friend, in this case, Renée de Saussine, to see the book to completion. *Au piano avec Fauré,* compiled in collaboration with Janine Weill, came out in 1963, and was dedicated to Long's friend and an admirer of Fauré's music, Germaine de Jouvenel.

A physician from Bordeaux, Pierre Laumonier, had heard Long play the Fauré C minor Quartet in front of the Church of Saint-Michel in Menton. A few years later, when he was visiting friends on the Riviera, Long was staying with Germaine de Jouvenel, a neighbor of his hosts. Laumonier was still moved by Long's performance and had read *Au piano avec Debussy.* He asked to meet the artist, and the two conversed for hours with great animation. Long was still working on her Fauré volume, and she asked Laumonier if he would help her put together the last piece of the trilogy, *Au piano avec Ravel.* Honored and thrilled by such a prospect, he accepted, but unfortunately, "I was slow in my work. I thought that our time was infinite and our friend invulnerable; she left us before the task was completed but with the promise that it would be."[29] *Au piano avec Ravel* was published posthumously in 1971, under Long's authorship but stating, "Texts gathered and presented by Professor Pierre Laumonier." All three books have been translated into English.

Long's second book on piano technique, *La Petite Méthode de Piano,* published in 1963, was expressly designed for children. Long clearly stated in the Preface how she envisioned her work and how it diverged from traditional approaches practiced in France at the time:

> Elementary teaching of piano encounters two problems. It disappoints many students by its complexity and its slowness: complexity of theory and slowness of practice. . . . The two parts (theory and practice) should go hand in hand. Now, the mistake of separating them at the beginning of piano studies is made too often. The child is introduced to abstract theoretical concepts, he is taught solfège in the absolute, in a vacuum, without any contact whatsoever with the instrument he has chosen to discover. These rudiments are thus given a tedious and discouraging character. . . . To give a beginner all this heavy material is to disconcert him and discourage him. . . .
>
> Let us put our child in front of the keyboard and leave it up to the instrument to suggest, progressively, a certain number of enigmas which he will feel the desire to elucidate. . . . Interested and amused by his own discoveries, he will pursue willingly the road which will broaden his horizon. . . . It is in this spirit that this book carefully interweaves . . . the study of the keyboard and the development of the muscular mechanism with theoretical concepts. . . .
>
> To use solfège as a means and not as an end in itself, such is the method I propose in the following pages.[30]

Ravel often used to say: "Perhaps I have not had enough solfège." Long's response was: "No one should ever study solfège anymore if not studying it makes one into a Ravel!"[31] Fauré, walking out of solfège examinations at the Conservatoire, would exclaim: "If I had had to answer the questions that I was asked to pose to our students, I would not have been able to answer any one of them." Long would reply, "Let us give him a big *F* and let us kneel in front of his sublime *oeuvre.*"[32]

In devising her method for children, Long had another priority in mind: to incorporate as much contemporary music as possible in the earliest stages of learning. To that end, she commissioned very short pieces from many composers. Each piece was designed to illustrate a specific concept, pianistic or theoretical; as part of the fabric of the method, it was inserted in the appropriate section. The composers who contributed to *La Petite Méthode* included Federico Mompou, Jacques Castérède, Noël Gallon, Claude Pascal, Roger Boutry, Henri Sauguet, Pierre Petit, Daniel-Lesur, Henry Barraud, Francis Poulenc, and Darius Milhaud. To make the didactic purpose complete, a very short biography of the composer and a list of his major works followed each little piece. Six more composers—André Jolivet, Henri Dutilleux, Jean Françaix, Georges Auric, Jean Rivier, and Raymond Loucheur—were asked to write slightly longer pieces for the end of the book.

> I thought it was desirable to expose children to contemporary music, right from the beginning.
>
> Thus I wish to express my gratitude to all the composers who, upon my request, agreed with much kindness and modesty to put their great talents to the service of young pianists, by composing for them the short pieces which figure in this book.
>
> Finally, I want to thank particularly Jacques Castérède, for his valuable collaboration in the realization of this elementary piano method.[33]

The composer Jacques Castérède proved quite helpful, indeed, writing many letters to Long during the summer of 1963, giving her reports on proofs, and keeping track of the composers who had submitted their pieces. Castérède's correspondence provides a detailed account of every step involved in the publication of *La Petite Méthode.* While Long was resting in the south of France and working on her upcoming book on Ravel, she relinquished all responsibility to Castérède. On July 23, for instance, he brought up the question of Poulenc's piece (Poulenc had died the previous January 30):

> Dear Madam,
>
> I understood from your last letter that Poulenc had written the beginning of a piece for *La Méthode.* I do not know if he had time to finish it, but I never received a manuscript from Poulenc, and neither did the publisher Salabert. This is why he does not figure in the list of autograph manuscripts I gave you, and I did not think it necessary to put him on the list since, alas, it is too late to thank him. . . . I just received a third proof of *La Méthode:* it looks very good. Your Preface is perfect, there are no more mistakes and I will quickly send it to the publisher so that it can come out as soon as possible.
>
> Let me wish you . . . good rest, and all the necessary tranquility to make good progress on your Ravel book.
>
> Jacques Castérède[34]

Rested from the summer, Long returned to Paris in the fall of 1963 to prepare for the twentieth anniversary of her competition, November 12–30, and to enjoy the publication of *La Petite Méthode* and her book on Fauré. Later that winter she organized a recital of young children to present the entire collection of pieces commissioned for *La Petite Méthode.* Pierrette Mari dedicated a long column to this concert in *Lettres françaises* of March 19, 1964:

> Madame Marguerite Long constantly gives us evidence of her unflagging activity. . . . After the tenth Concours . . . after a book on Fauré, she just published a new *Petite Méthode de Piano* in which she joins to her renown the presence of famous contemporary composers. . . . It was moving to find in this collection Francis Poulenc's last message.
>
> In the presence of the Director of the Paris Conservatoire, who received Madame Marguerite Long in the Salle Berlioz, and with the witty introduction given by Pierre Petit, these charming little works were performed by ten children between the ages of five and twelve.

Well into her 90th year, Long was still the champion of contemporary music, always combining it with her pedagogical goals. Surrounded by devoted friends, she could continue to accomplish the tasks she set for herself, without ever losing an opportunity to maintain her public and political presence. She could retire to the south of France to work on one book, *Au piano avec Ravel,* in collaboration with her admirer Dr. Laumonier, while conducting from a distance the progress of another current project, *La Petite Méthode.* Long always had the reputation of being able to pursue several things at once, in day-to-day life as well as in the long term. This asset remained with her through her last years. Although her health and physical condition slowed her down, her mind and spirit never slackened.

Long's Last Two Years

The summer of 1964 was not as productive and cheerful as the previous one. In July, while visiting friends in the country, Long slipped on the gravel and fell. She broke her pelvis and was taken to the American Hospital in Paris to ensure the best care available. Letters and telegrams arrived from near and far. Her Soviet friends did not forget her and collectively signed a telegram:

> Dear friend,
>
> We are deeply saddened by your accident. With all our hearts we wish you the fastest recovery. Soviet musicians appreciate highly your exceptional merits in the development of the art of the piano and your great care for the friendship between our two people.
>
> Best wishes.
>
> Khrennikov, Shostakovich, Kabalevsky, Gilels.[35]

Her compatriots also expressed their sympathy. Among them was her old friend and colleague Nadia Boulanger, who wrote on August 8, 1964:

> Dear Friend,
>
> It was with profound emotion that I learned of your terrible accident and your extreme courage. . . . Please be assured that my thoughts are with you and that I do hope that this hardship will not last too long.
>
> Always your faithful,
>
> Nadia Boulanger[36]

Thanks to the abundance of mail she received and her eagerness to answer every piece of it with the help of a friend, Long was able to recover quite rapidly for a woman of her age. Her determination paid off, for though most people believed that she would never walk again, Long had decided that she would be on her feet for her 90th birthday.

On November 13, 1964, Long turned 90. She had far outlived all her contemporaries, pianists who were born in the 1870s: Godowsky, Skryabin, Rachmaninoff, Lhevinne, Bauer, Ravel, Viñes, Hofmann, Cortot, Landowska, and Dohnányi. She received an avalanche of greetings. Among the telegrams from musical organizations was one from the Chopin Society in Warsaw: "On your birthday, please accept, Madam, our warmest wishes and respectful homage for the eminent pedagogue and pianist you are, fervent propagator of Chopin's music and friend of his native land."[37] Typical of the messages from her innumerable disciples was this telegram: "Believe me to be very close to you on this beautiful birthday. Your always faithful, Samson François."[38]

Among letters from friends and colleagues was one from Nadia Boulanger:

> Called away from Paris to painful circumstances, I will not have the joy to celebrate with you on Friday. But you know that my thoughts are with you often, with much gratitude and faithfulness.
>
> Let me express my regret in being so far and my certainty of being present in spirit.[39]

Concert managers and theater directors were unanimous in acknowledging the day. The Director of the Théâtre des Champs-Elysées wrote: "Please receive my wishes for this great anniversary, Madam, to which I join all my congratulations and genuine thanks for the unforgettable hours of music that the Théâtre des Champs-Elysées owes you. Felix Valoussière."[40]

A birthday celebration was held in the Salle Berlioz, in the Paris Conservatoire, on November 13. In the opening speech, the Director of the Conservatoire, Raymond Gallois-Montbrun, announced that a room in the building would bear the name of Marguerite Long. Jacques Jaujard then told of the wonderful road that the Concours had traveled in over twenty years, and Louis Joxe spoke in endearing terms, not as a politician but as a close friend of the artist.

The climax of the evening was the presentation to Long of "Le Livre d'Or" (golden book).[41] Conceived by Darius Milhaud and Henri Sauguet, it contains expressions of friendship and recognition from those whose lives had been touched by Marguerite Long. Milhaud and Sauguet gathered over 200 autograph messages from personalities ranging from President Charles de Gaulle to such stars of the stage as Maurice Chevalier, Régine Crespin, and Serge Lifar. The title page reads: "To Marguerite Long—Homage from her friends and admirers. For the twentieth anniversary of the Concours Marguerite Long–Jacques Thibaud. November 1963." The project had taken longer than anticipated so that "Le Livre d'Or" was not ready until Long's 90th birthday, exactly a year after the twentieth anniversary of the Concours.

Among the royalty who contributed to the book were Queen Elisabeth of Belgium, Prince Rainier of Monaco, Prince Pierre of Monaco, the Count of Paris, Prince Napoleon, and the Infante d'Espagne. Pablo Picasso, Marc

Chagall, and other artists not only signed their names but also drew little sketches. Among the writers were Marcel Achard, André Maurois, François Mauriac, and André Malraux. Politicians abounded, from Georges Pompidou (then Prime Minister) to Pierre Mendès-France, from Jacques Chaban-Delmas to Maurice Couve de Murville. There were tributes from living French composers and from such foreigners as Virgil Thomson and Dmitri Shostakovich; from conductors Lorin Maazel, Igor Markevitch, Ernest Ansermet, Jean Martinon, and other great maestros of the time. Yehudi Menuhin, Pierre Bernac, Wilhelm Kempff, Artur Rubinstein, Zino Francescatti, Leonid Kogan, Emil Gilels, Marcel Dupré, Mstislav Rostropovich, Henryk Szeryng, and Mieczyslaw Horszowski were among the long list of performing artists represented in this precious volume of homage. Some wrote a few words, others several pages filled with anecdotes and reminiscences. A few composers, such as Henri Dutilleux and André Jolivet, drew staves in the shape of garlands and took the opportunity to write one more tune for Madame Long. "Le Livre d'Or," bound in parchment and gold, is an astounding symbol of the far-reaching, fulfilling life of Marguerite Long, and of its ultimate consecration. In the words of François Mauriac: "All the world's music has passed through you and your disciples."

Even though Long tried very hard to be on her feet for this important moment, her accident during the summer of 1964 had severely diminished her physical endurance. In planning her activities, every effort had to be balanced by a great deal of rest. Yet she was never absent from the world of music. In the spring of 1965, Long was the subject of six television interviews. In her witty, very slight southern accent, she recounted memories of the past.[42] At each interview she was assisted by one of her current favorite disciples: Bruno Gelber, Yuri Boukoff, Marie-Thérèse Fourneau, Samson François, Aldo Ciccolini, and "Il bambino"—Daniel Wayenberg. Each one played during the program, enriching Long's reminiscences with music associated with her.

Long was asked to serve on the jury of the 1966 Tchaikovsky Competition. The invitation, dated August 25, 1965, was translated by the Soviet Embassy in Paris and forwarded to her:

> Madame Marguerite Long,
>
> I have the honor to forward to you the invitation from the Organizational Committee of the International Tchaikovsky Competition, signed by Mr. Shostakovich, to be part of the jury of this competition.

> The Committee expressed the hope that you arrive in Moscow toward the end of May 1966.
>
> B. Tchervov, First Secretary of the Embassy[43]

Sadly, when the competition began, Long had already passed away.

A few months before her death, another national honor was bestowed on Long. Just as she had been the first woman musician to receive the Cravate de Commandeur of the Légion d'Honneur in 1938, in the fall of 1965 she was the first woman to be awarded the Grand Croix de l'Ordre du Mérite, the highest insignia of this new order recently established by de Gaulle. For her last public celebration, Long stood among her friends at the reception in the Cercle Interallié, a sumptuous private club facing the Place de la Concorde in Paris. "None of the great honors she received ever could alter her two most striking virtues: forthrightness and good humor."[44]

With her energy dwindling, Long gave her final master class in January 1966, at her Académie de Piano, on Rue Freycinet. Two of her beloved disciples performed for her one last time: Daniel Wayenberg playing the solo part of Beethoven's "Emperor" Concerto, and Bruno Gelber the orchestral accompaniment. Long was moved to tears. Only a week before her death, Wayenberg called her about a new recording of his that had just been released, with music by Jolivet. She responded at once, "Come over and let us listen to it together. I want to hear it."[45]

Her death, on February 13, 1966, was very peaceful. Long left this world serene and submissive. Her heart simply stopped. In accordance with her frequently expressed wish, music from Fauré's Requiem was performed at her funeral: "The songs of his Requiem are without fear, they do not express terror, but rather, a gentle belief in mercy. . . . This Requiem is lit by the eternal ray of hope of its 'In Paradisium.' "[46] Long's friends gathered for their last farewell at her neighborhood church. As Jacques Février wrote:

> A deep emotion reigned this morning at Saint-Ferdinand-des-Ternes, where we came to render our ultimate homage to Marguerite Long—an emotion which grabbed us all when the Reverend Father Carré told us of the words of Mozart, who was uneasy about death and feared it: "If God wants it, I want it." Madame Long repeated those very words to Father Carré before she left for eternity.
>
> In the presence of such a noble attitude, we can only bow with respect and admiration before the towering personality who dominated the music world for so many years.[47]

Long was buried in the cemetery of Sainte-Baudrille, near Nîmes, according to her own wish that she be close to her family and under the Mediterranean sun of her childhood.

Emil Gilels was deeply moved by her loss:

> I am incapable of expressing in words the emotion I felt when I learned of the death of Marguerite Long. I knew her rather late in life, but she seemed to hold the secret of eternal youth, so enthusiastic about all that concerned our art. . . . Whoever had the honor of approaching her was struck by her human warmth.
>
> This year, we were expecting her for our Tchaikovsky Competition. She promised she would come and we wanted to fête her. Alas. . . .[48]

Daniel Wayenberg, whom Long enjoyed calling "Il Bambino," expressed the feelings of many:

> We knew that the page, harshly turned, would never be torn from our hearts. . . . At each one of our encounters with Marguerite Long, we experienced such a feeling of energy and vitality that it seemed unthinkable that such news could ever come to us.[49]

Notes

1. Marguerite Long's Youth

1. I.N.A. Archives: 1954–55 radio talks referred to in the Preface. Unless otherwise specified, all quotations from Long in this chapter comes from this source.

2. Autograph letter, Long Archives, BMGM, Paris.

3. Personal autograph notes and manuscripts, Long Archives, BMGM, Paris. This source refers to numerous random papers where Long jotted down thoughts and ideas. Often they were on the back of a program. Occasionally they might be a composed paragraph that may have been intended for a project of some kind.

4. "Hommage du monde musical à Marguerite Long," *Journal des jeunesses musicales de France,* March 5, 1966.

5. Marguerite Long, *Au piano avec Fauré* (Paris: Julliard, 1963), pp. 11–12.

6. Joseph de Marliave, *Etudes musicales* (Paris: Félix Alcan, 1917). Marliave signed his writings with the pseudonym Saint-Jean, which was the name of his family estate in the Lauragais (southwest France, near Toulouse).

7. Personal autograph notes, Long Archives, BMGM, Paris. See above, note 3.

8. Joseph de Marliave, *Les quatuors de Beethoven* (Paris: Félix Alcan, 1925). Translated by Hilda Andrews (Oxford: Oxford University Press, 1928; reprint, New York: Dover, 1961). Gabriel Fauré wrote the Preface in April 1924, a few months before he died.

9. Ibid., pp. ii, iii, iv.

2. Marguerite Long and Gabriel Fauré, 1902–1912

1. Marguerite Long, *Au piano avec Debussy* (Paris: Julliard, 1960), p. 10.
2. Marguerite Long, *Au piano avec Fauré* (Paris: Julliard, 1963), p. 102.
3. I.N.A. Archives, Paris.
4. Ibid., repeated by many of the students I interviewed.
5. Long, *Fauré,* pl. 3. Letter reproduced in facsimile. It is not included in recent editions or in the English translation of the book.
6. Ibid., p. 31.
7. Ibid., p. 183.
8. Score in Long Archives, BMGM, Paris.
9. Long, *Fauré,* p. 65.
10. Ibid., p. 66.
11. I.N.A. Archives, Paris.
12. Long, *Fauré,* p. 28.
13. Ibid., p. 82.

14. Ibid., p. 57, also recounted in I.N.A. Archives, Paris.

15. Lecture notes from Long, Long Archives, BMGM, Paris.

16. Long, *Fauré,* p. 124.

17. Ibid., p. 148.

18. Ibid., p. 102.

19. I.N.A. Archives, Paris.

20. Gabriel Fauré, *Lettres intimes,* edited by Philippe Fauré-Fremiet (Paris: La Colombe, 1951), p. 186.

21. I.N.A. Archives, Paris. The entire anecdote is also found in Long, *Fauré,* p. 108.

22. Letter quoted in translation in H. H. Stuckenschmidt, *Maurice Ravel* (Philadelphia: Chilton Book Co., 1968), p. 94.

23. Robert Orledge, *Gabriel Fauré* (London: Eulenburg Ltd., 1979), pp. 23–24. Orledge himself quotes a few words by Fauré, from the journal *Comoedia,* April 20, 1910.

24. Jean-Michel Nectoux, *Gabriel Fauré,* translated by Roger Nichols (Cambridge: Cambridge University Press, 1991), p. 285.

25. Orledge, p. 29.

26. Vladimir Jankélévitch, *Gabriel Fauré, ses mélodies, son esthétique* (Paris: Plon, 1951), p. ii. Quoted in translation in Nectoux, p. 286.

27. Long, *Fauré,* p. 15.

28. Quoted in translation in Nectoux, p. 308, from *Lettres intimes,* p. 138.

29. Letter in the private collection of Dr. Vacher, Paris, published for the first time in Jean-Michel Nectoux, *Gabriel Fauré, les Voix du Clair-obscur* (Paris: Flammarion, 1990), pp. 310–11.

30. Quoted in Long, *Fauré,* p. 67.

31. Ibid.

32. Nectoux, trans. Nichols, p. 308.

33. Long, *Fauré,* pp. 178–79.

34. Ibid., p. 184.

3. *Other Musical Collaborations*

1. Unless otherwise specified, all subsequent quotations from Long in this chapter come from I.N.A. Archives, Paris.

2. Marguerite Long, *Au piano avec Fauré* (Paris: Julliard, 1963), p. 91.

3. Ibid., p. 92.

4. *Gabriel Fauré, His Life Through His Letters,* collected and edited by Jean-Michel Nectoux (London: Marion Boyars Publishers, 1984), p. 278.

5. Ibid., p. 277.

6. Long, *Fauré,* p. 89.

7. Score preserved at Long Archives, BMGM, Paris.

8. "Forty-four Unpublished Letters from Roger-Ducasse to Long and Her Husband, Marliave," compiled and annotated by Jacques Depaulis (Bordeaux, 1988), p. 15.

9. Marliave, *Etudes musicales* (Paris: Félix Alcan, 1917).

10. Depaulis, p. 51.
11. Ibid., p. 37.
12. Long, *Fauré,* p. 183.
13. Letters quoted in Jacques Depaulis, "Roger-Ducasse et Marguerite Long, une amitié, une correspondance," *Revue Internationale de Musique Française* 28 (February 1989):97–98.
14. Déodat de Séverac, "La centralisation et les petites chapelles," *Le Courrier musical,* January 1 and 15, March 1, 1908.
15. Marguerite Long, "Déodat de Séverac," *L'Information Musicale* 25, May 9, 1941. This short article honored Déodat de Séverac twenty years after his death.
16. Autograph letter, Long Archives, BMGM, Paris.
17. Autograph postcard, Long Archives, BMGM, Paris.
18. Letter read by Long during one of her radio interviews. I.N.A. Archives, Paris.
19. I.N.A. Archives, Paris.

4. *Marguerite Long and Claude Debussy*

1. I.N.A. Archives, Paris.
2. Ibid., also related in Marguerite Long, *Au piano avec Debussy* (Paris: Julliard, 1960), p. 17.
3. Ibid.
4. Ibid., p. 16.
5. Autograph letter, Long Archives, BMGM, Paris.
6. Long, *Debussy,* p. 21.
7. I.N.A. Archives, Paris.
8. Ibid.
9. Robert Orledge, *Gabriel Fauré* (London: Eulenburg Ltd., 1979), p. 15. Fauré also wrote his delicious suite for piano duet, *Dolly,* for Emma Bardac's daughter Dolly.
10. *Claude Debussy, Lettres 1884–1918,* compiled and presented by François Lesure (Paris: Hermann, 1980), p. 242.
11. I.N.A. Archives, Paris.
12. Videotaped interview with Cortot, Cortot Archives, BMGM, Archives, Bibliothèque Musicale Gustave Mahler, Paris.
13. Edward Lockspeiser, *Claude Debussy, His Life and Mind* (Cambridge: Cambridge University Press, 1978), pp. 223–24. Original French version in *Claude Debussy, Lettres,* pp. 286–87.
14. Long, *Debussy,* p. 21.
15. Autograph letter, Long Archives, BMGM, Paris. All subsequent letters in this chapter from Bruneau to Long come from this source.
16. Ibid.
17. Ibid.
18. This letter and the next two from Roger-Ducasse are quoted from "Forty-four Unpublished Letters from Roger-Ducasse to Long and Her Husband, Marliave," compiled and annotated by Jacques Depaulis (Bordeaux, 1988), pp. 23–25, 40–41, and 50–51 respectively.

19. Personal notes and manuscripts, Long Archives, BMGM, Paris.
20. Autograph letter, Long Archives, BMGM, Paris.
21. I.N.A. Archives, Paris.
22. Depaulis, p. 30.
23. *Claude Debussy, Lettres,* p. 279.
24. I.N.A. Archives, Paris.
25. Ibid.
26. *Claude Debussy, Lettres,* p. 257.
27. I.N.A. Archives, Paris. Also mentioned in Long, *Debussy,* p. 27. Long insisted that editions of Debussy's music were usually trustworthy, for the composer carefully supervised his publisher's work; she made the same claim for Ravel's music. Fauré editions, on the other hand, contained a deplorable number of mistakes.
28. Ibid.
29. Long, *Debussy,* p. 36.
30. Ibid., p. 37.
31. Interview with Long by Maurice Imbert for *Le Courrier musical,* 1932.
32. I.N.A. Archives, Paris. Explanation also provided in Long, *Debussy,* p. 126.
33. Ibid., p. 111.
34. Contrary to what Long claims in her book, at least one of these Etudes had been played in public previously. On November 21, 1916, George Copland premiered *Pour les arpèges composés* and *Sonorités opposées* in Aeolian Hall, New York (see *Musical America,* Vol. 25, No. 5); and Walter Rummel played four of the twelve Etudes on or about December 14, 1916 (see Charles Timbrell, "Claude Debussy and Walter Rummel, Chronicle of a Friendship with New Correspondence," *Music & Letters,* August 1992). *Pour les cinq doigts* may have been premiered by Long, since we do not know exactly which four Etudes were on Rummel's program.
35. Autograph letter, Long Archives, BMGM, Paris. All the letters from Emma Debussy to Long quoted in this chapter come from this source.

Debussy's wife, Emma Bardac, often signed herself Emma Claude Debussy, or the three initials, ECD. In many letters, she referred to her husband as the *Maître,* an honorific often used in France for great musicians, not unlike the Italian equivalent, *Maestro.*

36. Letter from Debussy to Chouchou, quoted in Long, *Debussy,* p. 99.
37. Debussy had given the first performances of eleven of his Preludes between 1910 and 1913. He had also given the première of his Cello Sonata, with Joseph Salmon, in March 1917. At his last public appearance, on May 5, 1917 at the Salle Gaveau, he gave the first performance of his Violin Sonata, with Gaston Poulet, and accompanied Rose Féart in a set of songs.
38. Autograph letter, Long Archives, BMGM, Paris.

5. *The Postwar Years and the Twenties*

1. I.N.A. Archives, Paris. Also discussed in Marguerite Long, *Au piano avec Ravel* (Paris: Julliard, 1971), pp. 141–47.
2. Long's lecture notes, Long Archives, BMGM, Paris.
3. Ibid.

4. I.N.A. Archives, Paris.
5. Paul Landormy in *La Victoire,* March 23, 1920.
6. "Forty-four Unpublished Letters from Roger-Ducasse to Long and Her Husband, Marliave," compiled and annotated by Jacques Depaulis (Bordeaux, 1988), p. 67.
7. Ibid., p. 74.
8. Reprint of an article by Emile Vuillermoz, November 28, 1925, Long Archives, BMGM, Paris.
9. Autograph letter, Long Archives, BMGM, Paris.
10. Roger-Ducasse in *Le Monde musical,* May 1921.
11. In the 1950s, Long recorded the Chopin Concerto again with the modern L.P. technology under the baton of André Cluytens.

6. The 1930s

1. Marguerite Long, *Au piano avec Ravel* (Paris: Julliard, 1971), p. 57.
2. I.N.A. Archives, Paris.
3. Ibid.
4. Ibid.
5. Ibid. Also recounted in Long, *Ravel,* p. 61, and told by her students.
6. I.N.A. Archives, Paris.
7. In *Ravel,* pp. 63–71, Long gives entertaining accounts of her travels with the composer.
8. I.N.A. Archives, Paris.
9. Long, *Ravel,* p. 65.
10. Ibid., p. 64.
11. I.N.A. Archives, Paris.
12. These songs were commissioned at the beginning of 1932 by a film company that planned to make a film of *Don Quixote* with Chaliapin. The project never came to fruition, but Ravel's three songs remained a truly beautiful set. See Marcel Marnat, *Maurice Ravel* (Paris: Arthème Fayard, 1986), pp. 664–65.
13. I.N.A. Archives, Paris.
14. Ibid.
15. Ibid.
16. Ibid. Alfred Cortot came close to publishing a two-hand transcription of the Concerto for the Left Hand, but its publication was vetoed; it appears that Long had something to do with the veto. The Cortot manuscript is stored in the Alfred Cortot Archives, BMGM, Paris.
17. Ibid. Also told in Long, *Ravel,* p. 25.
18. I.N.A. Archives, Paris.
19. Ibid.
20. Ibid.
21. Ibid.
22. Ibid.
23. Ibid.
24. Autograph letter, Long Archives, BMGM, Paris.
25. The score is presently housed at the Long Archives, BMGM, Paris.

26. Darius Milhaud, in *Jour,* June 11, 1934.
27. I.N.A. Archives, Paris.
28. Official letter from the Ministère de l'Education Nationale, dated February 4, 1938. Long Archives, BMGM, Paris.
29. Personal autograph notes, Long Archives, BMGM, Paris.

7. *Portrait of a Pedagogue*

1. Quoted in an interview with Long's physician, Dr. Jean Thin; also occurs in her radio interviews, I.N.A. Archives, Paris.
2. I.N.A. Archives, Paris.
3. Ibid. Also quoted in the Preface to Long's piano method book, *Le Piano* (Paris: Salabert, 1959), p. i.
4. Personal interview.
5. Extensive accounts of those master classes, each one described in detail, were published in *Le Monde musical* of July 1921.
6. The six performers were Nicole Henriot, Nanou Toinet, Odette Gartenlaub, Charlie Lilamand, Simone de Cachard, and Jacqueline Schweitzer. Program of the concert, Long Archives, BMGM, Paris.
7. Autograph letter, Long Archives, BMGM, Paris.
8. Flier in Long Archives, BMGM, Paris.
9. Interview with Maurice Imbert in *Le Courrier musical,* 1932.
10. Report on the three classes by E. Vuillermoz, *Excelsior,* January 22, 1934.
11. Interview with Maurice Imbert, *Le Courrier musical,* 1932.
12. Printed version of a lecture delivered by Long for Radio-Paris, entitled "The Piano, Its Technique and Its Teaching." Long Archives, BMGM, Paris.
13. Interview transcript dated March 1936, Long Archives, BMGM, Paris.
14. Ibid.
15. Typed letter, Long Archives, BMGM, Paris.
16. Henri Sauguet, in *Jour,* June 26, 1938; and Paul Landormy, in *Le Temps,* June 25, 1938.

8. *The War Years*

1. Long Archives, BMGM, Paris. All subsequent quotations of letters from Thibaud to Long come from this source.
2. Unidentified newspaper clipping, dated June 1941, Long Archives, BMGM, Paris.
3. The Premier Prix laureates were Jacqueline Bernard (now Latarjet), Françoise Soulé, Nicole Henriot, and Marie-Thérèse Fourneau.
4. Autograph letter, Long Archives, BMGM, Paris.
5. Autograph notes, Long Archives, BMGM, Paris. This remark was well remembered by her pupils.
6. Marguerite Long, *Au piano avec Fauré* (Paris: Julliard, 1963), p. 96.
7. Ibid., p. 172.
8. Ibid., p. 178.

9. Ibid., pp. 172–73.
10. I.N.A. Archives, Paris.
11. Autograph letter, Long Archives, BMGM, Paris.
12. Ibid.
13. Autograph notes, Long Archives, BMGM, Paris.
14. Autograph letter, Long Archives, BMGM, Paris.
15. Typed letter in Long Archives, BMGM, Paris.
16. Anecdote told by students who attended some of the rehearsals. Also partly recounted in Long, *Fauré,* p. 172.
17. Typed letter in Long Archives, BMGM, Paris.
18. *Parisien libéré,* November 9, 1944.
19. Long, *Fauré,* p. 177.

9. *The Concours Marguerite Long–Jacques Thibaud*

1. I.N.A. Archives, Paris.
2. Ibid.
3. Ibid.
4. Ibid.
5. Ibid.
6. Ibid.
7. Ibid.
8. Autograph letter, Long Archives, BMGM, Paris.
9. Olivier Alain, "L'Action des Jeunesses Musicales" *La Revue Musicale* 245 (1959):77.
10. Ibid.
11. Autograph letter, Long Archives, BMGM, Paris.
12. The typed transcript of this entire press conference is in the Long Archives, BMGM, Paris.
13. Long Archives, BMGM, Paris.
14. Autograph letter, Long Archives, BMGM, Paris.
15. Typed letter, Long Archives, BMGM, Paris.
16. Lengthy article by Pierrette Mari in an unidentified newspaper, spring 1961. Long Archives, BMGM, Paris.
17. Autograph notes, Long Archives, BMGM, Paris.
18. Carbon copy of a letter from the office of the Prime Minister, Long Archives, BMGM, Paris.
19. Interview with Long by Claude Samuel, *Paris-Presse,* November 29, 1962.
20. Quoted by René Dumesnil in *Le Monde,* February 19, 1963; and by Pierrette Mari in *Le Journal musical français,* November 7, 1963.
21. Autograph letter, Long Archives, BMGM, Paris.

10. *The Postwar Decade*

1. Personal interview with Ventsislav Yankoff.
2. Ibid.
3. Pierre Barbizet wrote a beautiful essay honoring his mentor: "Marguerite Long," *La Revue musicale* 245 (1959): 25–28.

4. France-musique, "Désaccord parfait," 1986. A radio show which gathered several pianists and journalists in honor of the twentieth anniversary of Long's death.

5. I.N.A. Archives, Paris. On the last broadcast of the 1954–55 series of twenty radio shows, three of Long's former pupils were invited to contribute reminiscences.

6. Ibid.

7. Autograph letter, Long Archives, BMGM, Paris.

8. Autograph postcard, Long Archives, BMGM, Paris.

9. Unless otherwise specified, this and other quotations in this chapter were collected during personal interviews with Long's students.

10. Magda Tagliaferro, "Hommage du monde musical à Marguerite Long," *Journal des jeunesses musicales de France,* March 1966.

11. Barbizet, p. 25.

12. I.N.A. Archives, Paris.

13. Autograph letter, Long Archives, BMGM, Paris.

14. Ibid.

15. Ibid.

16. Interview with Jean-Paul Léon, son of Paul Léon, member of the Institut de France, Director of the Académie des Beaux-Arts, and a lifelong friend of Long. See above, p. 000.

17. Autograph letter, Long Archives, BMGM, Paris.

18. Historical note on the Concours, pamphlet in Long Archives, BMGM, Paris.

19. "Désaccord parfait," France-musique radio show.

20. Unpublished interview conducted by Charles Timbrell, July 1986.

21. Autograph letter, Long Archives, BMGM, Paris.

22. I.N.A. Archives, and confirmed by Long's pupils.

23. Interview with Lucette Descaves.

24. The interviewees who contributed the following anecdotes asked to remain anonymous.

25. Autograph letter, private collection of Philippe Rougier, Paris.

26. Both lectures were published in the journal associated with the lecture series: Marguerite Long and Bernard Gavoty, "Deux aspects de Chopin," *Conferencia* 10 (October 15, 1949): 397–419.

27. Typed text of the speech, Long Archives, BMGM, Paris.

28. Autograph notes, Long Archives, BMGM, Paris.

29. Title of the program, Long Archives, BMGM, Paris.

11. *Ambassador of French Music*

1. Autograph letter, Long Archives, BMGM, Paris.

2. Ibid.

3. The complete program of courses as well as Long's handwritten notes give ample detail on the subject and style of her lectures. Long Archives, BMGM, Paris.

4. Autograph notes, Long Archives, BMGM, Paris.

5. Ibid.

6. Magda Tagliaferro, "Homage du monde musical à Marguerite Long," *Journal des jeunesses musicales de France,* March 1966.

7. Autograph letter, Long Archives, BMGM, Paris. Unless otherwise specified, subsequent letters in this chapter between Long and her Brazilian friends come from this source.

8. Villa-Lobos, *Francette et Pià,* pièces faciles pour piano sur des thèmes populaires français et brésiliens. Pour le cours d'enfants de Madame Marguerite Long (Paris: Max Eschig, n.d.).

9. Typed transcript of a translated Brazilian radio report describing this formal reception in Long's home. Long Archives, Paris.

10. Autograph letter, private collection of Philippe Rougier, Paris.

11. Autograph manuscript of Long's speech. Long Archives, BMGM, Paris.

12. Autograph letter, private collection of Philippe Rougier, Paris.

13. Autograph postcards, Long Archives, BMGM, Paris.

14. Typed text of Long's opening speech at the Academy of Fine Arts in Rio de Janeiro. Long Archives, BMGM, Paris.

15. Partly typed, partly autograph list of the persons who were present at the party, with each one's title, position, or profession handwritten on the right-hand side. Long Archives, BMGM, Paris.

16. Autograph letter, private collection of Philippe Rougier, Paris.

17. Ibid.

18. Ibid.

19. Autograph letter, Long Archives, BMGM, Paris.

20. Ibid.

21. Ibid.

22. Ibid. The reference to "the best possible health" is a reminder that Long was 87 years old at the time of this letter.

23. Marguerite Long, *Au piano avec Fauré* (Paris: Julliard, 1963), p. 62.

24. Typed letter, Long Archives, BMGM, Paris.

25. Personal interview with Louis Joxe. The official document, dated April 19, 1955 and stamped with the Conservatory's seal, is in the Long Archives, BMGM, Paris.

26. Typed letter in Long Archives, BMGM, Paris.

27. Ibid.

28. Autograph letter, Long Archives, BMGM, Paris.

29. I.N.A. Archives, Paris; see above, Preface.

30. Ibid.

12. *The Last Ten Years of Long's Life*

1. Program of the June 4, 1956 concert at the Sorbonne, Long Archives, BMGM, Paris. The "braided garland of homage" refers to these composers' collective composition, *Variations sur le nom de Marguerite Long.*

2. Claude Rostand, in *Carrefour,* June 16, 1956.

3. Autograph manuscript of the score owned and housed by Salabert. The work was never published.

4. Telegram, Long Archives, BMGM, Paris.

5. Ibid.

6. Ibid.

7. Autograph letter, Long Archives, BMGM, Paris.
8. "Gaveau aujourd'hui," article by Claude Rostand printed in the program of the concert. Long Archives, BMGM, Paris.
9. Typed transcript of this speech in Long Archives, BMGM, Paris.
10. Autograph text of Long's response, Long Archives, BMGM, Paris.
11. Personal interview with Dr. Jean Thin.
12. *Le Gard à Paris,* March 1959.
13. Autograph letter, Long Archives, BMGM, Paris.
14. Typed letter, Long Archives, BMGM, Paris.
15. Autograph notes, Long Archives, BMGM, Paris.
16. Quoted in Bernard Gavoty's notes on the program of the April 1, 1960 concert. Bernard Gavoty, a musicologist and critic, is the author of *Frédéric Chopin* (Paris, 1974; English translation, 1977).
17. Hélène Jourdan-Morhange, "Gala Chopin à l'Opéra," *Lettres Françaises,* April 7–13, 1960.
18. Ibid.
19. Notes by Long in the program of the concert, Long Archives, BMGM, Paris.
20. Autograph postcard, Long Archives, BMGM, Paris.
21. Personal interviews with her physician, Dr. Jean Thin, and the composer Daniel-Lesure.
22. Marguerite Long, *Le Piano* (Paris: Salabert, 1959), frontispiece, unnumbered.
23. Ibid., Preface, p. 1.
24. Ibid., Foreword, p. ii. All following quotations in this section come from the Foreword.
25. Ibid., p. xi.
26. Ibid., p. 97.
27. Autograph letter, Long Archives, BMGM, Paris.
28. Ibid.
29. Marguerite Long, *Au piano avec Ravel* (Paris: Julliard, 1971), Foreword by Laumonier, p. 10. Long spent many summers as a guest of her friend Germaine de Jouvenel, in St. Jean Cap Ferrat, on the French Riviera.
30. Marguerite Long, *La Petite Méthode* (Paris: Salabert, 1963), Preface, pp. 1–2.
31. Quoted in Long's personal autograph notes, Long Archives, BMGM, Paris.
32. Ibid.
33. Long, *La Petite Méthode,* p. 2.
34. Autograph letter, Long Archives, BMGM, Paris.
35. Telegram, Long Archives, BMGM, Paris.
36. Autograph letter, Long Archives, BMGM, Paris.
37. Long Archives, BMGM, Paris.
38. Ibid.
39. Autograph letter, Long Archives, BMGM, Paris.
40. Telegram, Long Archives, BMGM, Paris.
41. "Le Livre d'Or" is securely kept at the Long Archives, BMGM, Paris.
42. Six television interviews with Long, conducted and produced by Claude Santelli in the spring of 1965. I.N.A. Archives, Paris.
43. Typed letter, Long Archives, BMGM, Paris.

44. Magda Tagliaferro, in "Hommage du Monde Musical à Marguerite Long," *Journal des jeunesses musicales de France,* March 1966. This issue published homages to Long from nearly 50 personalities of the music world.

45. Personal interview with Daniel Wayenberg, also told in "Hommage."

46. Marguerite Long, *Au piano avec Fauré* (Paris: Julliard, 1963), p. 177.

47. Jacques Février, in "Hommage."

48. Emil Gilels, in "Hommage."

49. Daniel Wayenberg, in "Hommage."

Glossary

This glossary gives a brief profile of musicians prominent in France in the first half of the twentieth century who had personal connections with Long. It does not include those who had extensive relationships with her, for they are discussed in detail in the text.

Büsser, Henri (1872–1973), composer and conductor, studied at the Ecole Niedermeyer, as did Fauré. He furthered his musical training at the Conservatoire under Franck and Widor. A 1893 Prix de Rome laureate, Büsser became Professor of Composition at the Paris Conservatoire in 1931. At Debussy's request, he conducted the fourth and subsequent performances of *Pelléas et Mélisande* at the Opéra-Comique in 1902, when Messager was called to London's Covent Garden. In 1905, he became conductor of the Paris Opéra.

Capet, Lucien (1873–1928), is remembered chiefly for the string quartet he founded in 1893, immediately after receiving his Premier Prix in violin at the Paris Conservatoire. This quartet lasted until 1899. In 1903, Capet gathered a new group, of which Louis Hasselmans was a member. It was disbanded in 1910, and Capet founded a third quartet in that year. Capet's quartets were well known throughout Europe for their beautiful tone, unity of spirit, technical polish, and faithfulness to the composers' scores. In 1924 Capet became director of the Institut de Violon in Paris, after having had a brilliant career as soloist and chamber player.

Casadesus, Henri (1879–1947), was a member of an exceptional musical family, which included nine renowned musicians spanning three generations. Composer and violist, Henri was a member of the Capet Quartet from its inception in 1893 through World War I, surviving the many personnel changes that the quartet underwent. He founded the Société des Instruments Anciens in collaboration with Saint-Saëns, and his collection of rare instruments is now owned by the Boston Symphony Orchestra. His brother, Francis, was responsible for founding the American Conservatory in Fontainebleau. The well-known pianist Robert Casadesus was his nephew.

Chevillard, Camille (1859–1923), composer and conductor, was the son-in-law of Charles Lamoureux, who founded the Orchestre Lamoureux in 1881. He succeeded Lamoureux in 1899 as musical director of the orchestra. Chevillard collaborated with Debussy for the première of *La Mer* on October 15, 1905. He was a strong advocate of German music though, and founded the Société Beethoven in 1889. Trained as a pianist at the Conservatoire, he formed a trio with Maurice Hayot and Joseph Salmon in 1895. He was awarded the rosette of Chevalier de la Légion d'Honneur in 1903, and was appointed professor of instrumental music ensemble at the Paris Conservatoire in 1907.

Concerts Colonne were given on Sundays by the Orchestre Colonne, one of the three best orchestras in Paris. Edouard Colonne (1838–1910), a violinist, founded the orchestra in 1871 and was its music director until his death in 1910. He was succeeded by Gabriel Pierné; the present music director is Philippe Entremont.

Dubois, Théodore (1837–1924), composer, organist, and teacher, served for a time as Inspecteur des Beaux-Arts pour l'Enseignement Musical. A Prix de Rome laureate in 1861, he was *maître de chapelle* at Sainte Clotilde in Paris from 1861 to 1869; then he replaced Saint-Saëns as organist of the Madeleine, holding that post until 1877. From 1871 to 1896 he was Professor of Harmony and Composition at the Paris Conservatoire; he became its director in 1896, succeeding Thomas, and served until Fauré's appointment in 1905.

Dumesnil, René (1879–1967), was an academician and a very influential music critic. His books on musical subjects range from Wagner to the history of French music. He received the coveted Prix National de Littérature for his critical edition of the works of Gustave Flaubert, published in 1949.

Gaubert, Philippe (1879–1941), was extremely active in France at the turn of the century. He became Professor of Flute at the Paris Conservatoire in 1919. As a composer, he won the Prix de Rome in 1905; he wrote many operas and works for the stage, as well as chamber music, including three sonatas for flute and piano. He is remembered mostly as a conductor, for he was André Messager's successor at the Orchestre de la Société des Concerts in 1919 and became music director of the Opéra in 1920. He is featured in several of Long's concerto recordings.

Hasselmans, Louis (1878–1957), one of the foremost cellists of the period, was a member of the Capet Quartet for six years. He was the dedicatee of Fauré's First Cello Sonata, Op. 109. His posts as conductor included the Concerts Hasselmans, the Opéra-Comique, the Montreal Opera (1911–1913), the Chicago Civic Opera (1918–1919), and New York's Metropolitan Opera for its French repertory. Hasselmans came from a notable family of musicians active in this period, and his sister, Marguerite, was Fauré's intimate companion from 1900 on.

Hayot, Maurice (1862–1945), a prominent violinist, resigned in 1896 from his position as Professor at the Paris Conservatoire to devote his time exclusively to his concert tours and to the string quartet he had founded. He also played in a trio with Camille Chevillard and Joseph Salmon. In July 1907, Hayot played Fauré's First Violin Sonata with Marguerite Hasselmans at the piano, at a dinner given by Marcel Proust at the Ritz, in honor of Fauré.

Inghelbrecht, Désiré-Emile (1880–1965), French composer and conductor, was the founder of the Orchestre National. Early in his career he became a friend of Debussy, whose music he championed all his life. He directed the chorus for the première of *Le martyre de St. Sebastien* in 1911, and for the first French production of *Boris Godounov,* at the Théâtre des Champs-Elysées in 1913. He was conductor at the Opéra-Comique, the Orchestre Pasdeloup, and the Paris Opéra. His output as a composer is substantial, of a highly refined French character, inspired by Fauré and Debussy.

Landormy, Paul (1869–1943), was a composer and a musicologist. A graduate in Letters of the Ecole Normale Supérieure, he also taught philosophy and wrote on Socrates and Descartes. His many writings on music were published in *Le Temps* and *La Victoire.*

Landowsky, Marcel (b. 1915), is a composer and a prominent music administrator. As a child, he was a student of Long. At the Paris Conservatoire he studied composition with Büsser and conducting with Gaubert. He was music director for the Comédie Française from 1962 to 1965; in 1966 he was appointed to the Ministère des Affaires Culturelles to be in charge of music. In this position, Landowsky was responsible for significant musical reforms in France: he created the Orchestre de Paris, reformed the Paris Opéra, and fought to include serious music curricula in the public schools. He married one of Long's pupils, Jaqueline Potier, who had earned her Premier Prix at the Conservatoire in the 1930s.

Maréchal, Maurice (1892–1964), was a solo cellist who traveled throughout the world, performing with leading orchestras in the U.S., the Soviet Union, and Japan. He became Professor of Cello at the Paris Conservatoire in 1942. At the end of his life, Fauré was particularly fond of Maréchal's interpretations of his music.

Messager, André (1853–1929), composer and conductor, was a pupil of Saint-Saëns and Fauré at the Ecole Niedermeyer. He directed the first performances of *Pelléas et Mélisande,* which Debussy dedicated to him. He was primarily a composer of operettas. His conducting responsibilities included the directorships of the Opéra-Comique (1899–1901), Covent Garden (1901–1907), and the Société des Concerts du Conservatoire (1908–1919). He is also renowned for his direction of Wagner's *Ring* cycle at the Paris Opéra in 1909.

Monteux, Pierre (1875–1964), had an illustrious career, which began when he shared a Premier Prix in violin at the Conservatoire with Jacques Thibaud in 1896. He was principal violist at the Opéra-Comique (playing the first performances of *Pelléas et Mélisande*), and later in the Orchestre Colonne. His conducting career was launched when he directed Diaghilev's Russian Ballets (1911–1914), conducting the premières of Stravinsky's *Rite of Spring* and *Petroushka.* He founded the Monteux School for conducting in Paris, in 1932, which he subsequently continued in Hancock, Maine. André Previn and Neville Marriner are among his pupils. In 1961, Monteux accepted his final apointment: at 86 he signed a 25-year contract with the London Symphony Orchestra.

Münch, Charles (1891–1968), a native of Strasbourg, was trained as a violinist. He succeeded Philippe Gaubert as Director of the Société des Concerts du Conservatoire in 1937. Münch toured widely in Europe and the U.S. and was music director of the Boston Symphony Orchestra from 1948 until 1962, where he gave many American premières of French works. Upon his return to France, he was instrumental in forming the Orchestre de Paris in 1967. He died in Virginia in November 1968, while on tour with his new orchestra.

Pierné, Gabriel (1863–1937), was a conductor and a composer. Although he was a disciple of Franck, he also studied at the Conservatoire. He won the Prix de Rome in 1882, at the age of eighteen. In 1910 he became Director of the Orchestre Colonne, succeeding the founder, Edouard Colonne. Pierré was a friend of Debussy, whom he knew as a student at the Conservatoire and later as a laureate in Rome; Pierné conducted the premières of *Iberia* and *Jeux*.

Rabaud, Henri (1873–1949), won the Prix de Rome in 1894. He was mainly an opera conductor, but he also conducted the Boston Symphony Orchestra in 1918. In 1920 he succeeded Fauré as Director of the Paris Conservatoire.

Risler, Edouard (1873–1929), was a pianist of the same generation as Marguerite Long and Alfred Cortot. He premiered many contemporary works, notably Dukas's Piano Sonata and Variations on a Theme by Rameau. Risler became Professor of Piano at the Paris Conservatoire in 1907.

Vieux, Maurice (1884–1951), was principal violist in the Opéra Orchestra and the Société des Concerts, in addition to teaching at the Paris Conservatoire. Fauré expressed the wish that Vieux play the viola part in his String Quartet at its Paris première. This wish was realized posthumously, on June 12, 1925, when Thibaud, Krettly, Vieux, and Hekking performed the work at the Société Nationale. Vieux had also performed in the première of Fauré's Second Piano Quintet, in May 1921, to great acclaim.

Viñes, Ricardo (1875–1943), pianist, was of Spanish origin. A childhood friend of Ravel, he premiered many works by Debussy and Ravel. Granados, Albeniz, and Séverac were his close friends, and he championed their music as well. He gave the first performances in France of many great Russian works, including Musorgsky's *Pictures at an Exhibition*, Balakirev's *Islamey*, and Prokofiev's *Sarcasm*. He was the dedicatee of Debussy's *Poissons d'or*, Ravel's *Oiseaux tristes*, Falla's *Nights in the Gardens of Spain*, and other works. Francis Poulenc was his most famous pupil, and he had many friends among writers and artists, including Colette, Cocteau, Max Jacob, Picasso, and Redon.

Vuillermoz, Emile (1878–1960), was trained as a composer in Fauré's class at the Paris Conservatoire and was instrumental in creating the Société Musicale Indépendante with his mentor, in 1909. Abandoning composition, he became an eminent musicologist, published numerous books, and was appointed editor-in-chief of the *Revue Musicale* in 1911. The bulk and scope of his writings, along with his efforts on behalf of contemporary music, earned him the title of Officier de la Légion d'Honneur. Debussy, Ravel, and Schmitt, and later Schoenberg, Stravinsky, Bartòk, Malipiero, and Szymanowski were among his friends.

Wittgenstein, Paul (1887–1961), Viennese pianist and pupil of Leschetizky, lost his right arm during World War I. In addition to Ravel's famous Concerto for the Left Hand, he commissioned left-hand works from Strauss, Britten, and Prokofiev (Fourth Concerto), among others. The philosopher Ludwig Wittgenstein was his brother. In 1938 Paul Wittgenstein emigrated to New York, and in 1946 he acquired American citizenship.

Discography

The following recordings by Marguerite Long were issued on 78 rpm. Unless otherwise indicated, they were all pressed by Columbia; recording dates are given when available.

BEETHOVEN:

Third Piano Concerto, C minor, Op. 37, with Félix Weingartner conducting the Orchestre de la Société des Concerts du Conservatoire (June 10, 1939). LFX 581-4.

Fifth Piano Concerto, E-flat major, Op. 73, with Charles Münch conducting the Société des Concerts. LFX 679-83.

CHOPIN:

Fantasy in F minor, D 13112-13; American issue, 17018/9-D.

Waltz, Op. 64, No. 3.

Waltz, Op. 70, No. 3. LF 7.

Concerto in F minor, with Philippe Gaubert conducting the Société des Concerts du Conservatoire; and Mazurka, Op. 59 No. 3. D 15236-9; American issue, Set 143 (67800/3-D).

Barcarolle. LFX 325.

Second Scherzo. LFX 513.

Berceuse

Fantaisie Impromptu. Distributed in Japan.

DEBUSSY:

La plus que lente

Jardins sous la pluie (1929). LFX 24.

First and Second Arabesques (1930). LF 55; American issue, 17033-D.

FAURÉ:

Second and Fifth Impromptus. LF 126

Sixth Nocturne and Second Barcarolle. LFX 437

Sixth Barcarolle and Fourth Nocturne. LFX 567; American issue, 69 063-T.

Ballade for piano and orchestra, Op. 19, with Philippe Gaubert conducting the Société des Concerts (1931). LFX 54-55; American issue, MX-62 (70490/1-D).

First Piano Quartet, in C minor, Op. 15, with the Pasquier Trio, Jean (violin), Pierre (viola), and Etienne (cello) (recorded by Pathé Marconi on LP in 1956; see below).

Second Piano Quartet, in G minor, with Jacques Thibaud, Maurice Vieux, and Pierre Fournier. La Voix de son Maître DB 5103-6.

"Les Berceaux," Op. 23, No. 1, with Ninon Vallin. LF 125.

HALFFTER:

Rapsodie Portugaise, with Charles Münch conducting the Société des Concerts. LF X 629-30.

D'INDY:

Symphonie sur un chant montagnard, with Paul Paray conducting Orchestre Colonne. LFX 352-4; American issue, set 211 (68279/81-D).

MILHAUD:

First Piano Concerto, with Darius Milhaud conducting the Orchestre National de France; and "Paysandu" (from *Saudades*) and "Alfama" (from *L'Automne*) (1935). LFX 375-6; American issue, set X-67 (68737/8-D).

MOZART:

Concerto in A major, K. 488, with Philippe Gaubert conducting the Société des Concerts. LFX 408-10; American issue, Set 261 (68566/8).

Sonata for violin and piano, in B-flat major, K. 378, with Jacques Thibaud.

Sonata for violin and piano, in A major, K. 526, with Jacques Thibaud. (Both sonatas were recorded in July 1943, but were never issued on 78rpm. They were later pressed on LP, see below.)

RAVEL:

Concerto in G major, with Ravel conducting Orchestre Lamoureux (Freitas-Branco actually conducting, April 1932). LFX 257-9; LX 194-6; American issue, set 176 (68064/6-D).

The following works were recorded by Long on LP.

CHOPIN:

Concerto in F minor, with André Cluytens conducting the Société des Concerts (1953). Pathé Marconi FC 25010, FCX 193.

FAURÉ:

First Piano Quartet, in C minor, Op. 15. FC 1057.

Ballade, with André Cluytens conducting, and Ravel, Concerto in G major, with Georges Tzipine conducting; Orchestre de la Société des Concerts. (1952). Angel 35013.

Works transferred from 78 rpm to LP (not re-recorded by the artists).

BEETHOVEN:

Third Piano Concerto. FHX 5007, and Angel GR 2196.

Fifth Piano Concerto. FHX 5006.

DEBUSSY:

La plus que lente, Jardins sous la pluie, First and Second Arabesques. Pathé Marconi 2 C 051-16349.

FAURE:

Second Piano Quartet, in G minor. COLC 76, and Pathé Marconi 2 C 051-12815.

New issue of the First Piano Quartet. Pathé Marconi 2 C 051-12815.

Second and Sixth Barcarolles, Second and Fifth Impromptus, and Fourth and Sixth Nocturnes (reference not available).

MILHAUD:
First Piano Concerto, with "Paysandu" and "Alfama." Pathé Marconi 2 C 051-16349.

MOZART:
Sonatas for violin and piano in B-flat major, K. 378, and in A major, K. 526, with Jacques Thibaud (1943). HMV COLH 312.

RAVEL:
Concerto in G major, 1932 recording. Pathé Marconi 2 C 051-16349.

Recordings available as of 1992.

FAURE:
Two Piano Quartets. Compact Disc: EMI CDH 769794-2.
"Les Berceaux," with Ninon Vallin. In a large collection of songs entitled *The Record of Singing* (Vol. 3, "The French school"). LP: EMI EX 290 169-3.

RAVEL:
Concerto in G major.

MILHAUD:
First Piano Concerto, with "Paysandu" and "Alfama."

DEBUSSY:
Two Arabesques, *Jardins sous la pluie,* and *La plus que lente.* LP: EMI C051-16.349M.

Bibliography

Alain, Olivier. "Les Jeunesses Musicales et le Concours M.L.-J.T." See *Revue musicale.*

Barbier, Jean-Joël. "Les enregistrements de M. Long et de J. Thibaud." See *Revue musicale.*

Barbizet, Pierre. "Marguerite Long." See *Revue musicale.*

Brody, Elaine. *Paris, the Musical Kaleidoscope 1870–1925.* New York: George Braziller, Inc., 1987.

Cooper, Martin. *French Music from the Death of Berlioz to the Death of Fauré.* London: Oxford University Press, 1951. Reprinted 1969, 1974, and 1978.

Cortot, Alfred. *La musique française de piano.* 3 vols. Paris: Editions Reider, 1930–48. Translated by Hilda Andrews, 1977.

———. *Principes rationnels de la technique pianistique.* Paris: Salabert, 1928. Translated by R. Le Roy-Metaxas, 1937.

Debussy, Claude. *Claude Debussy, Lettres 1884–1918.* Compiled and edited by François Lesure. Paris: Hermann, 1980.

Depaulis, Jacques. "Forty-Four Unpublished Letters from Roger-Ducasse to Marguerite Long and Her Husband, Joseph de Marliave." Compiled and annotated by Depaulis. Manuscript. Bordeaux, 1988.

———. "Roger-Ducasse et Marguerite Long, une amitié, une correspondance." *Revue internationale de musique française* 28 (February 1989):79–98.

Escholier, Raymond. "Marguerite Long, son enfance nîmoise." See *Revue musicale.*

Fauré, Gabriel. *Lettres Intimes* [selected letters to his wife, 1885–1924]. Edited by Philippe Fauré-Fremiet. Paris: Grasset, 1951.

Fauré-Fremiet, Philippe. *Gabriel Fauré.* Paris: Albin Michel, 1957.

Gerig, Reginald. *Famous Pianists and Their Technique.* Washington and New York: Robert B. Luce, 1975.

Jankélévitch, Vladimir. *Gabriel Fauré, ses mélodies, son esthétique.* Paris: Plon, 1951.

"Liste des membres du Jury et des Lauréats année par année." See *Revue musicale.*

Lockspeiser, Edward. *Debussy, His Life and Mind.* 2 vols. London: Cassell and Co. Ltd, 1966. Reprinted with corrections, London: Cambridge University Press, 1978.

Long, Marguerite. *Au piano avec Debussy.* Paris: René Julliard, 1960. Translated by Olive Senior-Ellis, London: Dent, 1972.

———. *Au piano avec Fauré.* Paris: René Julliard, 1963. Translated by Olive Senior-Ellis, New York: Taplinger, 1981.

———. *Au piano avec Ravel,* compiled by Pierre Laumonier. Paris: René Julliard, 1971. Translated by Olive Senior-Ellis, London: Dent, 1973.

———. *La Petite Méthode de Piano.* Paris: Salabert, 1963.

———. *Le Piano.* Paris: Salabert, 1959.

Marliave, Joseph de. *Etudes Musicales.* Paris: Félix Alcan, 1917.

———. *Les Quatuors de Beethoven.* Introduction and Notes by Jean Escarra and Preface by Gabriel Fauré. Paris: Félix Alcan, 1925. Translated by Hilda Andrews, London: Oxford University Press, 1928; reprint, New York: Dover, 1961.

Marnat, Marcel. *Maurice Ravel.* Paris: Arthème Fayard, 1986.

Nectoux, Jean-Michel. *Gabriel Fauré: A Musical Life.* Translated by Roger Nichols. Cambridge: Cambridge University Press, 1991.

———. *Gabriel Fauré, His Life Through His Letters.* Translated by J. A. Underwood. New York and London: Marion Boyars Inc., 1984.

Orledge, Robert. *Gabriel Fauré.* London: Eulenburg Books, 1979.

Revue musicale, La. Numéro special, No. 245, 1959. Special issue devoted to the Concours International Marguerite Long–Jacques Thibaud and its founders. Contains twenty articles by many of the principal players of the competition, disciples, and friends. Provides historical information as well as homages to Long and Thibaud.

Schonberg, Harold C. *The Great Pianists.* New York: Simon and Schuster, 1963.

Stuckenschmidt, Hans Heinz. *Maurice Ravel.* Translated by Samuel R. Rosenbaum. Philadelphia: Chilton Book Company, 1968.

Timbrell, Charles. "Claude Debussy and Walter Rummel, Chronicle of a Friendship with New Correspondence." *Music & Letters,* August 1992.

Weill, Janine. *Marguerite Long: une vie fascinante.* Paris: René Julliard, 1969.

Editions of Music by Marguerite Long:

Mendelssohn, *Songs Without Words.* Edited and annotated by Long. Paris: Maurice Sénart et Cie., 1918.

Mozart Piano Concertos in D minor, K. 466; in A major, K. 488; in C minor, K. 491, and in B-flat major, K. 595. Edited and with fingerings by Long, orchestral reduction for second piano by Henri Büsser. Paris: Choudens, 1935.

Complete Mozart Piano Sonatas, with Preface, editing, and fingerings by Long. Paris: Choudens, 1934.

Index

Index

Cecilia Dunoyer IS MUSIC ADVISOR AT THE CENTER FOR PERFORMING ARTS AT PENN STATE UNIVERSITY. SHE COMBINES THE CAREERS OF PIANIST AND SCHOLAR, GIVING LECTURE-RECITALS ON FRENCH AND RUSSIAN MUSIC AND CONCERTIZING TO CRITICAL ACCLAIM IN BOTH EUROPE AND AMERICA. SHE IS AUTHOR OF MANY ARTICLES IN FRENCH AND AMERICAN JOURNALS.